Unlocking Wealth

Secret to Market Timing

By John Crane

Copyright © 2007 John Crane. All rights reserved

Published by Tradenet Publishing, Loveland, Colorado

ALL RIGHT RESERVED. No part of this publication may be reproduced, stored in a retrieval system, or transmitted in any form or by any means, electronic, mechanical, photocopied, recorded or otherwise, without prior written permission of the publisher and the author.

This publication is designed to provide accurate and authoritative information in regard to the subject matter covered. It is sold with the understanding that the author and the publisher are not engaged in rendering legal, accounting, or other professional services.

Authorization to photocopy items for internal or personal use, or for the internal or personal use of specific clients, is granted by Tradenet, provided that the U.S. $10.00 per page fee is paid directly to Tradenet, 1-800-831-7654.

Limit of Liability/Disclaimer of Warranty: While the publisher and author have used their best efforts in preparing this book, they make no representations or warranties with respect to the accuracy or completeness of the contents of this book and specifically disclaim any implied warranties of merchantability or fitness for a particular purpose. No warranty may be created or extended by sales representatives or written materials. The advice and strategies contained herein may not be suitable for your situation. You should consult with a professional where appropriate. Neither the publisher nor author shall be liable for any loss of profits or any other commercial damages, including but not limited to special, incidental, consequential, or other damages.

Printed in the United States of America.

All charts used in this manual are furnished courtesy of DTN Corporation and were produced by their ProphetX charting software.

Disclaimer

It should not be assumed that the methods, techniques, or indicators presented in this book will be profitable or that they will not result in losses. Past results are not necessarily indicative of future results. Examples in this book are for educational purposes only. This is not a solicitation of any order to buy or sell.

The NFA requires us to state "HYPOTHETICAL OR SIMULATED PERFORMANCE RESULTS HAVE CERTAIN INHERENT LIMITATIONS. UNLIKE AN ACTUAL PERFORMANCE RECORD, SIMULATED RESULTS DO NOT REPRESENT ACTUAL TRADING. ALSO, SINCE THE TRADES HAVE NOT ACTUALLY BEEN EXECUTED, THE RESULTS MAY HAVE UNDER OR OVERCOMPENSATED FOR THE IMPACT, IF ANY, OF CERTAIN MARKET FACTORS, SUCH AS LACK OF LIQUIDITY. SIMULATED TRADING PROGRAMS IN GENERAL ARE ALSO SUBJECT TO THE FACT THAT THEY ARE DESIGNED WITH THE BENEFIT OF HINDSIGHT. NO REPRESENTATION IS BEING MADE THAT ANY ACCOUNT WILL OR IS LIKELY TO ACHIEVE PROFITS OR LOSSES SIMILAR TO THESE SHOWN."

Acknowledgements

This book would never have made it all the way to publication without the helping hands of many individuals. In particular, I am extremely grateful for all the help that I received from Joseph Kellogg, Kathleen Marusak and to my two daughters, Anastasia and Holliston for all of your contributions to this book. A special thanks to my wife Angela for all the patience and support you offered during the several months it took to complete this book.

John Crane

Contents

Preface

Introduction

CHAPTER 1 – Order out of Chaos – 5

A discussion of market behavior and how it is effected by human emotions and economic supply and demand.
How the Action/Reaction theory of a reoccurring cycle circulates throughout the market.

CHAPTER 2 – Time – Trend Reversal Pattern - 21

The Trend Reversal Pattern marks the beginning and end of major trend change.
The Reaction swing is the central point of the Action/Reaction trading method.
It is where the Action ends and the Reaction begin.
Rules to identify Reaction swings and use them to project future turning points in the market.

CHAPTER 3 – Time – Trend Continuation Pattern - 87

The Trend Continuation Pattern occurs inside a trending market and identifies the center of the longer-term cycle.
Rules to identify the Trend Continuation Pattern and project future turning points in the market.

CHAPTER 4 – Price – Trend Reversal Pattern - 105

Where and when is the right time to enter or exit the market? An easy and reliable way to determine future support and resistance price levels for entry or exit.

CHAPTER 5 – How are they connected? - 149

How to identify the difference between a major turning point and a short-term swing pattern.

CHAPTER 6 – Market Tells - 169

Price patterns exhibit specific characteristics and foretell future market action.

CHAPTER 7 – Options with Action/Reaction - 217

Combining options with the Reaction swing projections can enhance gains.

CHAPTER 8 – Combining Technical Indicators with Action/Reaction - 237

Using technical indicators in conjunction with the Reversal Date Indicator. Rules to help identify major turning points in the market.

CHAPTER 9 – Trading with different time frames - 253

What is a hidden Reaction swing? Sometimes patterns can be hidden in a longer-term time frame, but revealed in the intra-day chart.
How to find the hidden Reaction swing and use it for an early entry.

CHAPTER 10 – Final word - 269

Some final words or wisdom and common sense trading rules to live by.
A list and description of trading tools that will enhance your trading skills and help you shorten your learning curve.

Resources for Traders - 270

INDEX - 276

Preface

The continual need to expand one's knowledge or to improve an existing idea is an inherent one in all of us. After finishing my last book "Advanced Swing Trading", I had many requests for more specific signals for entry and exit. I continued to work on my theories of Action/Reaction, with the objective of finding new ways to expand and to improve this unique trading approach and share with you my favorite strategies.

This book deals with the Action/Reaction theory by combining price levels, timing methods and confirmation patterns that strengthen the predictability of future market moves. I take a step-by-step look at the Action/Reaction theory and illustrate how to identify the key trading opportunities. I explain the step-by step process I use to determine my entry and exit of the positions and how to use the information provided by the market to project the next market movement.

One of the unique techniques described in this book is the method of projecting future prices. I have not seen this incredible technique published before. By using my Action lines and Reaction lines, within the Reaction cycle, I illustrate how to project the time and price of major market reversals. This cycle tells the trader if the market is going to make a major turn or if the market is only going to make a small correction against the prevailing trend.

Since writing my last book, one of the most frequent questions people asked me was "Does this method also work for Stocks?" The answer is - Yes, it does! I have included several examples showing how the Reversal dates work just as well for Stocks as they do for futures. Since most of my experience has been in the futures market, the majority of the examples in this book are from futures markets. However, this in no way means that this technique can only be used in the futures markets.

My hope is that the information in this book will increase your awareness of the market's true behavior and serve as a confirmation of your own market analysis.

I offer help throughout every step of your learning process. My specially trained staff is available to answer questions and guide you through the rough stops. You can also follow my daily updates and compare your results with mine. See the appendix for more information on how to take advantage of this valuable resource.

Introduction

I am sure many of you have heard the story told by Joe Kennedy about the time he got his shoes shined at Grand Central Station. As he was sitting and reading his newspaper, the young man who was shining his shoes told Joe that he had bought some stock for himself, which meant that he now had himself a piece of the American dream. This conversation convinced Joe that the bull market of the 1920s was over. He reasoned, "If the shoe shine boy is in the market, who is left to buy? If everyone is in the market, there is nowhere for it to go but down." The story goes on to tell how Joe Kennedy pulled his money out of the stock market and avoided the disastrous crash of 1929. This is typical market behavior after any extended market move. It can happen after a long-term bull market in the stocks or even a short-term swing trade in the futures market.

Much of this distress and financial loss can be avoided if investors take the time and a little effort to educate themselves on market behavior. Inexperienced traders tend to hesitate when it comes to entering markets near the beginning of a trend but are more than willing to jump into markets near the end of the trend, just as professional traders are exiting their positions.

In February of 2000, just before the stock market climax, I was speaking at a seminar in San Francisco about the Reversal Date and Action/Reaction Theory (the subject of this book). After the presentation, I was approached by one of the attendees whom I knew from one of my previous seminars. He pulled out a chart of the Dow Jones Index, on which he had applied some of my timing indicators and reversal patterns. Based on this analysis, he said that he had just pulled all his money out of the tech stocks and was going to short the Dow Jones futures. This man offers a perfect example of what we should strive to emulate. He took the necessary time and effort to educate himself on market behavior and he was rewarded when he closed his long position near the top of the market and was prepared to enter a short positions. He was aware of the market behavior, but more importantly, he had the discipline to act on the information. He did not get caught in all the market hype that was being spewed daily from the business news shows.

All too often traders seem to be in a hurry; we're all seeking instant gratification. We have learned as traders, this type of thinking often leads us away from success. If you study the path of successful traders from the past to the present, you will find each had much in common. The most important of these similarities are patience, discipline and a willingness to work as hard and as long as it takes to succeed. Successful traders realize that the pathway to continued success comes not from "inside information" or even from an overabundance of knowledge, but from the understanding of human behavior and how it translates into the market. This formula has not changed since the early 1800s, when U.S. futures trading began on the Midwestern frontier and can probably be traced back as far as 1640, when trading took place in Bulb futures, and it will continue long into the future. In other words, a little education and practice will benefit you forever.

Jesse Livermore, one of the great traders during the early twentieth century, stated that one of the most important keys to his success as a trader was understanding market behavior and knowing when to cut his losses quickly. Jack Schwager, in his book "Market Wizards," interviews Paul Tudor Jones, who is possibly one of the most successful traders of recent time. Paul Tudor Jones insists that a huge part of his success is cutting his losses quickly. He said one of the most important secrets to his trading success is, "If the market is not behaving the way I think it should, I get out!"

Of the millions of people involved in speculative markets, only a small percentage will spend the time and effort needed to learn how to trade. Although there is no Holy Grail to trading success, there are road maps and warning signs available to guide you toward your desired destination.

Yes, there are many stories of traders who made a killing off one trade, or maybe even a string of trades. This will always be the case, as it is the nature of the markets to offer these opportunities. However, you need to be ready to take advantage of such opportunities when they are offered, because the market can take

Introduction

them away just as quickly if you do not practice pro-active money management. Unfortunately, for every lucky trader, there are countless others who are not so lucky. The good news is that long-term success is available to everyone who has desire, dedication and a strong worth ethic.

A few years ago, a young man from our town was preparing to ski in the Olympics. He and his older brother had been skiing since they were very young. A friend asked the older brother how he felt about his younger brother being an Olympic skier and a top contender for the gold medal. He replied, "I'm a better skier than he is, but I quit skiing a long time ago, I got tired of all the work. To me it was not worth all the effort." This statement says volumes about the difference between success and failure. You have to believe the rewards will outweigh the effort.

Any investment that offers the potential of high return offers the potential for high risk...they go hand-in-hand. The trading patterns and methods described in this book have served me well and I have no doubt that they will continue to do so. It will require study and concentration on your part, but I believe with hard work, you will quickly realize the tremendous value of reversal timing and trading techniques.

This book is about Time, Price and Patterns, and their reflection on market behavior. The Reversal Date trading indicator is not meant to be a turnkey system, but it can be used by itself or incorporated into other trading strategies. Flexibility is one of the strongest features of the Action/Reaction trading approach. I describe this method in a clear concise manner that should help you understand market behavior and enable you to use what you have learned with a high degree of reliability.

My goal is to provide you with the knowledge, confidence and ability to add what you learn from this book to whatever trading approach you are most comfortable with. Since most of the information in this book is designed to anticipate trend exhaustion or trend reversals, it may strike you as unconventional, but I believe we must think out of the box to be more successful.

The Reversal Date indicator and the Action/Reaction techniques described in this book can be applied to stocks or commodities. In addition, they work equally as well on daily or intra-day charts. I strongly encourage you to apply them both.

I believe learning the methods described in this book will give you a tremendous edge, as well as reduce the stress of blindly trading without a defined plan or the knowledge of market behavior. The ability to look at the market and have confidence in your trading decision is worth its weight in gold.

Trading offers one of the last great frontiers of opportunity. It is one of the very few avenues that offers everyone equal opportunity. There are very few venues where an individual can start with a relatively small bankroll and actually become a millionaire. While I hardly expect all readers of this book to suddenly transform into super traders, I do believe this information will open your minds to a new way of looking at the market and improve your personal trading performance.

Chapter 1

> *"The girl who can't dance says the band can't play."*
> Yiddish Proverb

Trading is Easy – Anyone Can Do It!

Almost anyone can open a stock account or commodity trading account. All you need is to be old enough and meet the financial requirements. You don't need a license, a certificate, or a degree. It doesn't require any advanced training, an apprenticeship or a college education and trading does not discriminate when it comes to gender, race, religion or age. Unlike other businesses, competition is good when it comes to trading; the more people that trade, the better it is for the business...it is the perfect business.

On the other hand, becoming a consistently successful trader is a completely different story. For example, as when opening a trading account, almost anyone can buy a set of golf clubs and attempt to play golf, but very few people can buy a set of clubs and immediately compete at a professional level. It takes training, dedication and practice...lots of practice to become proficient at the game. Even then, very few can step onto a golf course and compete with Tiger Woods, but that is exactly what many novice traders attempt to do on a daily basis. They step into the trading arena to compete with the seasoned professionals without learning the proper technique, discipline or a trading strategy that will help them understand market behavior.

But the good news is, trading is the one arena where this can be possible. If you have the knowledge of market behavior and discipline to stick with a trading plan you can go head-to-head with the professional traders and still come out ahead. It's not easy, but it is possible.

Chapter 1 – Trading is Easy – Anyone Can Do It! 6

Confusing a Trending Market with Trading Skills

In the later part of 1999, I was at a small neighborhood gathering. One of the women at the gathering was giving out stock advice to anyone willing to listen and she had quite a gathering. She was telling the group about how well her investment club was doing (the club was a small group of women from her work at a local computer company) and about how she and her husband were moving the majority of their retirement savings into the tech stocks, because the move was just beginning. "This is the new economy," she said. "And if you don't buy now, you will be left behind!"

About the same time the business channel had profiled a young market analyst, granting him almost celebrity status. This analyst's stock recommendations had been on target over the past two years and had registered double-digit returns. He was a brash 28-year-old and had been in the business for just six years. He predicted the Dow at 15,000 in the next six months.

It was a crazy time. Day trading had become the new pastime and internet stocks were the super highway to wealth. It seemed everyone had become a stock expert. Whenever the market staged a small correction, the cry was "Buy more, it will go back up!" This strategy was the only one that most of these new investors knew and it was the only one they needed; or so it seemed.

The rest, of course, is history. Shortly thereafter the internet bubble burst. Before long all the gains made during the runaway bull market had been lost and the buy-every-dip crowd were wiped out!

It's interesting how history repeats itself. At the beginning of 2006, at the height of the energy bull market, I read an article in "Trader" magazine regarding the top young trader that year. He was described as a very astute trader and a master at the energy markets. The previous year he had made an incredible sum of money for his firm's hedge fund and had been rewarded handsomely. Of course, he was bullish in the energy markets and had been buying every dip, believing there was no end in sight. He

Chapter 1 – Trading is Easy – Anyone Can Do It! 7

was touted as one of the best and brightest...but the bull market ended.

By September 2006 the market had reversed but the young man kept buying. The market behavior had changed, but he failed to recognize it. He was finally forced to liquidate his long position at a $6 billion dollar loss for the firm. Traders often confuse a bull market with intelligent trading skills, but understanding market behavior and being able to recognize and adjust to change is necessary to becoming a consistently successful trader. Remember, price is the final arbitrator and the market will always win if you choose to fight it.

The least understood part of your trading could be costing you money.

Traders spend a vast majority of their learning curve on market entry. Timing the entry has always been the most exciting part of trading. It's the moment you decide to take action and enter the market and from that time on there is no turning back. The adrenaline is pumping as the trade begins to unfold. If the market moves in the correct direction you feel satisfied; if it moves the wrong way you feel anxiety. Either is an emotional rush.

In reality, the entry is the easiest part of the trade. The decision to enter a trade is clear-cut, you either do it or you don't. Once you have entered the trade, everything changes. Your money is on the line and emotions can overtake rational thinking and quickly destroy a well-thought-out trading plan. This can cause a trader to exit early or too late. Either way, it can take away from the profit potential. Most traders spend very little time on the exit, but a bad exit strategy can cost hundreds of dollars.

For example, suppose you are long a position and the market reaches a new high and reverses and quickly drops through your stop, causing a loss on the trade. So you make a rule that the next time you have a profit you will exit quickly, because you reason that you can't go broke taking a profit. The next trade comes along and your position is showing a slight profit so you exit the trade with a gain. You're happy until you notice the market continuing to climb higher and higher as you stand on the sidelines. The potential for a large profit was missed. So you change the rule again, and the cycle continues.

A simple trading plan of entering the market and following with a protective stop is better than no plan, but you will give up a lot of profit potential when the market pulls back from a high or low and triggers the protective stop. Don't get me wrong, protective stops are necessary for equity preservation and timing the entry is important, but timing the exit can add greatly to your bottom line. This is what I hope to teach you: timing the entry and the exit to increase the consistency and add to the bottom line.

The Three Ingredients.

Making money consistently in the market requires a good deal of education and the right psychological makeup. But to enter the realm of the professional traders there are three more ingredients you need.

1, A trading method – This means an objective trading approach with definable trading rules that offers a defined entry method and can be easily illustrated and explained. This is not to say the method cannot be refined and improved, but the essential basis behind the method should remain the same. To trade the method successfully, you have to accept the premise that it is not infallible; nothing works 100% of the time. Losing trades happen; learn to accept them because if you keep looking for the Holy Grail, you will fail.

2. Discipline - Without discipline you won't be successful. Having the discipline to follow the method really comes from having confidence in the method. Confidence is what allows the trader to keep the discipline when the markets are not as friendly as they should be.

Money management could have its own category, but I included it under the category of discipline because they go hand-in-hand. A good trading approach will have money management built in to the method, but it still takes discipline to implement the strategy.

3. Practice – Just like with any other skill, practice will help improve your trading skills. "Paper trading" will help refine your skills and build confidence in your method, but it will not provide the true value learned from actual trading. Paper trading lacks the very thing that can harm a trader, the emotional stress of having your money on the line. Having had a successful run at paper trading does not translate into becoming a successful trader. Markets are not just an intellectual exercise, they are emotional and they can be very stressful. They are not without risk and risk can cloud your judgment. Only through experience can you begin to understand and control the emotions derived by having your hard earned money on the line.

Traders do many things in an attempt to remove the emotions from the formula, but in the end it is psychological. For example, when you go to Las Vegas and sit at the Blackjack table the first thing the dealer does is take your cash away and hand you a pile of chips. This removes the emotion attached to the cash. Gamblers are more willing to bet chips than their cash. The same can be said about trading. Instead of thinking about the price moves in dollar and cents begin to think of them in points or percentage. Removing the emotion allows you the discipline to follow your trading method without the stress. This can only be accomplished through practice and confidence in your trading method.

Practice means experience and experience takes time. Many new traders do not have the time or are unwilling to spend the time it takes to become a successful trader. They are always looking for the shortcut, but shortcuts in trading experience can lead to disaster.

Been There, Done That.
___

There is one way around this dilemma and that is to find a mentor, someone who has already been through the school of hard knocks and proven themselves over the years. Whether you sit next to them, attend a seminar or study a book or course, you may be able to jump some of the hurdles that novices or even seasoned traders experience along the path to successful trading. I have always believed there is no need to re-invent the wheel if someone has already been down that path and can stop me from making the same mistakes they have. Why not learn from their experience and move forward?

Hopefully, this book will prove to be your mentor when it comes to the Action/Reaction approach to trading, or at least provide you with a foundation to begin a successful trading career. The methods described have been refined through many years of trading and have progressed to where I feel very confident they can help any level or type of trader. Although not perfect, this trading approach offers a sound trading approach with built-in money management and timing techniques that can offer you that edge to help you come out on top when competing head-to-head with the professionals.

Order from Chaos.

Although price fluctuations may seem random, they are the result of many different market forces working together in a very efficient manner. Out of this apparent disorder, one begins to see a market that is moving in a very deliberate re-occurring pattern of that which is formed as buyers and sellers with different opinions about future prices act on their opinions.

Since my trading approach is technical in nature and chart based, it made it easier to implement. There are no outside distractions from subjective fundamental news stories and incomplete supply and demand figures. There is no need to try to interpret how the large commercial firms will react to a report or news story. Now, all I had to do is read the market reaction and let the world's best traders do my analysis for me.

Most of the current technical analysis is just a rehash of discoveries introduced years ago by great trading legends such as Gann, Elliott, Andrews and others. Although their trading approaches were different, the premise of their methodologies was the same. They all believed that there were natural cycles circulating throughout the markets.

Chapter 1 – Trading is Easy – Anyone Can Do It!

Of course the factors of supply and demand play a key role in market behavior. However, they do not play the role that most people think. You see the simplistic law of supply and demand is constantly subjected to a force that is equally powerful, hard to measure and infinitely less logical. While it is true that the fundamental factors of supply and demand control the long-term market trends, the short-term fluctuations are typically a response of a different force...human emotion. As a result of two of the strongest emotions (greed and fear), most traders have a tendency to over-react to market conditions. When things are going well, traders succumb to greed and overbuy in an effort to maximize profits. When the market is not going their way, fear kicks in, followed by a flurry of selling. These two opposing market forces are the reason markets fluctuate. Supply and demand figures may change, but human emotions remain constant.

Prices Lead Fundamentals.
_____

I not only believe price leads fundamental news, I have seen it happen more times than I can count. It is not uncommon for markets to top when the fundamental news is the most bullish and bottom when the news is the most bearish. I'm unable to count the number of times traders have asked me "How can the market be trading higher? We just had a very bearish report." The answer is simple – we are trading the futures market, not the current or past market. In other words, the futures price has already discounted the fundamental news. The large commercial firms and professional traders are already looking into the future when the news or market reports are released. While the unsuspecting trader is stepping into the market because of a news story or a government report, the experienced traders are stepping out because the recently released information has already been factored into the market and it is time to look forward.

Don't get me wrong. I am not saying that fundamentals do not influence market prices. In fact, they can have a dramatic affect on prices. Market fundamentals of supply and demand are the ultimate decision-makers in the marketplace. These forces will move the markets over the long-term, while the technical side provides entry and exit signals in the short-term.

Technical Analysis, What Is It?

Technical analysis is devoted to the internal studies of the markets, such as price, market momentum, chart patterns and market behavior, to name a few, and not the fundamental (or outside) forces that influence market movement. It looks at the forces that lie within the particular market activity and influence price activity. These forces are generally considered the human qualities and emotions.

When using technical analysis it is more important to look at what the market is doing rather than what the market should do. It is not important how much a commodity should be worth, but rather how much someone is willing to pay for it and the intensity of their belief. In a market based on supply and demand, the intensity of emotion will reveal which one is more powerful - those demanding the commodity or those supplying it.

A few years ago I was working with a trader who knew all the fundamental information concerning the hog market. He knew how many hogs were processed on a daily basis, how many hogs were on feed and how many were due to be processed as well as the number in cold storage – he knew it all. Based on his extensive knowledge of the current market he decided to short the market. His analysis was correct and the market dropped, but as the market moved lower he increased his position. After a couple of weeks he was sitting on a very large gain and his analysis was still bearish, but the market began to change direction. As the market rallied, he increased his position because, in his words, "the market is wrong." The market continued higher and yet he refused to exit his position. He complained that the market was being manipulated; his fundamental information told him the market should move lower. Before long all his profits were gone and he began to lose his initial investment. Yet, he still refused to believe he was wrong. In the end he was forced to liquidate the position with his account considerably smaller than before. All his information and analysis

Chapter 1 – Trading is Easy – Anyone Can Do It!

suggested the market should trade lower, yet the market rallied. The lesson here: If the market does not react as you anticipate, get out and re-evaluate. Do not get caught in an argument with the market, you can't win.

Every trader has their own reason for buying or selling a commodity, whether it is based on a technical signal or fundamental information or a producer offsetting his risk or even the end user locking his supply at a certain price. Whatever the reason, I believe it will be reflected in the price action. Outside influences affect the price and the net result is reflected in the market by the characteristics of the price action, the nature of the activity, when the action appeared and how much time it took to unfold.

Although the law of Supply and Demand should and does apply to all free markets, sometimes government regulations interfere for short intervals. But, as always, after this interference fails, the markets are given back to the people and the natural laws that govern them. I find it interesting how many times a market will make an unexpected large move for no apparent reason, only to be verified by some fundamental news released at a later date.

Jesse Livermore, a famous speculator once wrote,

"Remember there is always a reason for a stock acting the way it does. But also remember the chances are you will not become acquainted with the reason until some time in the future, when it is too late to act on it profitably."

Universal Laws of Price Action.

It is obvious that universal laws govern all aspects of life on earth, from the changing seasons, to the rise and fall of the tides, right down to the smallest atom of the universe. Since we accept this to be true, we also accept the premise that these laws may affect the actions of man and that under certain conditions, he will have similar or repetitive reactions. If so, it can also hold true in the markets that price patterns can and will repeat themselves as traders react to current patterns in the same way they did to past patterns. Therefore, the past can reflect the future.

The Action/Reaction theory suggests every trade needs three things in order to successfully identify a correct signal - *Time, Price and Pattern.* When all three components come together, the reaction can become very predictable. If you can improve the timing of your entry and exit price, it will enhance **any** trading method. That is what the Reversal Date indicator and the Reaction cycle can do for you. *It will tell you when a market should react and the price level the market needs to be at for it to react. It will even tell you what the market must do to confirm the trade signal!*

This is all based on the market theory that —"*For every action in the markets there is an equal and opposite reaction!"* Which means that if you can find the right *action* point in the market, you should be able to predict the *reaction.* Amazingly, you can predict when and where the market will likely reverse. *The key to all of this is the ability to find the end of the initial Action and the beginning of the Reaction.*

This may sound like a complicated and difficult task, especially to those not well versed in technical analysis. However, in reality it is very simple and easy to learn. This methodology is entirely based around one chart pattern that I call the *Reaction swing.* The Reaction swing is the first thing you will learn as it will lay the groundwork for your trading and allow everything else to simply fall into place.

There are many things that help a trader become more successful. These include common sense rules and sound techniques. However, I believe that two things are critical and must be possessed before anyone begins to trade in the market. These two things vital to any trader are *knowledge* and *confidence*; knowledge of how the markets work and confidence in the trading approach one has chosen to use. In this book, I give you the knowledge so you know how to identify when a major move in the market is about to begin or end, how to know what the market is telling you and how to react to the well defined patterns. However, you will have to build your own confidence. This is critical because without confidence in your ability to use it, knowledge is useless. Confidence comes from study and practice. The more you see the market react as you anticipate, the more you will believe.

Lagging Behind

My first introduction to trading was in the early 80s. I started simple by learning to use basic trend line and then moved up to classic chart patterns, such as Head and Shoulders, flags and pennant formations, and so on. These chart patterns had been used by traders for years and still remain very popular today.

Unfortunately, I experienced early success and became convinced that I knew it all. That quickly changed as reality taught me a hard lesson, but my short taste of success convinced me of the potential offered by trading. I became thirsty for more knowledge and went in search of more advanced indicators because I was convinced the more indicators I used the more successful I could become. I began to learn about momentum indicators, such as the Relative Strength Indicator (RSI), Stochastics and Moving Averages, to name just a few. I thought they were the answer to predicting major turning points.

Using these indicators did give me a good idea about the overall trend and strength of a market. This fit well with the teachings I found in the majority of the trading books I had read. I had read in several of these books that the only way to be a successful trader was to "take it out of the middle". They described the danger of trying to enter or exit at tops or bottoms; stating that the only safe and sane time to enter a trade is after the trend is established and well on its way. Even though there is a lot of wisdom in this trading philosophy, I always felt like I was starting a 100-yard dash 10 yards behind everyone else. It didn't fit my style.

Using these traditional technical indicators made it easy enough to enter a market in an established trend. However, several times I had to sit through large price fluctuations and take on more risk than necessary. The more I read and the more I traded, the more I knew I wanted to find a different way to analyze the markets. I wanted to find a methodology that would allow me to maximize profits and to reduce risk. This would require a way to enter a trade earlier and exit later or, in other words, catch the turns and improve my timing in the market.

Technical Indicators

There are so many technical tools available to traders today it can become confusing and make it easier to jump from one new indicator to the next, in an effort to find the one just right for them. New technology has made it easy to develop and test new indicators and has led to a surge of new systems available to the public. It was widely anticipated that new technology would open up the floodgates of prosperity to whoever was willing to pay the price for the system. However, the floodgates did not burst open. The computer made it easier, but not necessarily better.

The computer should be used as a tool to provide the information in the format you prefer, but it is not a substitute for experience and market knowledge. To be a successful trader, you need to get back to the basics and learn the characteristics of the market. All markets display certain inherent behavior. Learning to identify and exploit this behavior is essential in becoming a successful trader. It enables you to anticipate the market's movement and react in a purposeful way. Just like any other business, trading offers rewards to those who are willing to work hard, learn the markets and anticipate and react to changes quickly. Just as in business, traders who still look for the easy way to riches end up losers. I firmly believe that a trader will only experience real success if he learns the skills to trade, not from buying the latest system.

The Same, Only Different.

After some time it began to dawn on me, if I was reading all this information about the right way to trade, then other traders were probably reading and using the same information in the same way. If the saying was true, "80% of traders lose money," I quickly decided that I didn't want to look at the market in the same way the

80% looked at the market. That is when I started to look at the markets differently because someone had to have the information and expertise to trade the markets profitably. Instead of trading against these traders, I wanted to join them. We've all heard the old adage, "If you can't beat them, join them." I concluded, in order to do this, I'd have to start looking at markets differently and begin thinking "outside the box." I would no longer be able to be content to simply follow the mainstream and trade lagging and late indicators. The easiest way to accomplish this task was to know what the successful traders were thinking and then follow their lead. It all sounded so simple and I had my answer...price action.

It is said that the daily price action is the result of all the news and information and the analysis of how the information will affect the price of the underlying product. Based on all the information, the closing price is determined to be the fair price for that day. If the market closes higher, the bullish traders are in control and supply and demand warrants higher prices. When new or unexpected information enters the market, the large commercial firms and professional traders take action in the market, and that action is reflected in the price and that price action should tell me to buy/sell or stand aside. All I have to do is sit back and let the most successful traders do my analysis for me. Once they enter the market, the price action should alert me to the change of momentum so I can respond accordingly.

70% versus 30%

Markets have a tendency to only trend about 30% of the time while the other 70% of the time it is the accumulation phase of either consolidating in range or in a correction. I have never conducted a study of these facts, but I have been trading long enough to realize that it's probably true or very close to these percentages. When you look at a chart, you will see periods of consolidation, corrections or sideways movement. In between those consolidations there are periods when the market will break out and make an upward price movement or thrust (in a bullish market) or a downward price movement (in a bearish market) and then move into another corrective or consolidation phase. It is between the market consolidations – during the thrust - that a trader has the best opportunity to profit. Whether you are a swing trader (a person who tries to capture short-term swings in the market) or a trend follower, this is the price move traders are trying to capture.

Have you ever heard the old adage, "If you snooze, you lose"? It really holds true when it comes to trading. A trader has to be positioned and ready when the market makes its move. If you are not ready you will have to join the multitude of traders chasing the market who usually catch up at the end of the move. The market will not wait for you!

Without the knowledge or the proper preparation, you will not be ready and the market will leave you behind. It waits for no one. That is why understanding market behavior is so important. It gives you the "heads up" on what to expect next and prepares you to move at the appropriate time. I believe in trading the price action and patterns rather than the market news. I am always amazed by the ability of the market to respond to fundamental news before it happens or respond differently than anticipated because the report is already factored into the market. It seems the market has a sixth sense. So I make it a point to always remember, "What the market is doing is more important than what everyone expects it to do."

Swing traders or day traders have to be very careful and very patient. If they decide to concentrate on one market they are forced to make their profits during the 30% of the time the market is trending between consolidations periods. This can cause problems, because most traders don't have the discipline to sit and wait for the trade to set up properly. They feel the need for action and therefore tend to force trades that should not be taken. Trading is hard enough without adding this additional pressure and taking on unnecessary risks.

I have talked to many traders who think they are E-mini S&P traders and believe they can't look at other markets, because they don't understand them. I say, you don't have to know everything about T-Bonds, or Japanese yen, or even Coffee to trade them, all you need to know is market behavior and understand how to use the reoccurring price patterns on a chart. This allows you to

Chapter 1 – Trading is Easy – Anyone Can Do It!

diversify and look for the best sets up in several markets. Why force marginal trades in one market when you can find high probability trades in other markets? There are always markets setting up that offer great opportunities, all you have to do is find them. That's part of a trader's job.

The traditional way to enter a market is to wait for a breakout and buy the new high or sell the new low and follow with a protective stop, giving the market enough room to fluctuate and hopefully catch a big movement. This works fine, except a large portion of the potential gain is lost at the beginning of the trade and another large portion is given up at the end of the trade when the market pulls back to the stop price. If the trader has an advance idea where the correction will end and the new price move will begin, they can be ready to enter near the beginning of the move and exit near the end, before the market retraces.

Chapter 2

"The future is nothing but a repetition of the past."
W.D Gann

Time

I was first introduced to the concept of reoccurring cycles in the market over 20 years ago. Typically, cycles are determined by counting the days, or price bars, between two lows. It's generally accepted that all markets have certain defined cycles, such as a 28-day cycle in Cattle or a 21-day cycle in Soybeans. However, these cycles posed a problem for traders because sometimes they would bottom early or late and other times not at all and there was always the problem of longer-term cycles interfering with shorter-term cycles. This concept could be confusing to traders attempting to use cycles for timing and price projections. However, after reading about Roger W. Babson's theory of how Action/Reaction affected economic movements I began to look at the market from a different perspective.

Roger Babson was a highly successful entrepreneur, educator and philanthropist during the early 1900s. After graduating from the Massachusetts Institute of Technology in 1898 he was impressed with the teachings of the British scientist, mathematician, and philosopher Sir Isaac Newton, especially Newton's third law of motion—*"For every action there is an equal and opposite reaction."* He eventually incorporated Newton's theory into many of his personal and business endeavors.

He went on amass a considerable fortune –estimated at over $50,000,000—and was credited as the first investment advisor to warn of the 1929 stock market crash. Over the course of 33 years he authored 47 books, including his autobiography, *Actions and Reactions*. He also believed strongly in the need for specialized business education and established Babson College in Massachusetts and Webber College in Florida. Both are still using his philosophy of a specialized hands-on teaching approach.

Mr. Babson simply stated that economic phenomena move up and down. In other words, economic activity will not go in one direction without a movement in the opposite direction. From his statement about Action and Reaction, I theorized that market cycles could be looked at from a different point of view than the conventional approach. If the theory is truly based on natural reoccurring cycles one must only identify where the action ends and the reaction begins and use the past to project the future. So instead of looking from low to low, I should be looking for the exact center of the cycle.

What is a Reaction swing?

Turning a theory into a reality can be a daunting task. When one is introduced to the theory of A*ction/Reaction,* the first question that probably comes to mind is, "This all sounds great in theory, but can it be applied to real market situations?"

When attempting to solve a problem, the most difficult task is finding where to start. In this specific case, the problem was to identify what *Action* would lead to the *equal and opposite Reaction.* Markets will always have short-term fluctuations within a longer-term trend as buying and selling influences price action. It is within this price movement that I found the means to identify where the Action ends and the Reaction begins. Each time the market corrects (a short-term move in the opposite direction of the prevailing trend) and then resumes the current trend, an old cycle ends and a new cycle begins. This pattern occurs over and over again in every market, whether one is looking at individual stocks or commodity futures. I call this pattern the *Reaction swing.* See *Figure # 2.1*

Chapter 2 - Time

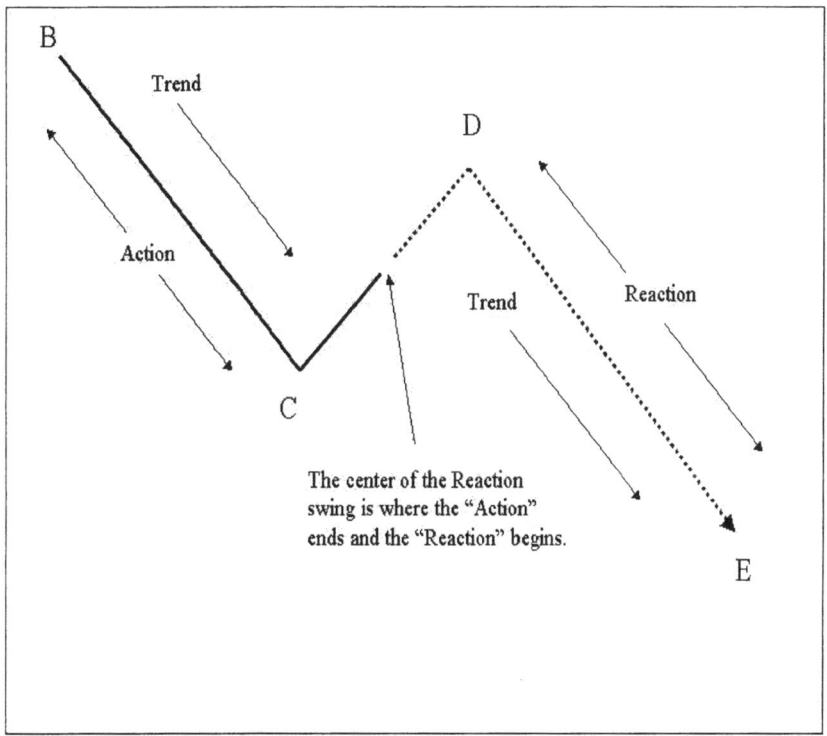

Figure # 2.1 – Action/Reaction

The Reaction swing is a reoccurring pattern that appears at the center of a cycle and divides the action segment from the reaction. Once this pattern is identified, all I need to do is look at *the past market action* and use that information to *project the future market reaction*. Because I can use this pattern to predict a future reversal – support or resistance - in the market, I call this the *Reversal date Indicator (RDI)*. Using this technique, I can use the market's own price action to predict and identify future support and resistance levels that act as price targets and possible turning points. This is important because, once a position is entered, I can project, with a high degree of accuracy, how long the current trend will continue. This advance knowledge of when a price move will most likely hit support or resistance. This information will help me determine the best time to adjust stops or exit at or near completion of the price move.

The *Reversal date Indicator* differs from many other technical trading methods because it uses the market's own predictive patterns to identify future market swings. Thus, it is a leading indictor that allows traders to trade from one market swing pattern to another with a high degree of confidence. Lagging indicators are based off past market action, but tend to confirm turning points after pivot point has been confirmed.

Having foreknowledge of a potential reaction point or Reversal date can give a trader a huge advantage in any type of market. The Reaction swing is the key to my methodology and it's where it all begins. If you can find the exact center of a cycle, you can look back at the beginning and then, based on this information, determine where the cycle (market price) will most likely go in the future and how long it take to get there.

A general observation of the markets shows that they do not trade in a straight line. There is always a struggle for control between the bears and the bulls. In this struggle, each side enjoys victories and suffers defeats, but one or the other will always win in the end.

For example, if a market makes a bottom formation after an extended downward move and then trades up to a price where many chart readers believe the market will run into resistance, the bearish traders will move in and sell. The bearish traders believe that the trend is still down and this correction provides a good selling opportunity. This, in turn, pushes the market down against the new upward trend. The result is a price correction also known as a retracement. When a new uptrending market corrects or retraces, the price will pull back to predetermined natural support levels. These price levels tend to support any market within any time frame. By using these support levels, I can determine when and where a correction will most likely begin or end before resuming the prevailing trend. It is this market action that forms a Reaction swing.

Natural Support and Resistance Levels.

The theory of natural support and resistance levels existing in the markets is not new. It has been discussed, argued over and interpreted for years with the Fibonacci theory being one of the most noted. Fibonacci is a centuries-old technical indicator that helps traders identify price fluctuations in non-random patterns. It evolved from a set of theories by Leonardo Fibonacci, a 12th century Italian mathematician whose research resulted in a set of numbers used today as a statistical tool for quantitative analysis.

My favorite Fibonacci (Fib) application is known as retracements. It is based on the observation that the market does not move in a straight line from point A to point B. Instead, along the way there will be ups and downs in the market price. Fibonacci retracement levels tell us in advance how far the price correction may go before it finds support or run into resistance.

After a significant move, prices will often retrace from the highs only to find support at the predetermined Fib support levels. Similarly, when a market bounces off a low, it will typically find resistance at the predetermined resistance levels.

To put these retracements on a chart, you have to identify a peak (high) and a valley or trough (low) on the chart. Between the high and low the most popular Fib retracements levels are 38.2%, 50%, 61.8%, and 78.2%. Knowing the Fib levels in advance allow me to determine where a market will most likely find support or meet resistance. I am a true believer that if something works then there is no use in "re-inventing the wheel" and since the Fib numbers are popular with traders the predetermined levels tend to be self-fulfilling and work well with the Reversal date Trading Indicator.

Combining the Fib retracement levels with a Reaction swing allows me to predetermine the buy and sell levels and project the price level at which the correction should end or begin. Therefore, I can take the theory and put it to good use by combining it with the Reversal dates. On the other hand, I can also take this information and put my own twist to it, as you will see later in this book.

Much has been written about the 50% retracement level. This means that the market will retrace 50% of the original move, find support, and then resume the current trend. Although I think this is a good rule of thumb, I have found the strongest reversals and largest moves begin beyond the 50% retracement level.

I have seen many times when an upward trending market retrace 50% of the original price move, find support, and then trade somewhat higher for a couple of days. Just as the trader begins to feel comfortable in his position, the market reverses again and trades to a new low.

Based on my research and experience, *I believe the strongest reversals take place between the 61.8% and 78% retracement levels. I call the price range between these levels buy/sell windows.* However, I have found the buy/sell windows works best if I give them a little wiggle room so I use 60% as the beginning of the window. Whenever a market enters a 60% buy/sell window, it is time to check for a Reversal date.

Using the buy and sell windows in conjunction with the Reversal dates provides a powerful blend of time and price. When a Reversal date occurs inside a buy or sell window, a strong price move can follow.

Action/Reaction Cycle

Since the Reaction swing is where the Action ends and the Reaction begins, it must be the center of a repetitive cycle. Therefore, the past should project the future. *Chart Figure # 2.2* better illustrates this concept. In this chart, the dominant trend is down and price movement between (B) and (C) is the Reaction swing. Mid-way in the trend, the market trades higher for a few days before turning lower and resuming the downward trend. The Reaction swing begins with the low pivot at (B) and ends with a high pivot at (C) and represents a minor price swing against the main trend. Once the market confirmed (see *Figure # 2.3*) the new pivot at (C) the *Reaction swing* from (B) to (C) is formed. As soon as the Reaction swing is established, I can determine the center of

Chapter 2 - Time

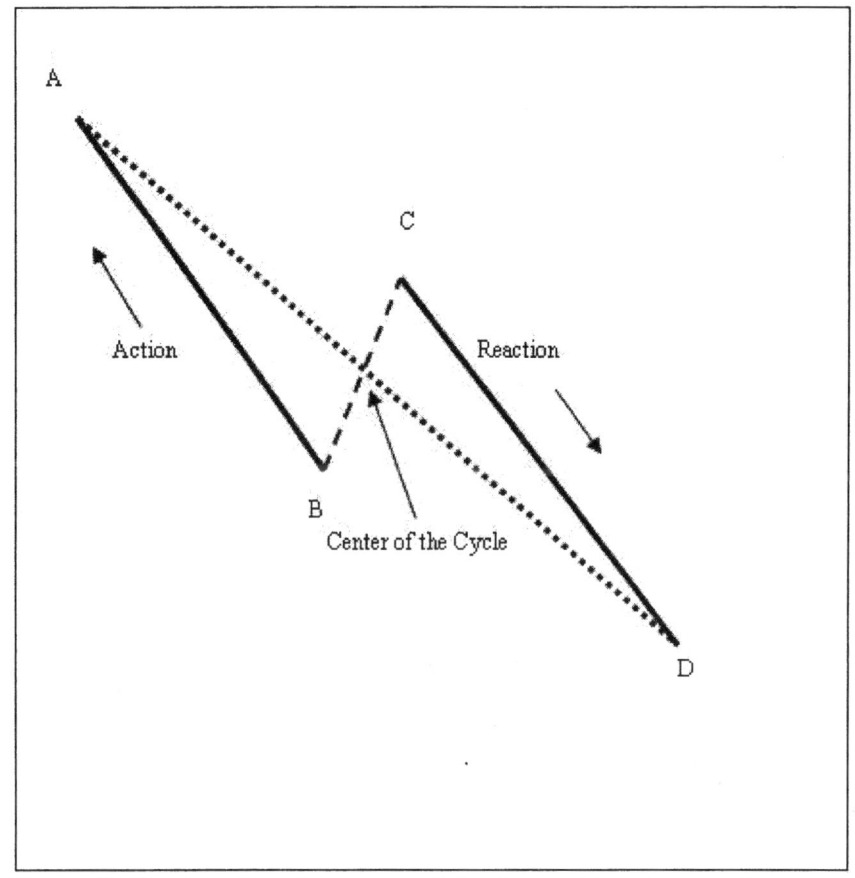

Figure # 2.2 – Finding the center of the Action/Reaction cycle

the Reaction swing by drawing a line from the high of the previous Reaction swing, marked as (A) in this example, through the center of the Reaction swing and find the exact center where the Action segment ends and the Reaction segments begins. *Figure # 2.2* better illustrates how to divide the *Action* segment from the *Reaction* segment.

Closing prices only

In traditional technical analysis, these chart patterns are called flags or pennants. Usually a trader will look at these patterns as a means to estimate the distance the market should move if and when it breaks out of the pattern. Although this method predicts a good target area, it is limited as it only offers a one-dimensional approach - that of Price alone.

A Reaction swing begins and ends with the *lowest* and *highest closing prices—always use the closing price*. For example, when a market is trending lower, it will always make a low closing price before it begins a corrective rally. This is the beginning of a possible Reaction swing. When this corrective rally comes to an end and then resumes the main downward trend, its pivot point is the highest closing price – and the end of the Reaction swing. The opposite occurs during an upward trending market.

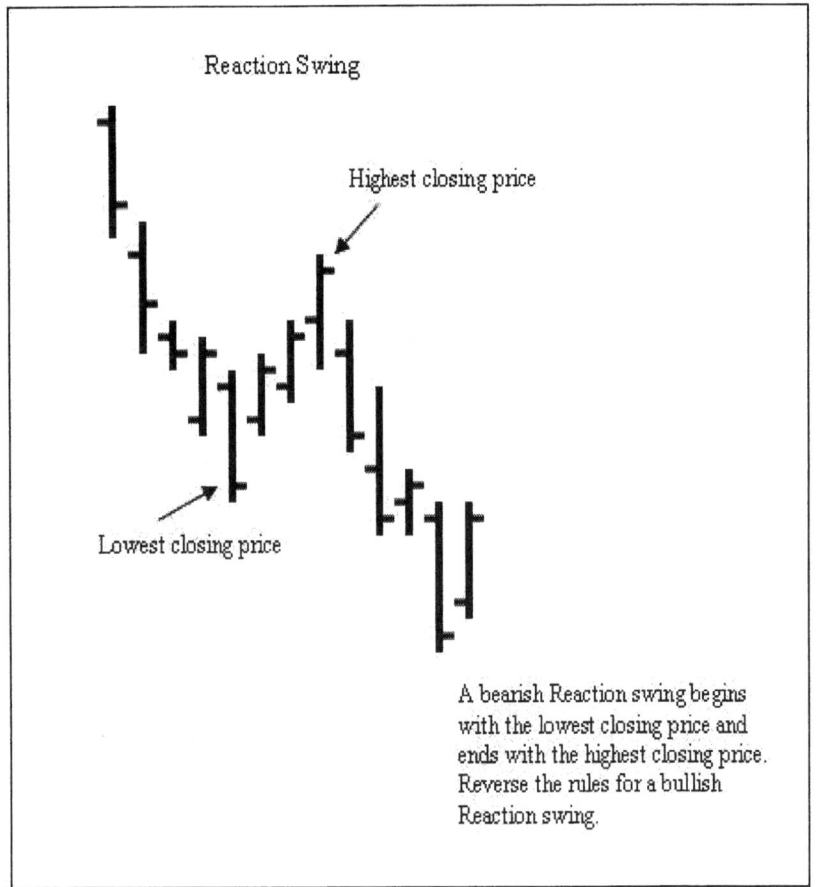

Figure # 2.3 –Reaction swing begins and ends with closing prices.

The beginning of the Reaction swing starts with the highest closing price before the resumption of the upward trend. Therefore, all you need to know are the dates of the highest closing price and the lowest closing price of the Reaction swing in order to move on to the next step - *projecting future turning points or reaction points in the market called Reversal dates. Figure # 2.3*

Pivot points

A Reaction swing consists of two pivot points, one at the beginning and one at the end. A price pivot contains a minimum of five consecutive price bars where the highest closing price (for a high pivot) is preceded by two consecutive price bars with lower closes and is followed by two consecutive price bars with lower closes. A low pivot is where the lowest closing price is preceded by two consecutive higher closes and followed by two consecutive higher closes. In other words, if the market is trending downward, a bearish Reaction swing forms when the market makes a low pivot and trades higher - against the prevailing trend - followed by a high pivot where the market reverses and resumes the downward trend without trading above the previous pivot high. See *Figure # 2.4.*

The low pivot is the beginning of the Reaction swing and the high pivot is the end of the Reaction swing. A sell signal is confirmed when a price bar trades below the pivot low, this is call the *Breakout bar.* (The opposite configuration would form a bullish Reaction swing and buy signal.)

A Reaction swing requires a minimum of three price bars, including the price bar with the **lowest closing price** and the price bar with the **highest closing price**, and at least one price bar in between. A Reaction swing can contain more than three price bars, but requires a minimum of three. See *Figure # 2.5.*

30   *Chapter 2 - Time*

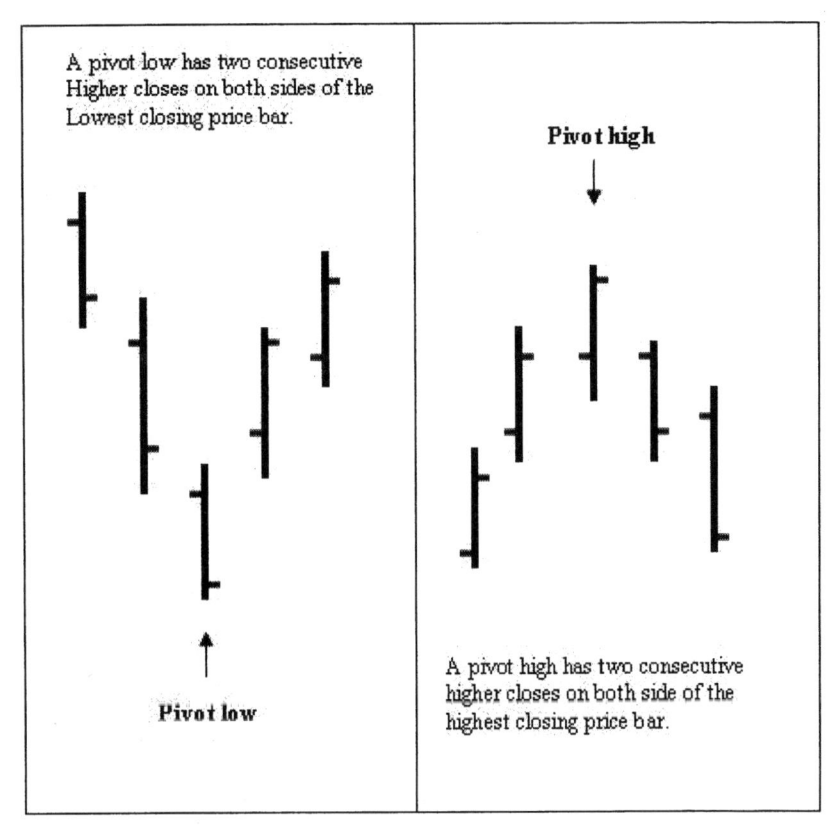

[Figure: Two panels illustrating pivot low (left) and pivot high (right). Left panel note: "A pivot low has two consecutive Higher closes on both sides of the Lowest closing price bar." Right panel note: "A pivot high has two consecutive higher closes on both side of the highest closing price bar."]

Figure # 2.4 –Pivot low and Pivot high

Reversal dates

Reversal dates and reaction points, are future dates where there is a high probability of a reaction in the market. The majority of the time, this reaction will be a reversal or a pause of the market's current trend. The reversal can be at either the end of a long-term price move or the beginning of a short-term price correction.

However, a small percentage of the time the market will not reverse on the predicted date. Instead, the market will begin to consolidate or form what I call a *continuation pattern*. This type of

Chapter 2 - Time 31

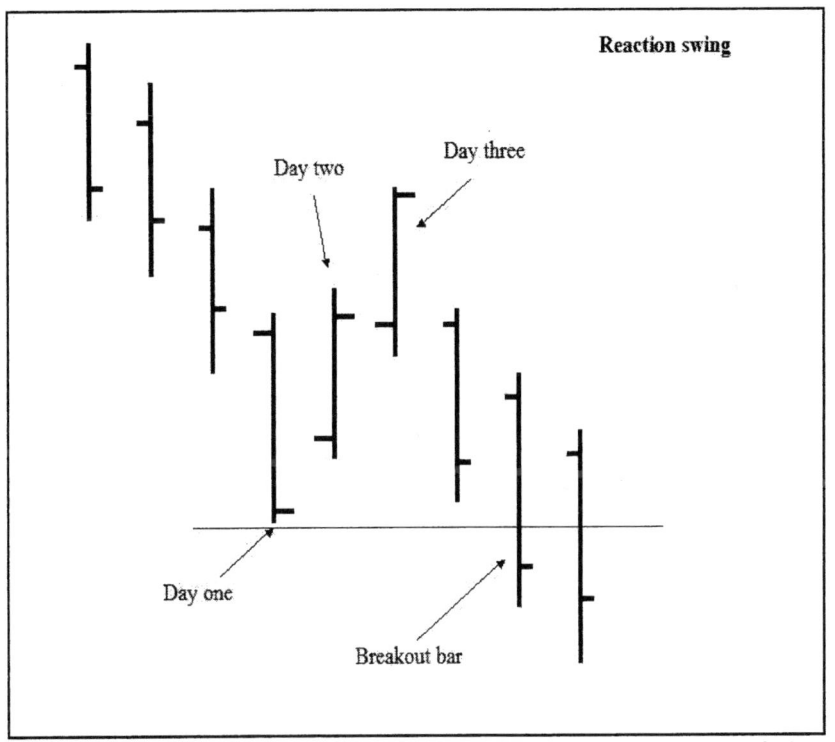

Figure # 2.5 – A Reaction swing consists of a minimum of three price bars.

pattern suggests that the market is not ready to reverse, but will continue to trade in the same direction as the current trend. This usually occurs when the market has been in a consolidation pattern (trading sideways).

On the predicted date, the market will generally break out of the consolidation pattern and continue the trend. Both the reversal and continuation patterns offer extremely important information to a trader.

Reverse/Forward Count

The key to predicting a future trend reversal is the reverse/forward count. I begin with the reverse count because it will give me the length of the action segment of the cycle. I can then use this information to forecast the reaction (future) market movement. The reverse count is a count of price periods backwards in time. The count starts at the beginning of the Reaction swing and counts in reverse to the beginning of the previous Reaction swing. This is the same whether in an advancing or declining market. In other words, in a downward trending market the reverse count will always begin with the first price bar to the left of the lowest closing price bar of the pivot at the beginning of the Reaction swing and count back to the lowest closing price bar of the previous Reaction swing. On the other hand, the reverse count, in an upward trending market, will always begin with the first price bar to the left of the highest closing price bar of the pivot that begins the Reaction swing and count back to the highest closing price bar of the previous Reaction swing. *(Please note: When a holiday falls on a trading day, it is counted as a regular day.)*

The forward count is simply the reverse count applied forward in time. The forward count begins with the first price bar after the end of the Reaction swing and goes forward in time the same number of price bars that the reverse count went backwards. *Remember, the end of the Reaction swing, in an upward trending market, is the lowest close of the downward price correction, and is the highest close of an upward price correction in a downward trend.*

Upward Trending Market

When the market is in an upward trend the reverse count will begin with the first price bar to the left of the highest close at the beginning of the Reaction swing. (In an upward trending market, the beginning of the Reaction swing is the highest closing price before the correction.) The count will continue in reverse to the highest closing price of the previous Reaction swing. The forward count begins on the first day to the right of the price bar with the lowest close at the end of the Reaction swing and counts forward the same number as the reverse count as shown in *Figure # 2.6.*

Chapter 2 - Time 33

September Dow Jones

The reverse count – in an upward trending market - begins on the first price bar to the left of the lowest close and counts back to the highest close of the previous Reaction swing.

The forward count begins on the first bar to the right of the lowest closing price and counts forward the same number of the reverse count.

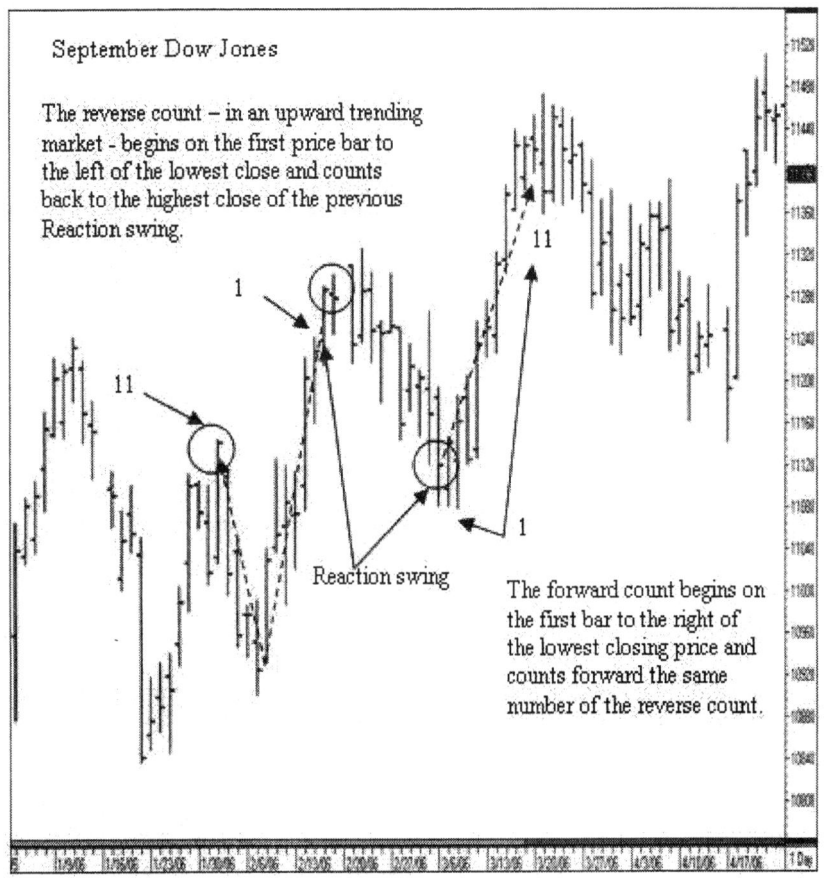

Figure # 2.6 – Reverse/Forward count in an upward trending market.

Downward Trending Market

The process is similar when the market is in a downward trend. The reverse count begins with the first price bar to the left of the beginning of the Reaction swing and counts in reverse to the lowest close of the previous Reaction swing. (In a downward trending market, the beginning is the lowest closing price of the low pivot point before the correction.) The forward count begins with the first price bar to the right of the highest close at the end of

Chapter 2 - Time

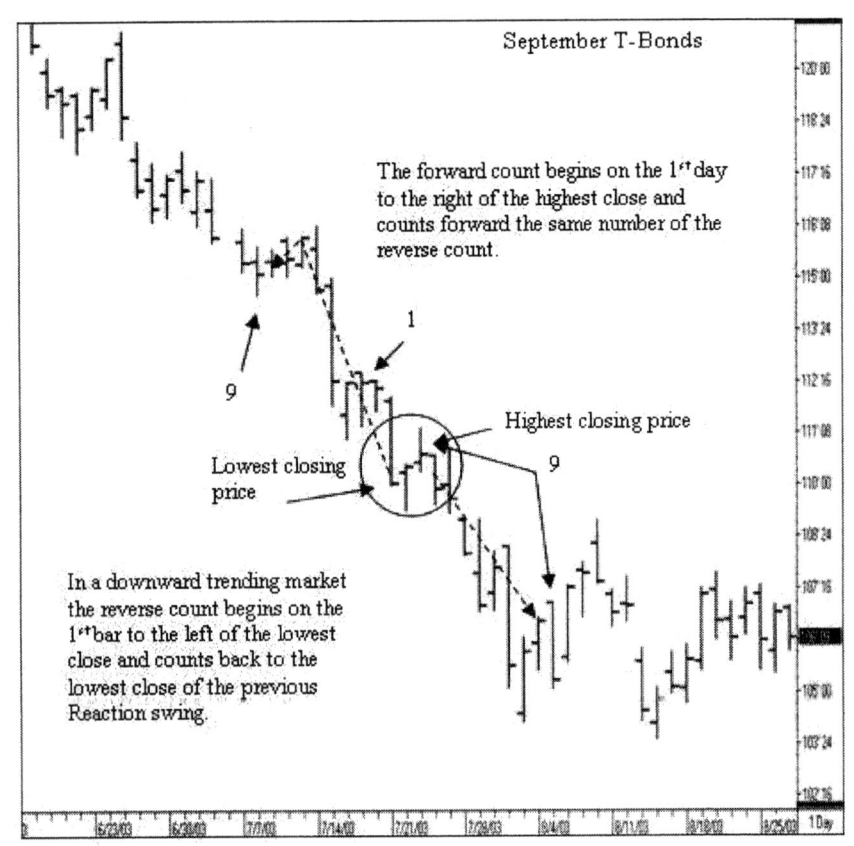

Figure # 2.7 – Reverse/Forward count in down trending market.

the Reaction swing and counts forward the same number as the reverse count as shown in *Figure #2.7*.

The end of a Reaction swing

The end of a Reaction swing is confirmed when there are two consecutive lower closes, thus confirming the high pivot, or two consecutive higher closes confirming the lower pivot of the swing pattern and the market continues in the direction of the main or longer-term trend. One knows for certain that the Reaction swing is confirmed, when the respective high or low pivot that marks the beginning of the Reaction swing is exceeded by the Breakout bar in the direction of the main trend.

Projecting Future Reversal dates.

It is not necessary to draw a line through the center of the Reaction swing when using it to project future Reversal dates. In order to project future Reversal dates, you only need to know the date of the highest closing price and the date of the lowest closing price. The rules for this process *in a downward trending market* are as follows:

1-Identify a Reaction swing. The beginning of a Reaction swing will be the price bar with the lowest closing price prior to a corrective rally and the end will be the price bar with the highest closing price.
2-Start on the first day to the left of this lowest close: consider it as day one and count each day or price bar going backwards.
3-Continue to count each day or price bar all the way back to the lowest closing price of the pivot at the beginning of the previous Reaction swing. (It is important to remember to count back to the lows in downward trending markets.) This is called the reverse count.
4-If a holiday falls on a trading day, it must be counted even if the market was closed.
5-Go to the end of the Reaction swing (in a downward trending market it is the day with the highest closing price) and complete the forward count as explained in rule # 6.
6-Begin with the first day to the right of the highest close and count forward the same number of days or price bars equal to the reverse count. For example, if the reverse count was 15 days, count forward 15 days.
7-Mark the date on the chart as the next potential Reversal date.
Note: Reverse the rules in an advancing market.

Common Mistakes

The most common mistakes that occur while using this trend reversal tool are usually the result of human error. Examples of human error include; miscounting periods, incorrectly identifying starting or ending periods of Reaction swings, misinterpreting a series of price bars as a Reaction swing, or trying to identify Reaction swings within trading ranges.

Misinterpreting a series of price bars as a Reaction swing may happen when you forget that the Reaction swings in a declining market are supposed to slant up, or that the Reaction swings in an advancing market are supposed to slant down. In other words, the group of price periods you identify as a Reaction swing may be slanting the wrong way.

Learning to correctly identify Reaction swings is vital when projecting future Reversal dates in the market. If you do not completely understand this process, go back and review this chapter and work through the examples before moving on to the next step. Without a complete understanding of the Reaction swing, the following information will not make sense. The next few examples will better demonstrate the identification process as it is applied in real market conditions.

Major Trend Reversals

Reaction swings can be part of larger price patterns consisting of a series of pivot points that are found in two different places of a market trend - each are treated differently. The first pattern we'll look at is the Trend Reversal pattern (TR) that occurs at major tops and major bottoms. The TR pattern consists of five pivot points occurring in a specific order with a Reaction swing being formed by the final two pivot points as shown in *Figure # 2.8*

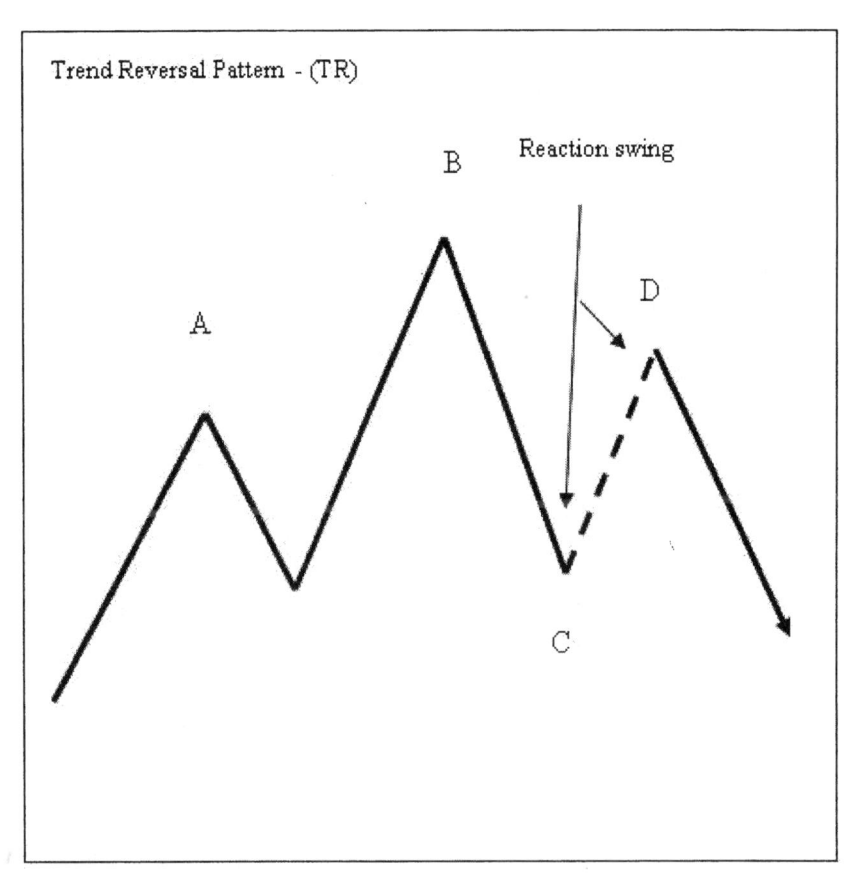

Figure # 2.8 – *Major Trend Reversal pattern (TR)*

This pattern may look familiar to many and is sometimes referred to by other names such as, Head and Shoulders top/bottom, M top or W bottom, or even as a1-2-3 top/bottom. However, I use the TR pattern in a very different way than what you may be accustomed.

The second pattern I like to use is called the Trend Continuation (TC) pattern and appears inside a strong trending market and follows a TR pattern. As the names states, this pattern signals a continuation of the current trend, but it also tells me much more. For example, a TC pattern can project how long the trend will continue and how far it may go. Like the TR pattern, the TC pattern also consists of five pivots, with the Reaction swing formed by the last two pivot points. However, for right now I want to concentrate on the Trend Reversal (TR) pattern.

I like to break the TR-pattern into two different types, based on how the patterns unfold. This is important because they have different rules to confirm an entry signal. As you read through the rules that define the two patterns you will notice I use a version of Fib numbers to identify retracement levels. I am making the assumption that you are familiar with the concept of Fib retracement levels.

When a market is at a major high or making a major turn, it will typically be followed by a pullback to support. This is where bullish traders tend to enter the market expecting another bullish leg and a run past the recent high. However, if the market is forming a TR pattern it will run into resistance somewhere between the 60% and 78% retracement levels and fail to move past the recent high. This swing pattern failure is the first sign of a market losing momentum and could lead to a shift in the trend. I call this pattern the Trend Reversal # 1 pattern or TR-1.

The TR-1 pattern requires the market to retrace over 60% of the initial price move from (B) to (C). At the 60% retracement level, I consider the market <u>inside the sell window</u>. The price bar that enters the sell window is called the *Signal bar*. When the price reaches the sell window, I will enter and order to sell when the price drops below the low of the *Signal bar* that entered the sell window. As soon as the price trades below the low of the Signal bar, the entry price is triggered and the sell signal is confirmed. As soon as the signal is confirmed a protective stop should be placed above the (B) high. (The rules are reversed for a buy pattern.)

Calculating Buy/Sell Windows.

The market enters into the buy/sell window when it has retraced 60% of the original move. In other words, if the prevailing trend of the market is down, the market would have to trade higher (against the trend) to enter the sell window.

Calculating the buy/sell window is a very simple and quick process – all you need is a calculator. Even though most, if not all technical charting software programs that can do this automatically, it is a good idea to know the process.

For a sell window, you take the high price of the current market swing and subtract the low price of the current of the market swing. The low is the price made just before the market began to trade higher against the prevailing downtrend. For example, if the high price is 7500 and the low price is 6500, the difference is 1000. Now calculate 60% of 1000. This equals 600.

Add the 600 points to the low price of 6500 to get 7100. This means that the market will need to trade up to 7100 before entering into the ideal selling window. Once the market has traded above 7100, a sell signal can occur anywhere between the beginning of the sell window and the recent high (in this case 7500). The following is a quick review of a sell window in a downtrend:

1-Once the market establishes an intermediate low and starts to trade higher from this low, subtract the high (the high price at the beginning of the prevailing trend prior to this intermediate low) from the low. This will equal the total price range of the original move, i.e.: 7500 – 6500 = 1000

2-Now multiply the range by 60%, i.e.:
1000 x 60% = 600

3-Add this total to the low.
6500 + 600 = 7100

4-This price (7100) is the beginning of the sell window.
To calculate a buy window, follow the same process except subtract the 60% total from the high price. When the market is in the sell window, in conjunction with a TR pattern, a major turn in the market can occur.

The Sell Window in the March Crude oil.

In *Figure # 2.9*, I use the March Crude oil chart to illustrate a sell window and Signal bar. The Crude oil topped at 69.15 (B) and then began a new downward trend. Crude oil continued to trade lower until it hit an intermediate low at 65.45 (C). The low was followed by a correction against the current downward trend. A quick calculation determined that 67.67 was the beginning of the sell window.

From the low at (C), the Crude oil traded higher over the next five trading days where it entered the sell window and identified a Signal bar when it reached a high of 69.00 - well inside the sell window. After the third day of trading inside the sell zone, Crude oil formed an outside day and broke sharply lower. This reversal was confirmed when the market broke below the low of the Signal bar, confirmed the TR-1 pattern and triggered the beginning of a substantial downward move. *Knowing in advance where a market is likely to reverse or at least run into support or resistance can only help give any trader an edge when entering or exiting a trade.*

Let's look at some examples of the TR pattern in action. *Figure # 2.10* features the March 2006 Crude oil and offers a good example of the TR-1 pattern. The March Crude had peaked at 69.15, but closed at 68.48 on January 20. The high close was followed by three consecutive lower closes that confirmed (B) as the high pivot. Crude rebounded with three consecutive higher closes - confirming a low pivot at (C) – and ended with a high closing price of 68.35 on January 30, putting the market inside the sell window.

(B) High – 6915 – (C) Low – 6545 = 370
370 x 60% = 222
6545 + 222 = 6767
The Buy window begins at 6767.

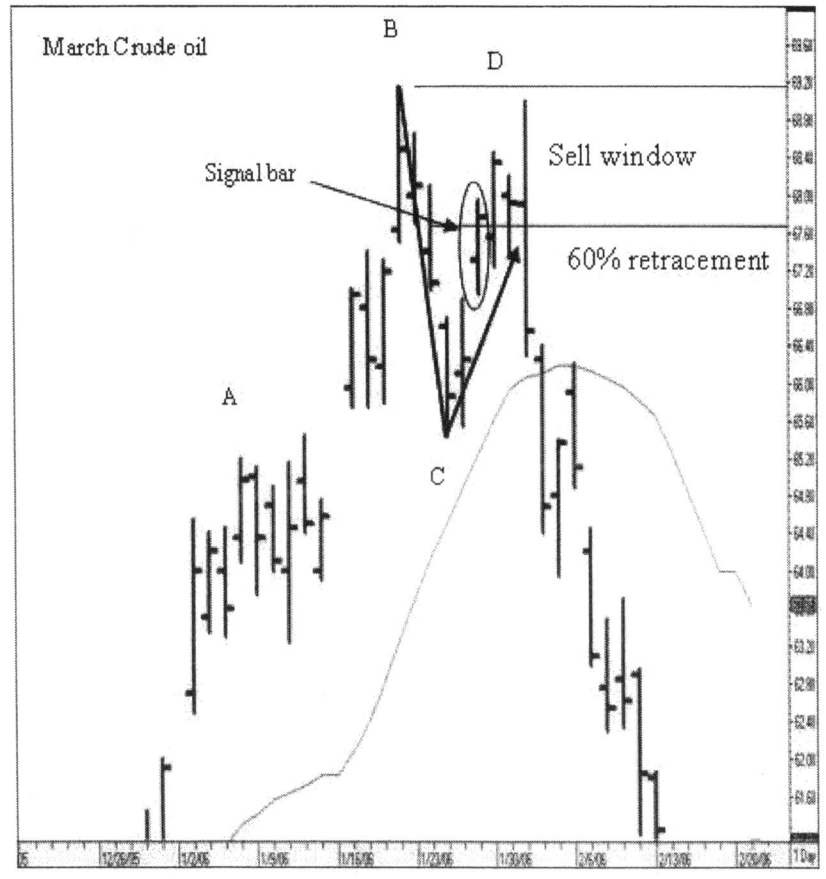

Figure # 2.9 – Finding the Buy/Sell windows

Since the market was within the sell window it was time to enter an order to sell if the March Crude oil traded below the low of the Signal bar inside the sell window. Since the January 30th price bar (D) was the price bar that entered the sell window it was considered the Signal bar, the order should be placed below the low of 67.25. Since the low was 67.25, the sell stop order should be placed at 67.20. Two days later (February 1) Crude oil reached a high of 69.00 but quickly lost momentum and turned lower. The 67.20-trigger price was reached and confirmed the reversal and sell signal.

The reverse/forward count began at (C) and went back to the beginning of the TR pattern (A). The count was 13 bars. I counted forward 13 days from (D) and determined a future Reversal date of February 16. In other words, the newly established downward trend should continue sideways or lower over the next 13 days, until it reaches the next Reversal date due on February 16. As you can see from the chart, March Crude oil fell over $17.00 before time ran out on February 16 and the market turned higher. The projected Reversal date identified the beginning and the end of a dramatic price collapse!

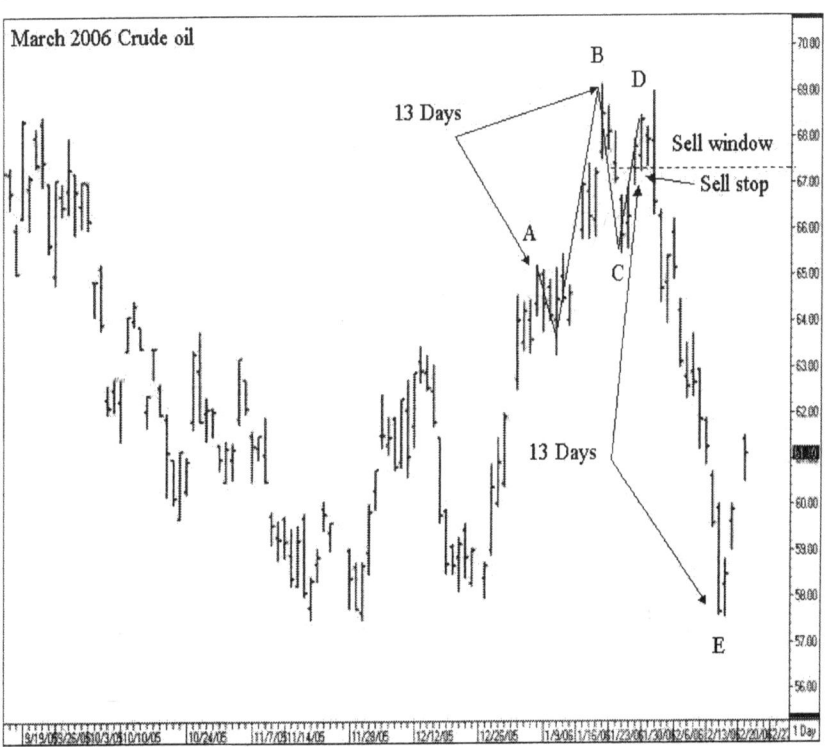

Figure # 2.10 – March 2006 Crude oil

Managing the Trade

Money management differs from trader to trader. Some traders are willing to take more risk than others who prefer to keep the stops very tight. This also happens on the other end of the trade, where traders differ in their exit methods. I believe one of the many benefits of the Reversal date Indicator trading methodology is that it allows all traders to incorporate their own preferences of money management.

Having said that, I would like to outline the way I like to manage the risk. As soon as the short position is triggered I suggest placing a protective stop above the beginning of the Reaction swing. (This is marked (D) on the Crude oil chart.) After the market has two consecutive lower closes below the trigger price – marked (C) – I will move the stop to just above the price bar the traded through the trigger price, the Breakout bar. After three consecutive closes below the pivot point the protective stop can be moved to the entry price. After the protective stop is at the entry price I will allow the market room fluctuate until the market approaches the projected Reversal date. At this point, I will tighten the stop by moving it underneath the low of the Reversal date. If the Reversal date closes higher, the stop is to just underneath the Reversal date price bar. At this point I can either choose to exit the position or continue to move the stop on a daily basis until the stop is hit and the position is closed.

20-Day Simple Moving Average

The Reversal date Indicator is based on market action and price behavior; therefore I use very few other technical or momentum indicators. Since most technical indicators are based off an average of past market action they are lagging in nature so their confirmation signals typically confirm after the market has reversed and moved beyond the high or low pivot. However, I will use the 20-day SMA (Simple Moving Average) as another confirmation tool when looking for a valid Reaction swing. I have found the best Reaction swing patterns form around the 20-day SMA. They may form below the 20-day SMA and break through to confirm the pattern, or form above the 20-day SMA and pull back to test the SMA before moving on. Either way, I believe it makes a stronger confirmation.

December Hogs

On August 26, December 2004 Hogs, *Figure # 2.11*, dropped below the pivot low of 62.10 made on August 17 (A) and closed at 61.17 marked (B). The following two sessions closed above 61.17, and confirmed August 26th as a pivot low. A couple of days later the market traded above the 20-day SMA (Simple Moving Average) and posted a pivot high of 64.37 on September 9 (C), before it entered a five-day correction that ended with a low close at 62.50 on September 8, marked as (D). The pullback from the (C) high had retraced below the 20-day SMA and more than 60% of the price move from (B) to (C), therefore the market was inside the buy window and the set up was complete and ready for me to enter an order to buy if the market traded above the Signal bar that entered the buy window. In this case the Signal bar was the fifth price bar from the September 1 pivot high. *(Remember, I treat a holiday the same as a trading day. Although the market was closed for the Labor Day holiday I will still count it as a trading day.)* The primary Reaction swing formed between (C) and (D) also completed the TR-1 pattern and set the stage for a rally when the Reaction swing buy signal is triggered.

It didn't take long for the buy signal to be triggered as the Hogs rallied the following day and closed above the previous two closes. This market action confirmed a longer-term TR pattern and triggered the buy signal to enter a long position at 63.15. As soon as the long position was triggered a protective stop was entered below (D).

Of course, the next step was to determine the projected Reversal date to see how long this bullish leg should last. When I do a reverse/forward count I count backwards from the beginning of the Reaction swing (C) to the pivot low that occurred before the major low, marked as (A). The reverse count equaled 11 days. Counting forward 11 days, from the price bar with the lowest close at (D), projected a future Reversal date of September 23. The December Hogs continued to trade higher into the September 23rd Reversal date with only one, two-day pause. The highest closing price was 71.20 and occurred on September 23, one day before a

Chapter 2 - Time   45

significant correction began. This date was predicted two weeks earlier.

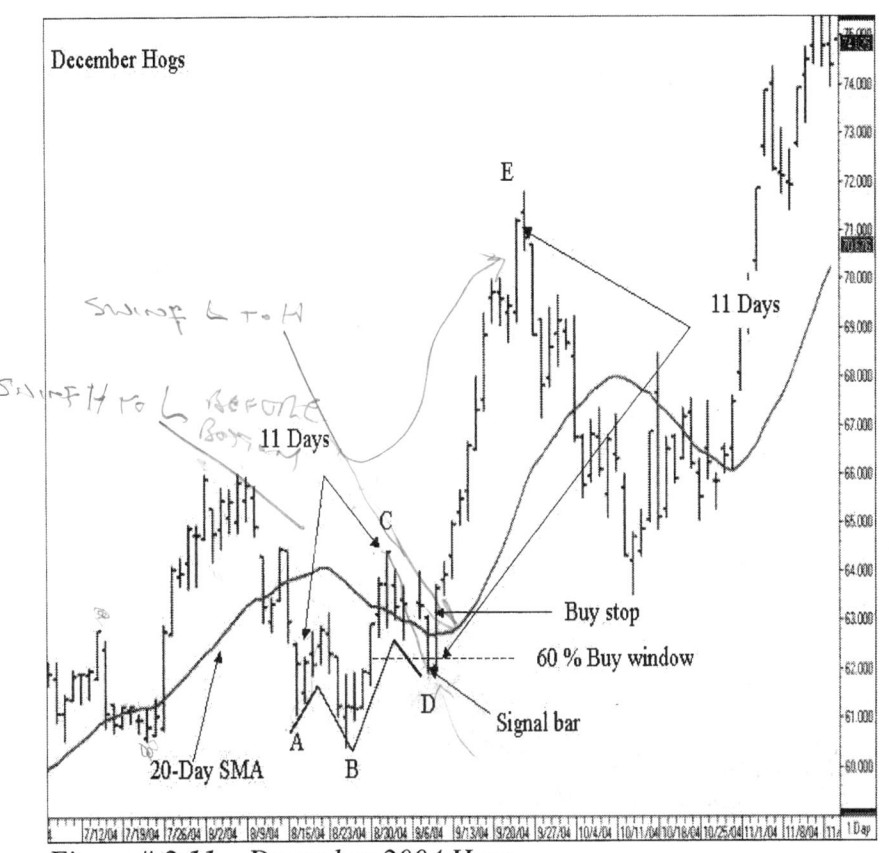

Figure # 2.11 – December 2004 Hogs

December 2005 Dow Jones

Figure # 2.12 - After a low close at 10,216 on October 13, the December Dow Jones futures shifted from a bearish market and began a new bullish trend. During the first couple of weeks the market was choppy, but it did form a bullish Reaction swing between October 19 and October 21. The beginning of the

Reaction swing is marked (C) with a high close at 10,447 and the end of the Reaction swing, with a low close of 10,240, is marked as (D). The low was inside the buy window; therefore the TR-1 pattern was in play. The Dow continued its erratic path over the next six days until it finally broke above the 20-day SMA and traded above the Reaction swing pivot high of 10,447. This price action confirmed the Reaction swing and triggered a buy signal for the Dow. As soon as the buy signal was triggered a reversal/forward count was done and the count was determined to be 20 days. The forward count of 20 days projected a future Reversal date on November 18.

The Dow continued higher, with only a couple of short-term pauses between the confirmation of the Reaction swing and the November 18 Reversal date. Four days before the Reversal date, the Dow Jones formed a small consolidation pattern when the market posted two consecutive lower closes. This was short-lived and the market broke to a new contract high of 10,795, on November 18...the Reversal date predicted three weeks earlier when the Dow was trading at 10,450.

The Dow Jones had rallied over 340 points – following the bullish TR-1 pattern confirmation - and posted a new high on the November 18th Reversal date. This is where the individual trader has to make a decision. They can exit with a very nice gain and look for the next pattern to unfold, or place a protective stop underneath the low of the Reversal date. Moving the stop would keep the long position in place as long as the market continued higher. If they elect to place the protective stop and stay with the position, the protective stop should be moved after the close of every day and placed underneath that daily low.

September T-Bonds

Figure # 2.13 - On June 13, 2003, the September T-Bonds closed at 122-21 (B). This high was above the previous pivot high posted on May 23 (A) and was followed by five consecutive lower closes that ended at 118-18 (C). A two-day bounce confirmed (C) as a

Chapter 2 - Time 47

Figure # 2.12 – December 2005 Dow Jones

low pivot and suggested the beginning of a bearish Reaction swing. June 25, started with a higher opening and reached a high of 120-30 (D) early in the session. The 120-30 high was more than 60% of the price swing from (B) to (C), putting the T-Bonds inside the sell window and established June 25 as the Signal bar. However, the rally faded quickly and turned lower where it dropped below the previous day's low of 119-03 and finally closed at 118-27, well below the previous pivot high. The following day began with a lower opening that triggered the sell signal and confirmed the TR-pattern at a major high.

The (D) to (C) swing pattern formed the primary Reaction swing and the last swing of the TR-1 pattern. As soon as the T-Bonds reached into the sell window a sell stop should be entered below the Signal bar that entered the sell window. However, in this case the low of the Signal bar was not known until the close. As soon as the T-Bonds triggered the sell signal a protective stop should be placed above the pivot high at (D). The next day, a sharp sell-off in the T-Bonds triggered the sell and pushed the market below the (C) low and closed at the bottom of the daily price range. After the market closed below the (C) low for two consecutive days, the protective stop should be lowered down to just above high of the Breakout bar. (The Breakout bar is the price bar that broke the support provided by the (C) pivot low. If a market closes below/above the pivot low/high for three consecutive days, it will most likely continue in the direction of the breakout.)

Now that I'm in a short T-Bond position I will use the information from the reverse/forward count to project how far and how long the next downward swing will most likely continue. The reverse count from the (C) low to the (A) high equaled 20 days. I used this information to project forward 20 days from the June 24th pivot high at (D)...the forward count projected a future Reversal date of July 22. As predicted, the T-Bonds continued to trade lower into the July 22 Reversal date. The T-Bonds dropped close to 10 basis points without any significant correction.

The value of this trading technique is in knowing - with a high degree of confidence - how long the market will continue in the current direction. One of the most costly mistakes a trader can make is to hold on to a winning position too long or exiting a position too early. With the Reversal date Indicator I can make a reasonable Time projection of when the trend will most likely end or begin a correction, allowing for a timely exit. Later in this book I will illustrate how to use the Action/Reaction method to make price projections in conjunction with the Time projections. It's just as simple and as effective.

Chapter 2 - Time   49

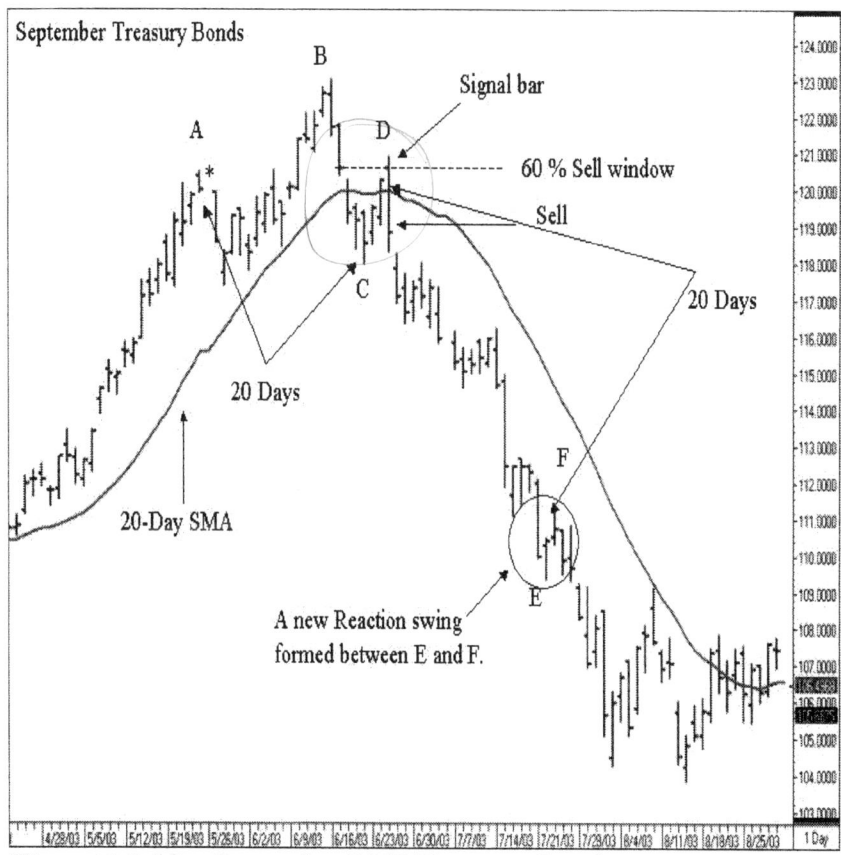

Figure # 2.13 – September 2003 Treasury Bonds

When the Trend Continues

Although the name Reversal date may imply the market will reverse on that day, that is not necessarily the way it works. What really happens is there is usually a reaction on or near the projected Reversal date. A high percentage of the time, the reaction results in a change of the existing trend or the beginning of a market correction (Reaction swing). On the other hand, a small percentage of time the reaction results in a continuation of the existing trend. Later in this book I discuss how to identify the difference between a reversal pattern and a continuation pattern. Both can be very helpful in your trading.

All of the chart examples I have shown so far have made either a major top or bottom on or near the projected Reversal date. This makes it very simple; I just exit the trade and wait for the next set up. However, nothing is that simple, but it doesn't have to be difficult or complicated either. Many times the market will just pause and form a new Reaction swing pattern near the Reversal date before continuing the trend. Even though the market has just offered a great trading opportunity from the TR pattern, if there is more to the trend I want to take advantage of the new opportunity... and there is a way to do just that. It is called the *Trend Continuation pattern (TC)* and - like the TR pattern – it can be a very useful and sometimes amazing tool for a trader who understands market behavior.

Since I am still talking about the TR pattern in this chapter, I don't want to get into the specifics of the Trend Continuation yet, but I did want you to be aware that there is a very simple way to take advantage of the extended market move as illustrated in this example of the September T-Bonds. The TR pattern triggered a very nice trade, but it was not the end of the move. I think you will be amazed at the information it provided.

December Coffee

Figure # 2.14 - After a sharp rally, the December 2004 Coffee peaked with a high closing price at 9030 on May 28. This high was quickly confirmed as a high pivot when the market pulled back to establish a low on June 7, followed by a three-day rally into June 10. The June 7 pivot low was the beginning of a new Reaction swing and the June 10 high was the end of the Reaction swing. This Reaction swing also completed a major TR-1 pattern and indicated the end of the upward trend and the beginning of a new downward trend.

Since the June 10 high peaked inside the sell window a sell order should be placed underneath the low of the June 10 Signal

Chapter 2 - Time 51

bar. The sell trigger price was hit the following day, when the market traded below the Signal day's low and closed below the (C) low. A soon as the 87.80 trigger price was elected, a protective stop was placed above the high of the June 10 price bar (D). The reverse/forward count from the (C) low back the pivot high (A) high equaled 19 days. (This TR-1 pattern is slightly different from others we have looked at so far, but it is treated the same.) The forward count from the (D) projected a future Reversal date of July 9.

The December Coffee plunged over 1,400 points in 19 days, before posting a low pivot on July 9...the Reversal date predicted almost three weeks earlier!

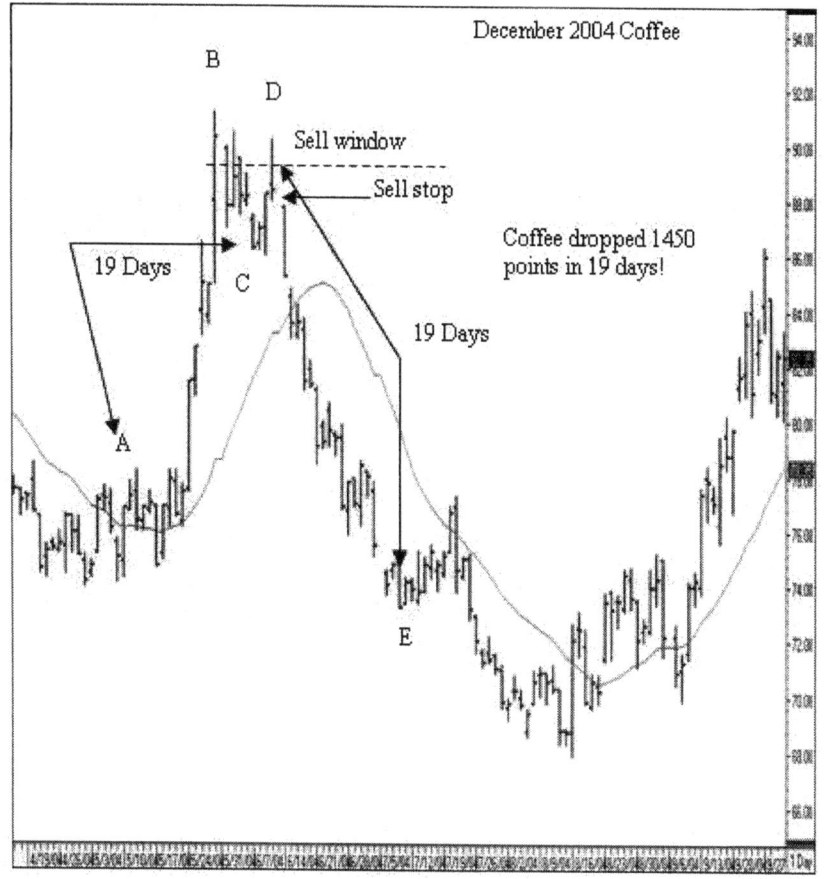

Figure # 2.14 – December 2004 Coffee

Trident Microsystems Inc. (TRID)

Figure # 2.15 - After several days of choppy trading, Trident Microsystems peaked at 31.47 before it closed at 31.07 on April 19, 2006. Two days later, the stock found support at the 20-day SMA and bounced higher over the next two days, confirming the April 19 low as a pivot low and the beginning of a Reaction swing. The rebound reached a high of 31.23 - well within the sell window that began at 30.52 – therefore I was looking at a TR-1 pattern. The sell signal would be triggered when the market traded below the low of the Signal bar that reached inside the sell window. In this case, the Signal bar it is the price bar of April 25 with a low at 30.03. On April 26, Trident Microsystems rolled over, traded through the trigger price of 30.00 and confirmed the sell signal that began a sustained price decline.

The reverse count, from the lowest close at (C) back to the lowest closing price at (A), equaled 12 days. The forward count of 12 days, from the highest close at (D), implied a futures Reversal date of May 11. TRID continued to trade lower and reached a close of 25.14 (E) on the May 11 Reversal date, followed by a six-day rebound to 28.07. Using the Reversal date Indicator the short position could have been closed near the low and before the sudden corrective rally!

Microsoft (MSFT)

Figure #2.16 – During the period between August 5, 2005 and November 18, MSFT offered two different views of the TR-1 pattern. After peaking at 27.94 on August 5, Microsoft traded lower until it found support at the 20-day SMA where it posted a low close of 26.72 on August 19. Eight days later the market peaked at 27.44 on August 31. This price was slightly above the 60% retracement level (27.42), therefore it is a TR-1 pattern. In this case the Signal bar occurred on August 31 with a low of 27.04 so the sell stop would be placed at 27.02.

Figure # 2.15 – Trident Microsystems (TRID)

Two days later the market dropped below 27.04 and closed at 27.02. The TR-1 pattern was confirmed and a short position triggered. Now for the reverse/forward count. The reverse count, from the pivot low at (C), back to the beginning of the TR-1 pattern, marked as (A) (July 21) – equaled 21 days. Counting forward 21 days from the end of the Reaction swing (August 31) marked (D) projected a future Reversal date of September 29.

Microsoft traded consistently lower over the next 17 days, finally hitting a low of 25.12 on September 23. From this low, the market traded higher over the next four days and peaked on September 29...the date projected over two weeks earlier. This is a little different look than I have shown you with the other examples

Chapter 2 - Time

(I will address this pattern in more detail in the Trend Continuation portion of this book), but I wanted to show what happens when the correction or retracement ended on a Reversal date. *(A market that makes a high pivot on a projected Reversal date will typically turn lower and a market that makes a low pivot on a Reversal date will typically turn higher. This can offer valuable information about the possibility of the trend continuing.)*

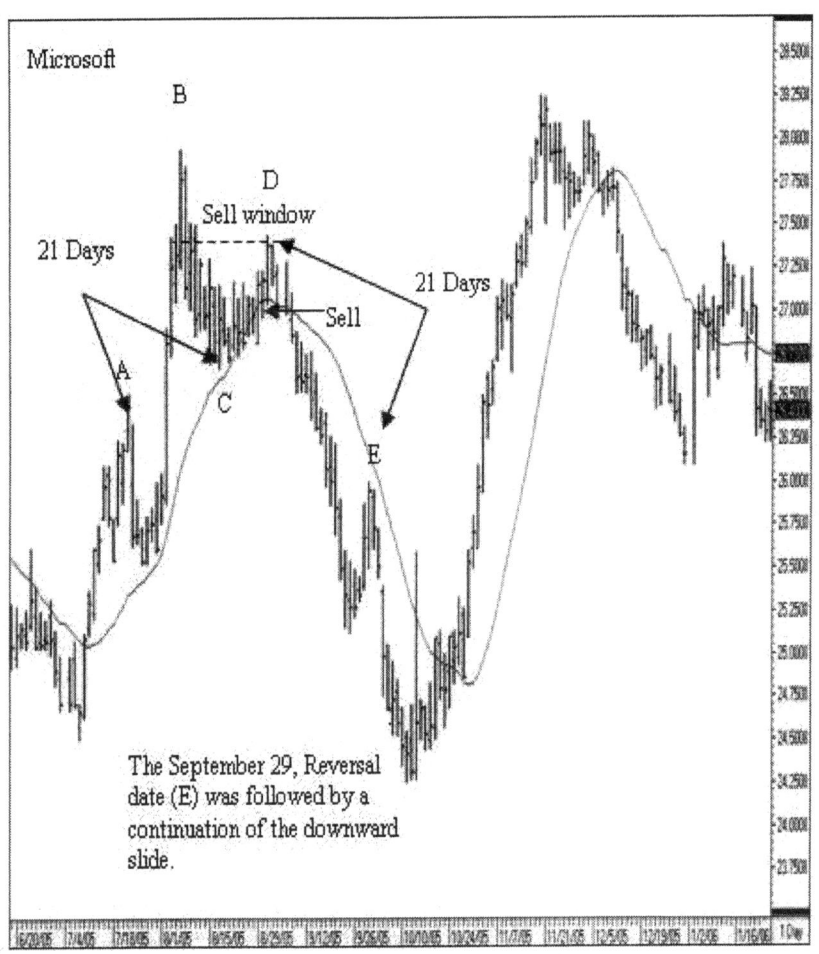

Figure # 2.16 – Microsoft (MSFT)

Buying Microsoft

Figure # 2.17 - The September 29th Reversal date, the highest closing price of the correction, was followed by a price collapse into October 11, where it finally bottomed at 24.25.

The October 11, low proved to be significant when the market turned higher and traded into the 20-day SMA where it posted a high close at 25.09 on October 19. This high was followed by two consecutive lower closes that confirmed October 19 as a high pivot point and the beginning of a new bullish Reaction swing. The two-day retracement ended with a low of 24.57, just slightly more than 60%. This put the market inside the buy window and confirmed the pattern sequence as a possible TR-1 pattern. The trigger price of 25.02 was hit on the following day and buy was confirmed.

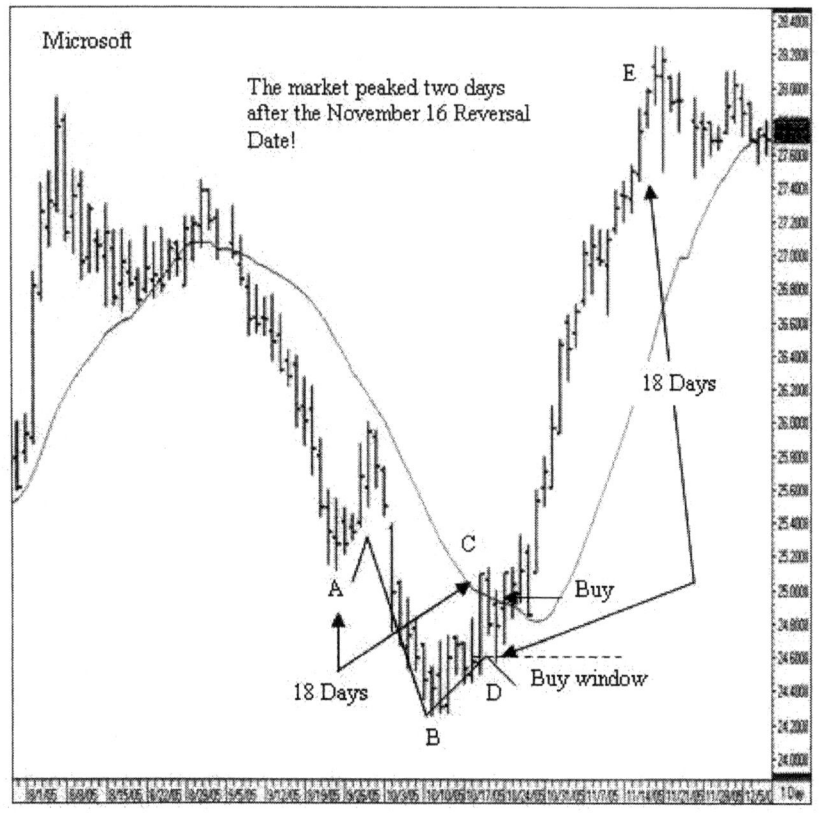

Figure # 2.17 – Microsoft – (MSFT)

The reverse count equaled 18 days, which in turn projected a future Reversal date of November 16. After triggering the buy signal at 25.02, Microsoft continued to move higher over the next 18 days and reached 27.88 on September 23. The Reversal date missed the major high by two days!

A major TR pattern generated a major sell signal followed by another TR pattern that generated a major buy signal, both offered significant trading opportunities with limited risk.

Identical Closes – Which One Should I Use?

Before I move on I want to talk a little about the reverse count to September 23, marked (A). The closing price on September 23 was 25.27. The next trading session was on Monday, September 26 and the closing price was also 25.27. When this happens I will always use the closing price that occurred first, in this case September 23. On occasion, a market will have three identical closing prices in a row. This is rare, but I have found the best results come by using the closing price in the center for your reverse count.

TR-2 Pattern

Market Corrections in a Strong Trending Market

There is always a "but" or "however" when dealing with the markets because nothing works 100% of the time. Using 60% retracements for buy and sell windows is an excellent technique for most markets. However, when the trend is extremely strong, the market will not usually retrace even close to the 60% level. Instead, the market will begin to make small and quick corrections that usually last three to seven days. The stronger the market, the shorter the correction time period. These strong trending markets will normally retrace between 30% to 40% of the original move - the Fib retracement number is 38.2%. In this type of market the retracement will typically fail to reach the 60% retracement level and therefore will not meet the criteria for the TR-1 pattern. Instead it forms the second type of Trend Reversal pattern I call the TR-2 and the entry methods are treated differently than the TR-1.

The TR-2 pattern is almost identical to the TR-1 pattern except the corrective rally off the (C) low—in a new downward trending market—does not reach the 60% sell window, therefore there is no Signal bar. Instead the corrective rally will fail early and turn in the direction of the newly formed trend. This is a sign of a strong trending market and subsequent price move following the pattern confirmation can be robust.

First, let's review the entry rules for a TR-2 pattern in a new downward trending market. As soon as the low pivot has been confirmed at (C), I enter a sell stop underneath the lowest low of the pivot. When the price penetrates the low and triggers the sell stop, a protective stop is placed above the high at (D). The price bar the breaks the support and triggers the sell signal is called the *Breakout bar*. The rules are reversed for a buy signal. Let's look at some examples of the TR-2 pattern in action.

I am a believer in using the market's own price behavior because it is a leading indicator that helps with two important aspects of trading; first, the market's own price behavior will provide signals that identify the beginning of a price move and secondly, it will let you know very quickly if the signal is correct. Other technical indicators such as Stochastics, RSI and Moving averages, etc., are considered lagging indicators because the entry signal typically occurs after the market move is already in progress and acts as a confirmation of the new trend. Don't get me wrong, there are certain times when I will us a Stochastic or a RSI to see if there is a divergence forming and use it as confirmation of my other signals and they can be very effective if used properly. However, the indicator I use the most, with the Reversal date Indicator, is the 20-day Simple Moving Average (SMA).

Although I look at the 20-day SMA in conjunction with the TR-1 pattern, I do put more emphasis on it when I am looking at a TR-2 pattern. I like to see the Reaction swing form around the 20-day SMA. For example, if the Reaction swing forms underneath the 20-day SMA the signal bar must trade through the 20-day SMA. On the other hand, when a market has already passed through the 20-day SMA and formed the Reaction swing above the 20-day SMA, it has a tendency to pullback to the 20-day SMA and sometimes penetrates the average before resuming the dominant trend and confirming the Reaction swing. Either way, I prefer to see the (C) to (D) Reaction swing form around the 20-day SMA.

May Soybeans

Figure # 2.18 is a chart of the May 2005 Soybeans. Between January 21 and February 17, the market completed a TR-2 pattern, ending with a Reaction swing. The pattern began with low pivot of $5.16 ¼ on January 18 marked (A) – which was followed by a five-day rally into a pivot high at $5.24 on January 25. The rally failed and the market dropped to a new contract low close of $5.02 ¼ on February 4 (B) before turning higher and confirmed the pivot low. The subsequent rally hit a short-term peak at $5.36 ¼ on February 14 (C) followed by a three-day correction that ended near the 20-day SMA and bottomed on February 16 (D). From here, the market posted a low close of $5.34 ¾ before resuming the new upward trend and forming a bullish Reaction swing. The five pivots I just described formed a TR-2 pattern and confirmed a trend shift from a downward trending market to an upward trending market. *(Note: The Reversal date Indicator uses <u>closing prices only</u>, when confirming price patterns and Reaction swings.)* Since the retracement from (C) to (D) was less that 60% it didn't meet the criteria for the TR-1 pattern, therefore the buy signal and entry will not be triggered until the Soybeans trade above the beginning of the Reaction swing at point (C).

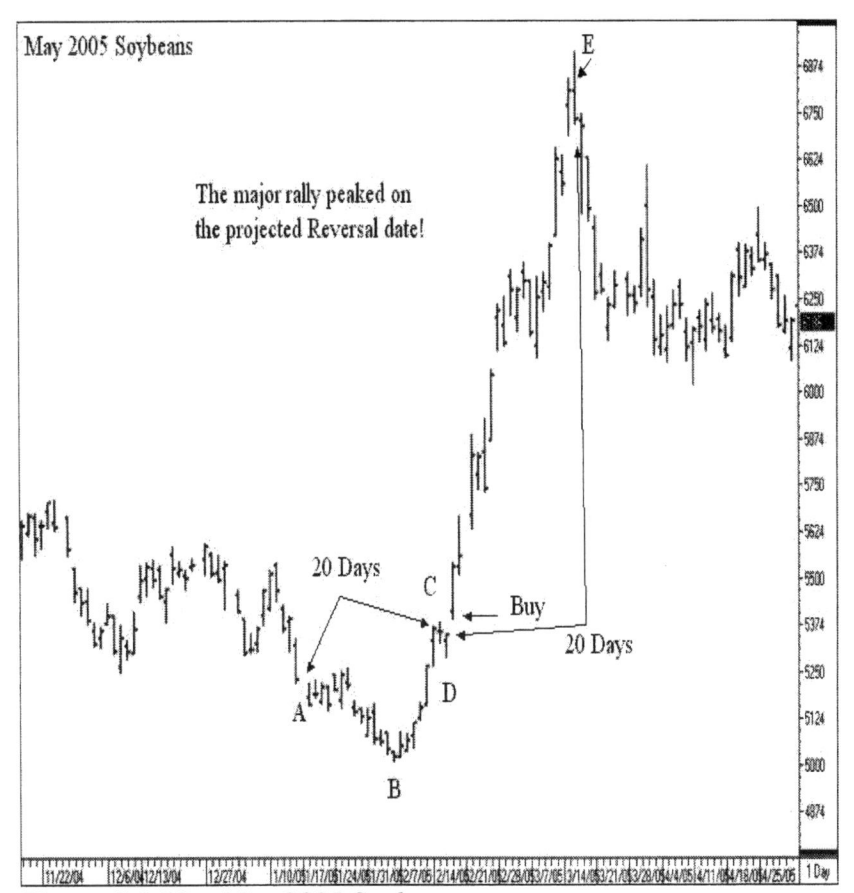

Figure # 2.18 – May 2005 Soybeans

Now, I concentrate on the price swing between the last two pivot points marked (C) to (D). This correction is the *Reaction swing*, which will be used to confirm the buy signal and identify the end of the TR-2 pattern.

On February 17, May Soybeans opened higher than the previous day's high and traded above the beginning of the Reaction swing (C) leaving a gap from $5.35 to $5.39 in the process. The Breakout bar confirmed the Reaction swing and the new upward trend. It is also a TR-2 pattern buy signal. The buy signal was triggered when the market traded above the pivot high of $5.36 1/2 (C). As soon as the entry is confirmed, a protective stop is entered underneath the pivot low at (D) and a reverse/forward count is completed to project the future Reversal date.

The first step in the reverse/forward counting process is to find the price bar with the highest closing price of the pivot at the beginning of the Reaction swing marked (C). Starting with the first daily price bar to the left of (C), begin counting the price bars in reverse until you reach the lowest closing price of the low pivot marked (A). The reverse count ends on January 17, but the market was closed on this date due to a holiday. *(Note: If a holiday occurs at the beginning of a Reaction swing I will consider the holiday as the pivot high or pivot low. A also count to this point because it is the beginning of the TR-2 pattern and represents the beginning of the current cycle.)* The reverse count equaled 20 days. Next, I went to the pivot point at the end of the Reaction swing (D) and began the forward count. Starting at the price bar with the lowest closing price I began counting forward 20 price bars, beginning with the first price bar to the right of the lowest closing price. (Note: *February 21st was a holiday that occurred during the week but I counted it as a trading day even though the market is closed.)* Counting forward 20 days suggested a reversal day was due to occur on March 16. In other words, the current market trend should continue for the next 20 days.

After the Reaction swing was confirmed the Soybeans remained in a strong upward trend for the next 20 days and reached $6.91 1/2 on the projected Reversal date of March 16. At this time I had to make a decision, I could either exit and close out a very profitable position or place the protective stop under the Reversal day low and continue to hold the long position.

The following day—called the Trail day—Soybeans traded below the previous day's low and continued lower for the next several days.

August 2005 Gold

Figure # 2.19 - On June 9, 2005, August Gold posted a low of $423.00 before it closed at $426.10. The low was right at the 20-day SMA. This pattern caught my attention because the market had closed lower over the previous three days and bounced off the support provided by the 20-day SMA. A possible Reaction swing had set up; if the market traded above the previous pivot high of $429.50—marked as (C)—the bullish Reaction swing and the major TR-2 pattern would be confirmed. In other words, a trade above $430.00 would confirm the Reaction swing and trigger the buy signal. It didn't take long for the Gold to reveal its intentions. The next day, gold traded through the $430.00 trigger price and closed at 431.10. Once the trade was entered the protective stop was placed underneath the pivot low price bar and the reverse/forward count completed. The reverse count from (C) to (A) equaled 10 days.

Projecting 10 days forward from the pivot low at (C) forecasted a future Reversal date for June 23.

After reaching the $430.00 trigger price, Gold continued higher and rallied over $14.00 dollars with only a one-day correction between the Reaction swing and the Reversal date! Right on schedule, Gold peaked at $444.20 on the June 23rd Reversal date, before beginning a 15-day correction that fell all the way back to $419.00.

62   Chapter 2 - Time

Figure # 2.19 – August 2005 Gold

December 2005 Gold

Figure #2.20 -The November 4th pivot low marked the end of an A-B-C correction and suggested the Gold was ready to resume the longer-term upward trend. However, it was the three-day consolidation at the 20-day SMA—marked (C) and (D)—that caught my eye. On Friday, November 11, Gold closed at $469.40

followed by a lower close of $469.10 on November 14 and $469.00 on November 15. This price action had formed a potential Reaction swing. It may appear to be a small pattern, but a small pattern can be just as explosive as a larger pattern.

Since the low of the swing pattern is well above the 60% retracement level, I set the buy stop above the (C) high. The very next day, Gold exploded at the opening and started trading at $473.70. The rally continued throughout the remainder of the session and finally closed at $479.10.

The reverse count from (C) to (A) equaled 16 days, therefore the forward count from the low at (D) projected a future Reversal date for December 7.

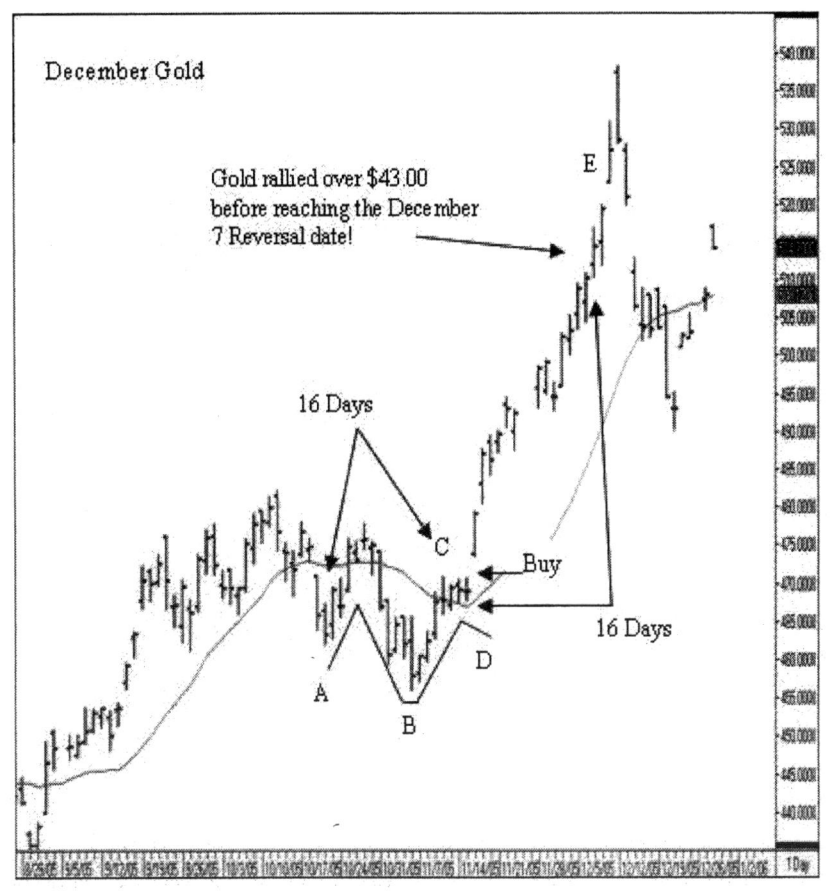

Figure # 2.20 – December 2005 Gold

The market followed the cycle like clockwork as it continued to climb into the predicted date. Sixteen days after the entry signal was triggered at $473.70, on November 16, Gold reached a high of $517.00 and posted a major high of $538.50 three days later. Gold had rallied over $43.00 in 16 days!

September 2006 Wheat

Figure # 2.21 - September Wheat formed a three-day Reaction swing between May 2 and May 4. Looking at the chart, in *Figure #2.21* you can see the Reaction swing formed around the 20-day SMA with the May 4th low just below the moving average. So far the market had retraced slightly more than 38% so it was considered a TR-2 pattern and a buy stop was placed above the pivot high of $3.82 ¾ at (C). The following day, May 5, Wheat gapped higher and began trading at $3.81, slightly below the pivot high of 382 ¾, but continued higher for the remainder of the day and finally closed at 386. This price action the price action had confirmed the bullish Reaction swing and triggered the buy signal. The reverse count from (C) back to the beginning of the TR-2 pattern (A) equaled 12 days. *(The lowest close was on Monday April 17, however the market was closed on the previous Friday and left a gap on the chart. If a gap appears at the beginning or end of a swing pattern, I consider it as the pivot high or pivot low. Therefore, the beginning of the TR-pattern was April 14.)*

The forward count from the low pivot at (D) projected a future Reversal date of May 22. September Wheat continued the strong rally and reached a high of $4.41 on the May 22nd Reversal date (E). The market opened higher on the trail day but failed to find new buyers and turned lower. The rally had ended and Wheat formed a new bearish TR-pattern that turned that confirmed a sell signal that was followed by lower prices over the next three weeks. The September Wheat is a good example of the type strong trending market action that typically follows a TR-2 pattern signal.

Chapter 2 - Time

[Chart: September Wheat]

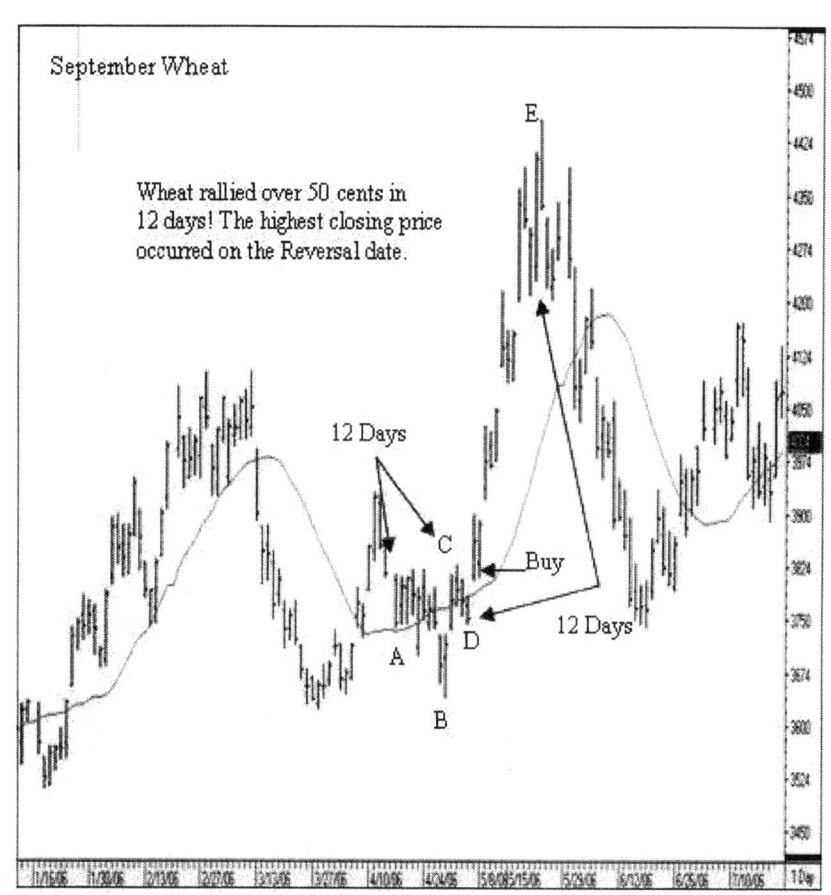

Wheat rallied over 50 cents in 12 days! The highest closing price occurred on the Reversal date.

Figure # 2.21 – September 2006 Wheat

September 2006 Cocoa

Figure # 2.22 - A soon as the September Cocoa confirmed a Reaction swing, with a pivot high on June 16 (C) followed by a pivot low on June 20 (D), it was time to do the reverse/forward count. The count from the high close at (C), back to the low at (A) equaled 14 days. (*The market was closed for Memorial Day and left a gap on the chart right in the center of the pivot low. Both the day before and the day after the holiday closed at the same price, 1,489, therefore, I will count the gap day as the low for the*

66 Chapter 2 - Time

reversal count.) Projecting forward, 14 days from the low of the Reaction swing indicated a future Reversal date due on July 10.

Four days after posting the low at (D) Cocoa traded above the previous pivot high at 1,555 – the beginning of the Reaction swing – and triggered a buy signal at 1560. During the following 10 trading days, Cocoa rallied to a high of 1,737. The high was reached on the projected Reversal date of July 10! Six days later, Cocoa was traded below 1,500; that's a 182-point rally into the Reversal date followed by a 237-point collapse after the Reversal date.

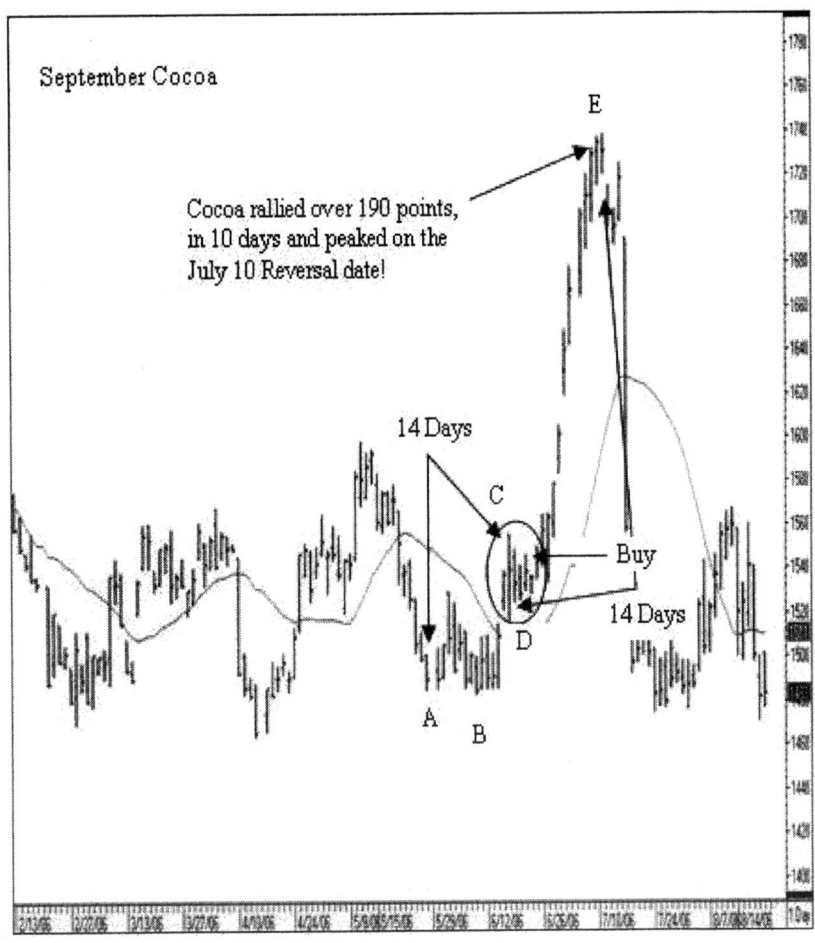

Figure # 2.22 – September 2006 Cocoa

July 2004 Silver

Figure # 2.23 - July Silver peaked at 8.235 on April 6. This high proved to be the end of a strong three-month rally and the point where Silver quickly rolled over and began to collapse. Six days after Silver posted the 8.235 high, the market hit a low of 7.020. However, the following three sessions posted three consecutive higher closes and confirmed a pivot low on April 14. This low also marked the beginning of the 1st reaction in the new downward trend and possibly the completion of a major TR-2 pattern. Since the corrective rally had not retraced at least 60% of the downward price swing from (C) to (B), I considered this a TR-2 pattern which means the sell stop was placed underneath the pivot low that marked the beginning of the Reaction swing marked (C) on the chart.

After the Silver fell more than a $1.20 in six days, most traders expected it to resume the upward trend, or were afraid to enter a short position right after such a large price move. However, the corrective rally failed on April 19, when the market tested the gap, but was unable to push any further. The following day began with a gap lower followed by a lower close. This price action confirmed the pivot high and marked the end of the Reaction swing. A break below the (C) pivot low was all that was needed to confirm the major TR-2 pattern and trigger a major sell signal.

One day later, Silver traded below the pivot low at (C), when the Breakout bar gapped lower and began trading at 6.50, followed with a close at 6.18. The price action had confirmed the bearish TR-2 pattern as well as triggered the sell signal. Now that the sell signal has been triggered and short position entered, timing of the exit and stop placement became extremely important, especially with the volatility Silver had been experiencing.

The reverse count began with the first price bar to the left of the pivot low at (C), back to the pivot high at (B) and continued on to the pivot high at (A)...the count equaled 16. With this information in hand I moved to the forward count and began on the first price bar to the right of the pivot high at (D) and counted forward 16 days. I came up with future Reversal date of May 11.

68   Chapter 2 - Time

Silver reached a low of 6.04 before it began a three-day bounce that ended on the April 24th where the market turned lower and resumed the downward trend. However, the most significant date was May 11. As you can see in *Figure # 2.23*, Silver chopped back and forth for several days before it bottomed at 5.52 on the May 11th Reversal date ... 98-cents below the trigger price of 6.50! Even after a very volatile beginning the TR-2 pattern and Reaction swing were able to pinpoint the exact low price bar in the July Silver.

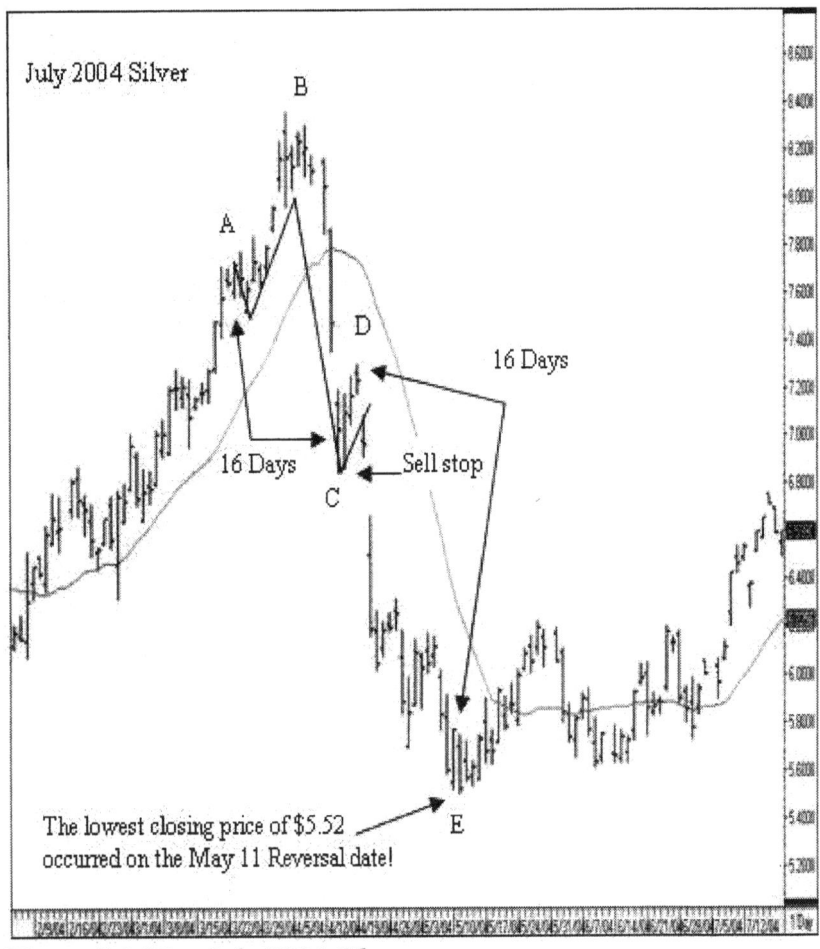

Figure # 2.23 – July 2004 Silver

December 2004 Japanese Yen

Figure # 2.24 - A major pivot low was confirmed on October 6 when December Japanese yen hit a low of .9617 (B), followed by a day with a higher close. A bullish wide range day followed and closed above the 20-day SMA. The next trading day was a Monday, but the market was closed for a holiday. Tuesday's session was a narrow range day and the close was below Friday's close. This market caught my attention because a bullish Reaction swing was forming above the 20-day SMA and above the 60% retracement level. Since the market did not pullback far enough to confirm a TR-1 pattern, I considered this a TR-2 pattern so the buy stop should be placed above the pivot high of .9182, marked (C).

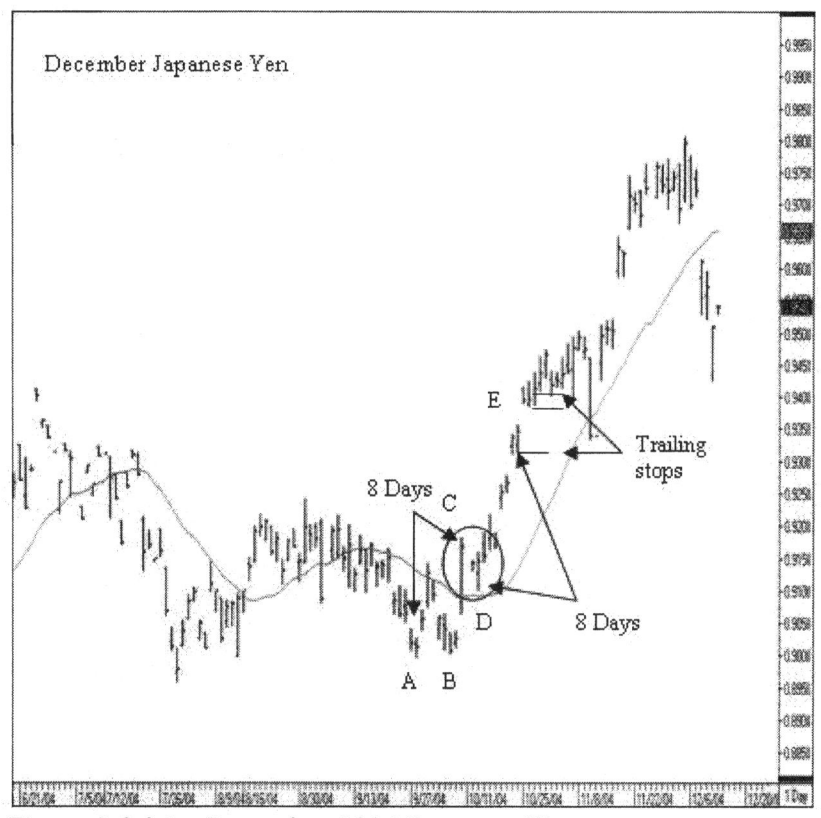

Figure # 2.24 – December 2004 Japanese Yen

It took two days for the market to break above the (C) pivot high and trigger the buy signal at .9185. The reverse/forward count from (C) to (A) equaled 8 days. The forward count projected a future Reversal date for October 22. The market continued to climb after the initial entry on October 14 and closed at .9347 on the October 22 Reversal date. It is decision time; do I exit at the close or adjust the protective stop and hold to see if the market will continue the trend?

If I elect to hold, I will place the protective stop 3 to 5 ticks underneath the Reversal date low; in this case the price would be .9310. Since the Reversal date had been reached the market was susceptible to a correction or a reversal. Therefore, it is necessary to be aggressive with the stop movement. Each day the market made a new high the stop should be moved just underneath the low of that price bar. The Japanese yen continued the upward trend for five more days before this method would have exited the trade at .9427.

June 2004 Japanese Yen

Figure # 2.25 - On April 1, 2004, the June Japanese Yen peaked at .9688 before turning lower. The market continued to trade lower into April 8th where the Yen found support at the 20-day SMA. The following session –April 9 – was a holiday (*even though the market was closed, I still count it as a trading day*) but the next trading session closed higher and confirmed the April 8th low as a pivot low and the beginning of a potential bearish Reaction swing. After the pivot was confirmed a sell stop should be placed underneath the April 8th low of .9413. The reverse count from (C) to (A) equaled 15 days. The forward count projected a future Reversal date for May 3. The market continued the downward trend into the May 3rd Reversal date, with only a couple of two-day corrections before it reached a low of .9043 on the predicted date. The June Japanese yen had completed a 320-point drop in 15 days! The next day began with a gap higher, followed by a fast run to .9245 two days after the Reversal date.

Chapter 2 - Time 71

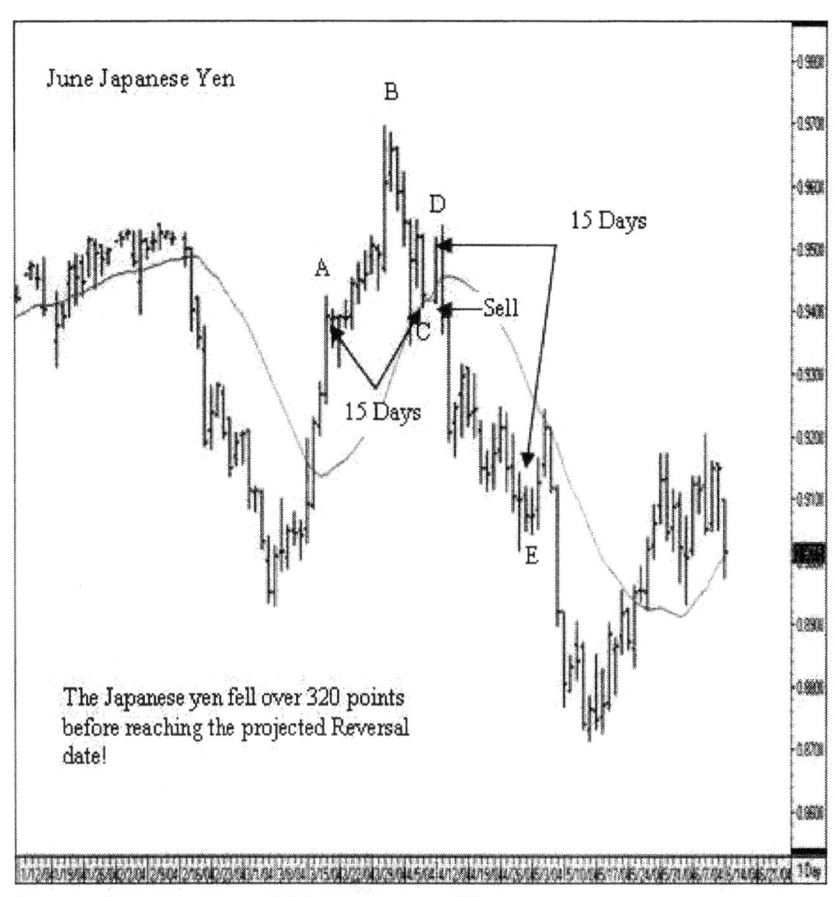

Figure # 2.25– June 2004 Japanese Yen

September 2006 Silver

Figure # 2.26 - On May 11, 2006 September Silver reached a new 23-year high at 15.157 (B) and closed near the top of the daily range. This proved to be the high of the move when the Silver collapsed and fell over $2.60 during the following six trading sessions, finally posting a low at 12.00 on May 22 (C) before it turned higher. The subsequent corrective rebound confirmed the beginning of a Reaction swing, but ended when the price reached the 20-day SMA at 13.418 on May 30 (D). *(The Memorial day holiday fell on May 29 and at the end of the Reaction swing. When a Reaction swing peaks on a holiday I consider it as the highest close. Therefore the forward count began with May 30 as day number 1.)* The resistance held and Silver reversed and resumed the downward slide. Two days later, Silver traded below the beginning of the Reaction swing - marked as (C) - and triggered the sell signal at 11.980 and confirmed the Reaction swing and the TR-2 pattern.

The reverse count from (C) to (A) equaled 13 days. The forward count, from the end of the Reaction swing (D), identified June 15th as the next potential Reversal date. Based on this information I felt fairly confident the downward swing should continue into or near the suggested Reversal date of June 15.

September Silver reached 9.627 on June 13th and closed at 9.724. Two days later – June 15, the predicted Reversal date – Silver posted a low of 9.720 before it closed at 10.063.

Never enter a pattern before its time.

Because the market traded higher into the Reversal date, I assumed the downward trend was about to resume; however, the Silver continued to trade higher over the next few days and never provided another sell signal confirmation. This is important, because even though the Reversal date Indicator may suggest the possibility of a continuation of the trend, it still needs to have a pattern confirmation before the signal is complete. In this case the Silver traded higher over the next three days before moving into a six-day consolidation pattern where it formed a new bullish Reaction swing. A buy signal followed on June 30, when the market broke above the beginning of the new Reaction swing and traded through the 20-day SMA. This is an important lesson: you never assume a pattern and never think you are going to get a jump on the trade by entering before the pattern is confirmed. I have always found it is best to give up a little on the entry price in order to get a stronger confirmation signal. This keeps me out of many bad trades and more than makes up for the extra price I give up on entry.

Figure # 2.26 – September 2006 Silver

Billiton (BHP)

Figure # 2.27 - On March 8, 2006, Billiton opened at a new 6-week low of 33.50 (B) and traded higher for the remainder of the day, finally closing at 34.22. The market continued to trade higher over the next six days where it crossed above the 20-day SMA before hitting resistance at 36.79 on March 17, marked as (C). The new high was followed by two consecutive lower closes that dipped below the 20-day SMA. The March 8th low (B) had been confirmed as a pivot low and (C) had been confirmed as the high pivot at the beginning of a possible Reaction swing.

At this point four of the five pivots were in place for a TR pattern. Since the current correction was less than 60% of the price move from (B) to (C), so a buy stop would be placed above the high at (C). On the second day – March 23 – BHP opened slightly higher and began trading at 36.90. The open was above the previous pivot high and the trigger price to confirm the buy signal and the TR-2 pattern. The reverse count, from (C) to the beginning of the TR-2 pattern, marked (A), equaled 13 days. The forward count of 13 days identified a future Reversal date of April 7.

After the buy signal was triggered at 36.90, BHP continued higher over the next 11 days, reaching a high of 44.00 one day before it closed at 42.45 on the April 7th Reversal date. As you can see in *Figure #2.27*, the Reversal date was also the lowest close and the end of a new Reaction swing. Remember, when a market trades lower into a Reversal date it will usually reverse higher. This new Reaction swing gave me a "heads up" that the trend would most likely continue the upward trend and that I should look for a Trend Continuation pattern to give me a new entry signal. I you are wondering what a Trend Continuation pattern is, I can tell you it is covered later in this book.

Dell Inc. (DELL)

Figure # 2.28 - From the low close of 34.83 posted on April 27, DELL rallied past the 20-day SMA before it reached a high on May 5. This high was followed by two consecutive lower closes before it found support at the 20-day SMA and resumed the newly formed upward trend. A potential TR-2 pattern had formed so a break above the pivot high at (C) would confirm the Reaction swing and the TR-2 pattern. On May 13, DELL gapped higher and

Chapter 2 - Time 75

began trading at 37.87 and closed at 39.33. The TR-2 pattern was confirmed and a buy signal triggered at 37.87.

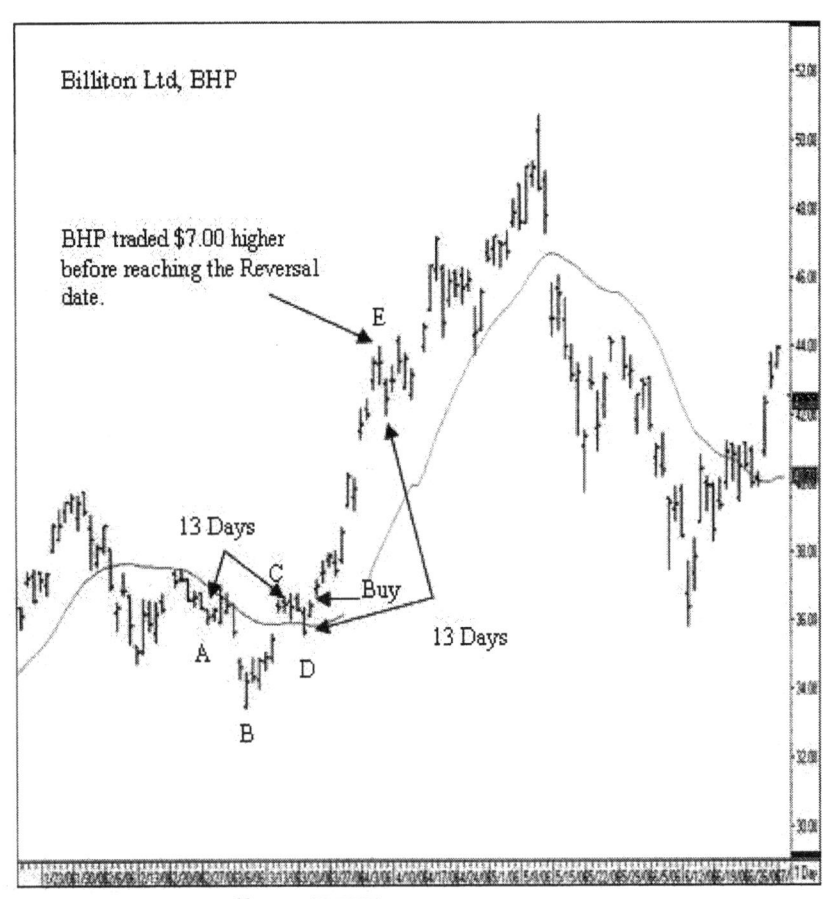

Figure # 2.27 – Billiton (BHP)

The reverse count from (C) to (A) equaled 14 days. Counting forward 14 days for the low pivot at (D) projected a future Reversal date of May 30. After the gap opening on May 13, DELL continued the rapid ascent and reached a high of 40.56 on May 26...just two days before the May 30 Reversal date. The market was closed on May 30 due to the Memorial Day holiday.

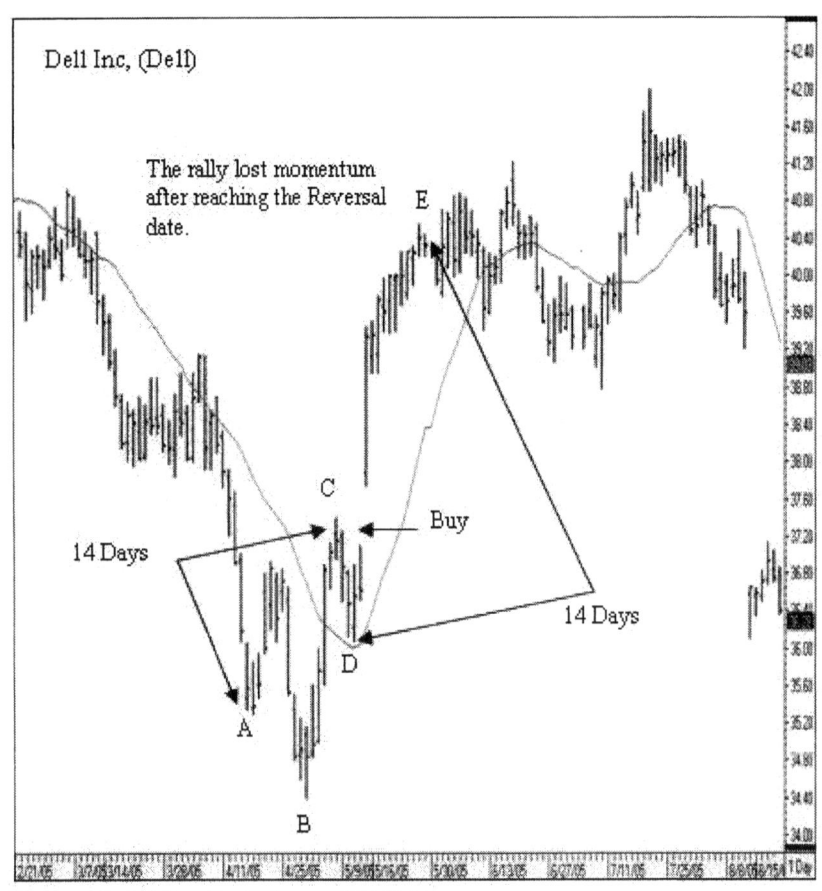

Figure # 2.28 – Dell Inc – (DELL)

Amazon.com (AMZN)

Figure # 2.29 - The chart of Amazon.com offers a different twist than the previous stocks I've illustrated. In this chart the market made a low at 32.79 on Friday, July 1, 2005. The following Monday is July 4th so the market was closed. However, July 5th closed higher than the July 1 close, but it ran into resistance at the 20-day SMA and peaked at 34.48 before it moved into a three-day consolidation. Inside the consolidation there were two consecutive lower closes that set up a possible Reaction swing. A break above

34.48 – the high of the Reaction swing at (C) - was needed to complete the TR-2 pattern and confirm the Reaction swing buy signal.

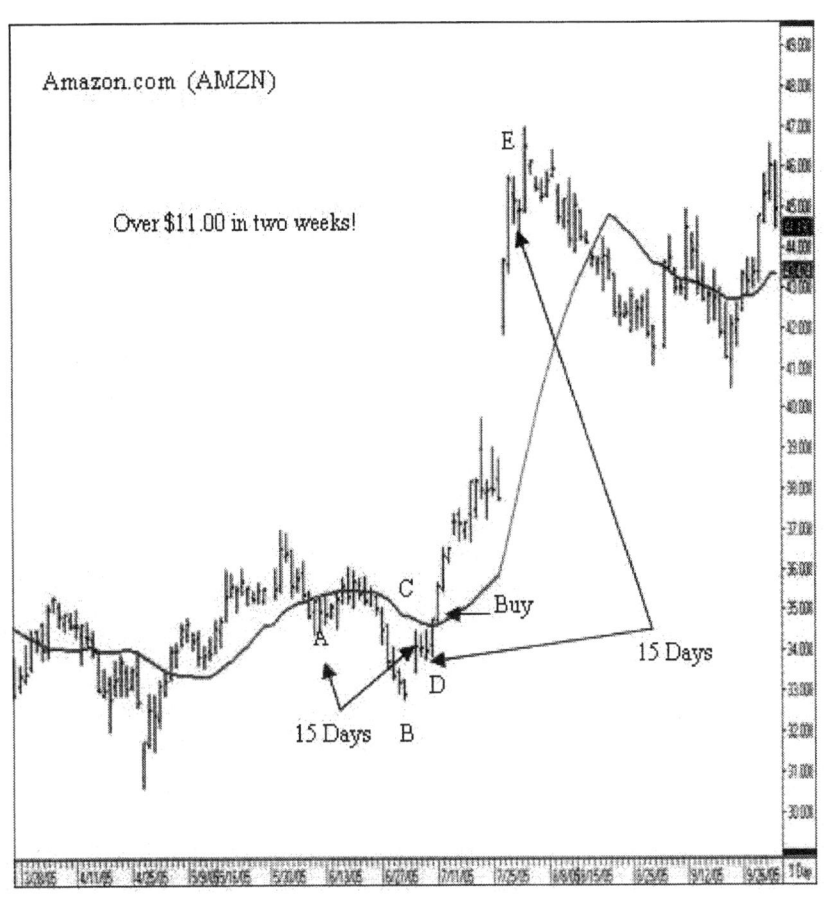

Figure # 2.29 – Amazon.com (AMZN)

July 8th opened steady, but ended the day at 34.75, slightly above the 20-day SMA and above the pivot high at the beginning of the Reaction swing, marked as (C) on the chart. The Breakout bar also pushed through the trigger price and confirmed the buy signal just above the previous high of 34.48. The reverse count from (C) back to the low at (A) equaled 15 days. I began the reverse count on July 1, because July 4th was a holiday and the market was closed. *(When a gap occurs at a major low or high, I have found it best to consider the gap day as the lowest or highest closing date.)* Counting forward 15 days from the low of the Reaction swing (D) projected a future Reversal date of July 28. Fourteen days after the initial buy signal was triggered at 34.50, AMZN reached a high of 45.81 on projected Reversal date of July 28.

Las Vegas Sands Corp. (LVS)

Figure # 2.30 - Two separate, but very effective TR patterns unfolded in the LVS chart between September 27, 2005 and January 20, 2006. The first pattern began with a pivot low on September 27 (A) followed by a lower pivot low on October 18 (B). LVS rallied off the October low and traded above the 20-day SMA, closing at 34.40 on October 24 (C). This pivot high was followed by three consecutive lower closes that ended on support provided by the 20-day SMA (D). This price action had confirmed the October 24 (C) high as the beginning of a bullish Reaction swing. The market did not pull back far enough to reach the buy window, so the buy stop was placed at 34.43, above (C) until it was triggered two days later.

The reverse count equaled 19 days, therefore the forward count projected the new upward trend to continue into November 23. Seventeen days after the entry, LVS closed at 45.83...$11.40 above the trigger price and on the November 23rd Reversal date.

LVS had been in a three-week correction before it posted a low close of 38.47 on December 19, 2005. Three days later it posted a high of 41.00 before it closed at 40.84 on December 22 and just above the 20-day SMA. From this high, the stock drifted lower over the next eight days before it made a low pivot on January 3rd and closed at 38.68. As soon as the market traded below the 60% retracement level (39.25) it had met the criteria for a TR-1 pattern. A buy stop should be placed above the high of the Signal entered the sell window. The high of the January 3rd was 39.74 therefore the buy stop would be above 39.74. (I typically like to place a stop 3 to 4 ticks above the high or below the low.)

Chapter 2 - Time 79

January 4th opened trading at 38.80 and began to rally, pushing past the high of the signal bar (39.74) where it triggered the buy signal before it closed at 40.09. The reverse count from (C) to (A) equaled 13 days and projected a future Reversal date of January 20. Twelve days after the Reaction swing was confirmed and the buy signal was triggered, LVS reached a high of 49.98 before it fell back to 46.05 on January 23…one day after the projected Reversal date and $6.31 above the entry!

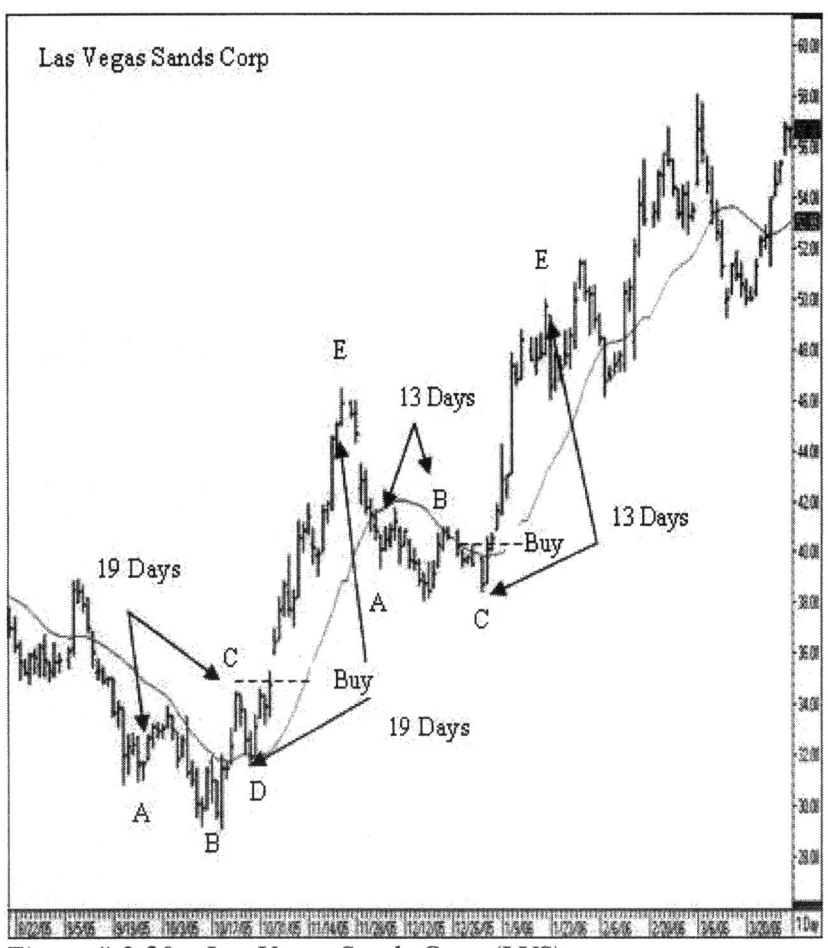

Figure # 2.30 – Las Vegas Sands Corp (LVS)

Baker Hughes Inc (BHI)

Figure # 2.31 - After an eight-day rally off the major low of March 21, BHI traded through the 20-day SMA before posting a high of 70.19 on March 30 (C). This high was followed by two lower closes and a retest of the 20-day SMA on April 4 – marked (D). The pivot high at (C) was the beginning of a new Reaction swing so a buy stop was entered at 70.22, above the (C) high. On April 5, BHI traded above (C) and hit the trigger price to confirm the buy signal and the entry. A protective stop was placed below the low at (D).

The reverse count from (C) to (A) equaled 15 days. The forward count projected a future Reversal date of April 24 (E). Thirteen days after the entry was triggered at 70.22 (C), BHI closes at 76.95 (E)... $.6.73 higher than the entry.

BHI only paused for a couple of days before resuming the upward trend. However, the two-day pause formed a new bullish Reaction swing before the trend continued. The new pattern was also a new signal and can be used in much the same way as the TR pattern. In other words, when a new Reaction swing is formed around a Reversal date projected from a TR pattern it is usually the center of a longer-term price swing. The new Reaction swing is the last pattern in a pattern series that I call a Trend Continuation pattern or a TC pattern. This pattern works just as the name implies, it identifies the center on a cycle and can be used to project out to the next high/low of consolidation.

December 2006 E-mini S&P

Figure # 2.32 - The Reversal date Trading Indicator can be a very versatile tool that works in both the commodity futures market and stock market in any time frame. The December E-mini S&P are a good example of how the RDTI can be applied on intra-day charts.

Figure # 2.31 – Baker Hughes Inc. (BHI)

A low pivot formed at 8:40 am (CST) before it rallied to a high of 1340.00 at 9:30 a.m., where it passed through the 20-bar SMA. The market retraced over the next forty minutes before it closed at 1338.00 at 10:10 a.m. The retracement was slightly more that 60% of the price move from (B) to (C), therefore the entry price was at 1339.00, just above the Signal bar that entered the 60% buy window. The very next price bar surged forward, triggered a buy signal and closed above the (C) pivot high.

The reverse count to (A) was 12 bars (10 x 12 = 120 minutes). The forward count projected an upward move into 12:00 p.m. The

Chapter 2 - Time

E-mini S&P peaked at 1347.75 at 12:00 p.m. - marked as (E). From this point on the market drifted sideways and lower.

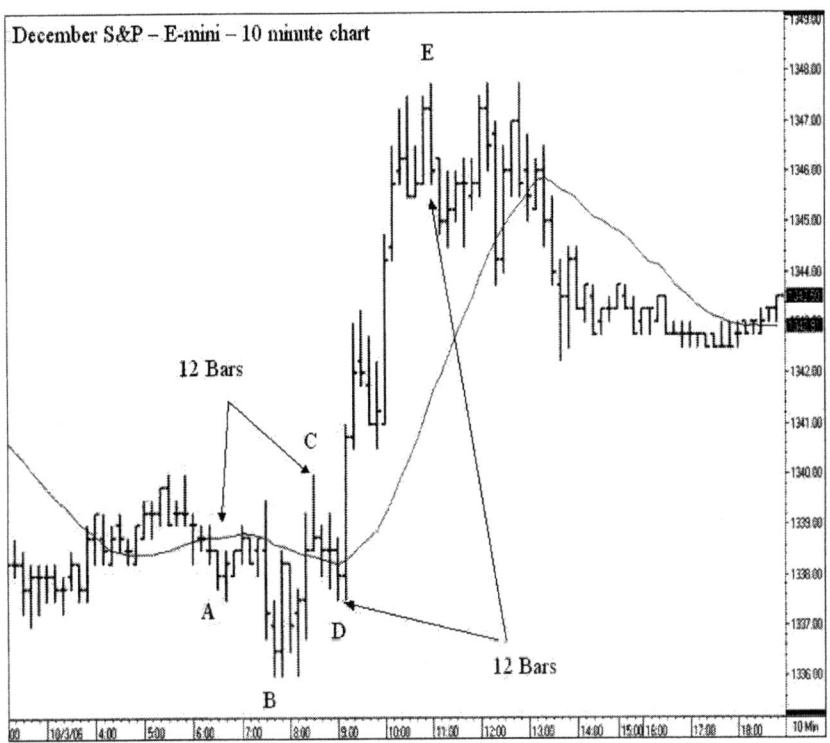

Figure # 2.32 – December 2006 E-mini S&P 500

December 2006 Dow Jones – E-mini

Figure # 2.33 - Most of the examples I have shown in this chapter begin at a major high or low in the market, however, I don't want you to get the idea this is only place that you will find a TR pattern. The 60-minute intra-day chart in *Figure # 2.33* offers a good example of what I mean.

The December E-mini Dow Jones posted a low of 11,565 at 1:20 a.m. CST on September 22, marked as (B). From this low, the E-mini Dow jumped to a high of 11,633 at the open of trading on September 25 (C). Three hours later the low of the Reaction swing

Chapter 2 - Time

was established and the Dow turned higher. Based on the 60% rule, a long position was triggered at 11,630 between 10:20 a.m. and 11:20 a.m. The reverse count to (A) equaled 28 bars or 28 hours. The forward projection of 28 hours predicted the future reversal bar between 1:20 p.m. and 2:20 p.m. on September 28.

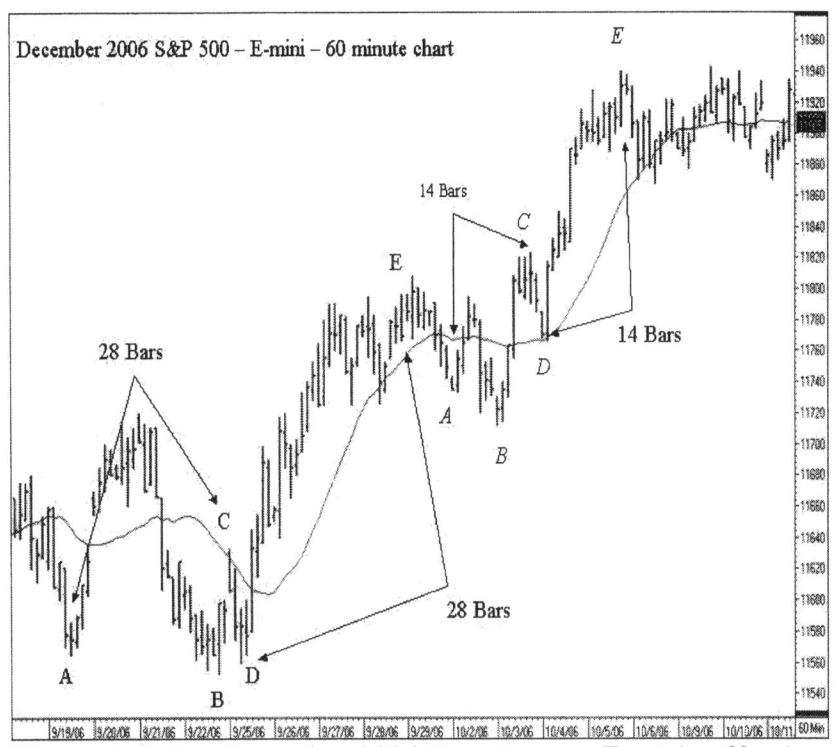

Figure # 2.33 – December 2006 Dow Jones – E-mini – 60-minute chart

Between the hour of 1:20 p.m. and 2:20 p.m., September 28, the E-Mini Dow Jones peaked at 11,796, right on schedule. From this point the Dow Jones traded sideways to lower until it closed at 11,735 on October 2 *(A)*. A three-hour rally followed before the Dow reversed and plunged to a new low of 11,712 during the first hour of trading on October 3 *(B)*. Six hours later, the Dow hit a high at 11,823 and pulled back during the next two hours of trading where it reached a low at 11,768 during the first hour of trading on October 4. The Dow Jones had formed TR pattern inside the longer-term upward trend. During the next two-hour period the Dow passed through the trigger price and initiated another buy signal at 11,825. The reverse count back to *(A)* equaled 14 hours and projected a future reversal bar between the hours of 1:20 p.m. and 2:20 p.m. on October 5. The highest price of the entire move was 11,940 and occurred at 2:15 p.m. on October 5.

The last TR pattern occurred at the end of a zigzag correction pattern, but still produced the same results as a TR pattern at a major low or high. The key is to look for the correct set up pattern at the end of a major trend or at the end of a three-wave or five-wave zigzag corrective pattern. There are constantly opportunities available if you know where to look and what to look for.

Forecasting the market

The TR patterns are great for forecasting future support or resistance levels in the markets that allow traders to know in advance when a market move is about to end. This goes a long way towards solving one of the most difficult tasks for a trader... knowing where to exit. Several of the examples I have just reviewed showed markets reaching a high/low on or very near the projected Reversal date before reversing and trading in the opposite direction. However, the market will not necessarily make a major top or bottom on every Reversal date identified by the TR pattern. Many times this consolidation or correction is only a pause in a longer-term trend, with more trading opportunities to follow.

One of the greatest benefits of learning the Reversal date Indicator and incorporating it into your trading is the paradigm shift you will experience in the way you look at the markets. You will forever have an understanding of market behavior and know when a market is unfolding properly or out of sync. This knowledge will allow you to avoid problematic markets and identify markets that offer the most potential with the fewest headaches. The increased confidence in yourself and your capability will allow you the capacity to trade more efficiently and reduce the stress you feel about which markets to trade and determining entry and exits. You will feel a sense of pride and accomplishment as you take these actions and see positive results on your own and no longer need to rely on outside "experts" or trading "gurus" to help you trade. This is a skill no one can take after from you and can be used for the rest of your life. So often I talk to traders who rely on outside information or chat rooms or "online trading advisors" for their trade recommendation and never learn the basics themselves. They are dependent on others to do what they should do themselves. If you want to follow others, at least understand the basics of market behavior.

Preparation is the Key to Success

The key to this type of trading is to have everything prepared before the signal is triggered. This trading approach is proactive. If you have to react to a signal, many times you will miss the trade altogether. The TR patterns and TC patterns are ideal for identifying the setups in advance of the signal. Once the set up is identified the orders can be placed before the open and all you have to do is sit back and watch the trade unfold. There is no guesswork or pressure to make a snap decision during a fast market. The signal is either triggered or not. This eliminates the subjectivity usually associated with trading.

This makes the Action/Reaction trading method a good candidate for traders who do not have the time to watch the markets closely once the trade is entered. The entry price and the stop placement are identified before the trade is entered. The protective stops are moved quickly to the entry price and then the market is allowed to fluctuate until the cycle is near completion where the stops are once again tighten before the anticipated reversal. Once the patterns have been identified and the parameters for the trade are set, the trader can concentrate on other things. This helps take the human emotions out of the equation because a good trade will take care of itself and a bad trade will be closed quickly.

Having a Game Plan

A successful coach will always have a game plan before the game even begins, a successful businessman will have a complete business plan before the doors are open and a successful trader needs to have a trading plan before the first order is placed. Eighty percent of all new businesses fail within the second year. The two main reason of failure are because they are undercapitalized and they fail to follow their business plan. The same can be said about trading. In order to succeed at trading you must follow your trading plan every step of the way. In addition to the actual setup, there is also the need for a solid foundation to manage the setup and the trade that follows. The foundation should be part of the trading plan and consist of the basic trading methodology, built in money management, and the knowledge of which market will respond best to the particular set up.

Chapter 3

"Time is on my side" -
The Rolling Stones

Trend Continuation Patterns

When I look at a trending market I can see two different types of trends. The first is a steady trend with overlapping waves. In other words, an upward trending market will move higher and then make a correction or retracement that is lower than the previous high swing point or pivot. An overlapping trend will typically retrace between 50% to 78% of the previous market upswing, before resuming the dominant upward trend. The pullback will usually last between 7 and 12 days. The other type of trend is a fast moving trend where the corrections or retracements are somewhere between 20% to 40% of the previous upswing. The correction will typically end at or above the previous pivot high before resuming the upward trend. The correction usually lasts between 3 to 4 days or sometimes can be as long as 7 days. This type of market is fast moving and can offer quick gains if played correctly.

Trading success depends on the strength or weakness of a market, as well as how well the trading plan is followed. The best trading opportunities generally appear early in a market trend. As the trend nears exhaustion, the odds for success decrease. At the end of a long-term trend, market momentum can disappear quickly. Sometimes, the market will even turn unexpectedly and dramatically against you. This can leave many inexperienced traders with the feeling that they've just been ambushed by the markets. Even though this change in market momentum seems sudden, there are usually warning signs that hint of a pending market direction change before it actually happens. It is here that

Chapter 3 - Trend Continuation Patterns

the TR pattern has its value. You may have noticed in most of the TR chart examples the trend would either end at the projected Reversal date or very soon after. Therefore, I would know in advance when the trend should be near exhaustion and therefore manage the position accordingly.

However, not all markets will peak at the end of the TR pattern projections. There are many times when the market will pause before continuing the trend. The pause will usually lead the market into a consolidation or correction phase before continuing the dominant trend, in other words, form a new Reaction swing. I call this type of market action a Trend Continuation pattern and it can be used in the same manner as the TR pattern. A Trend Continuation pattern (TC) always follows the TR- pattern and – as the name implies – portends a continuation of the current trend. But, the TC pattern does much more than just confirm a trend continuation; it can also be used to make Time and Price projections of the current trend. Just as the Reaction swing will fall in the center of a short-term market swing, the Trend Continuation pattern will fall in the center of a longer-term trend. Once again this falls in line with the Action/Reaction theory.

When a market trades higher into a projected Reversal date, the market has a strong tendency to reverse and trade lower. On the other hand, when a market trades lower into a projected Reversal date, the market has a strong tendency to reverse and trade higher. Therefore, if the prevailing trend is sloping downward and the market makes a low pivot a couple of days prior to a Reversal date and trades higher into that date, it would suggest the market is ready to reverse and resume the downward trend. This would be the beginning of a Trend Continuation or TC pattern. The opposite holds true if the market is trading higher and pulls back into the Reversal date; it would suggest a continuation of the upward trend. There are many warning signs that foreshadow trend exhaustion. These include: the end of a natural market cycle in a predetermined sequence, price patterns that foretell possible trend exhaustion, and momentum. These warning signals are enhanced when they occur on or near a predicted Reversal date. The following examples will illustrate what we are talking about.

Chapter 3 - Trend Continuation Patterns

The Trend Continuation (TC) pattern appears inside a strong trending market and follows a TR pattern. As the names states, this pattern signals a continuation of the current trend, but it also tells me much more. Such as, how long the trend will continue and how far it may go. Like the TR pattern, the TC pattern also consists of five pivots, with the Reaction swing formed by the last two pivot points, as shown in *Figure # 3.1*.

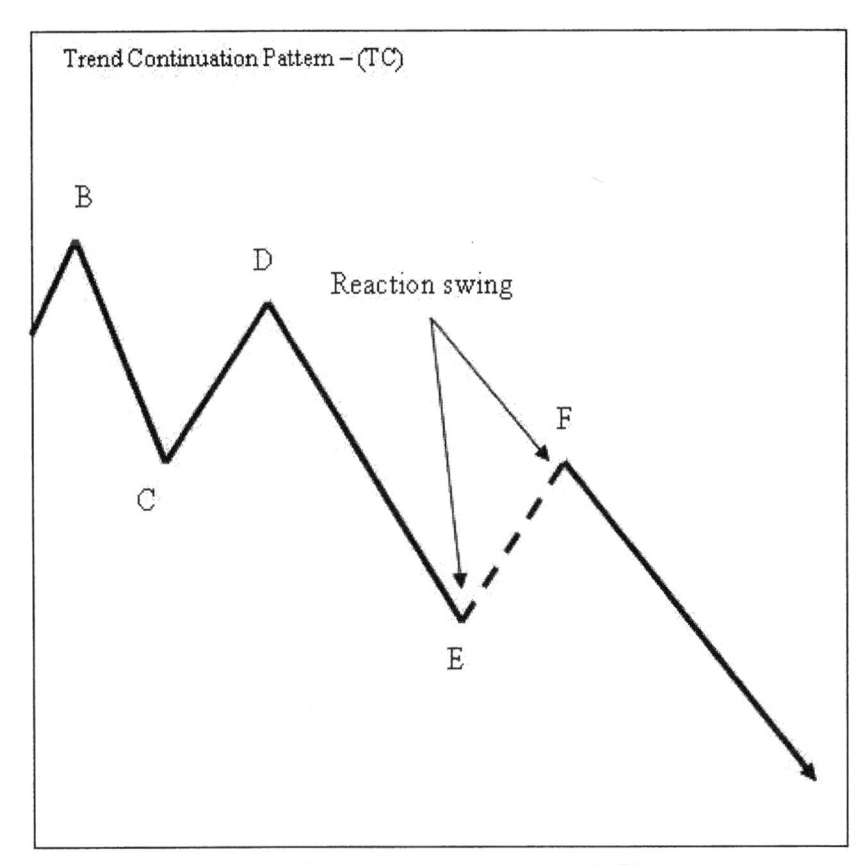

Figure # 3.1 – Trend Continuation Pattern – (TC)

Inside a trend the market will make a series of pivot high/lows, followed by a pullback to support or resistance. In an upward trending market, this is where bullish traders tend to enter the market expecting another bullish leg and a run past the recent high. In a downward trending market, this is when the bearish traders enter the market expecting another downward swing in the trend. If the market is forming a Trend Continuation pattern it will run into support or resistance somewhere between the 60% and 78% retracement levels or the 20-day SMA and fail to move past the recent high or low pivot point. This swing pattern failure is the first sign of the correction losing momentum and of a possible extension of the prevailing trend.

The same criteria I use for the TR pattern is also applied to the TC pattern. For example, as soon as I see a pivot point confirmed inside an existing downward trend I will consider this the beginning of a new Reaction swing and place a sell stop below the pivot point. If the market retraces more than 60% of the previous market swing from (D) to (E) I consider the market inside the sell window and the entry stop is moved to just below the low of the Signal bar that entered the sell window. As soon as a sell signal is triggered I will place a protective stop above the high at (F). I will usually place the protective stop 2 or 3 ticks above the high.

I also use the 20-day SMA in combination with the TC-pattern. The 20-day SMA acts as a resistance in downward trending markets and support in upward trending markets. If the corrective rally touches or penetrates the 20-day SMA the trigger price becomes the low of the price bar that touched or penetrated the 20-day SMA. This technique will provide an early entry in markets that have been in a steady downward trend where a 60% percent retracement would be hard to achieve. (The rules are reverse in an upward trending market.)

Instead of looking for new examples to illustrate the Trend Reversal pattern (TC), I will go back to the chart examples used to illustrate the TR patterns.

December Coffee

Figure # 3.2 - The December Coffee had reached a low of 73.75 on July 8 (E), the Reversal date projected from the TR-1 pattern, *(see Figure # 2.13)* and began to form another bearish Reaction swing where the market began a corrective rally after the July 8th

Chapter 3 - Trend Continuation Patterns 91

Reversal date. Eight days later, Coffee crossed above the 20-day SMA and finally closed at 76.65 on July 20 (F). The retracement had confirmed a pivot low on July 8 (E) and set up another selling opportunity and a possible TC-pattern. The high of the preceding pivot was 76.80 on June 30. The rebound from 73.75 (E) to the high of 76.65 was more than 60% of the previous price swing and above the 20-day SMA; therefore the sell stop is placed just below the Signal bar low (F). In this case the Signal bar occurred on July 20 and the low was 75.25.

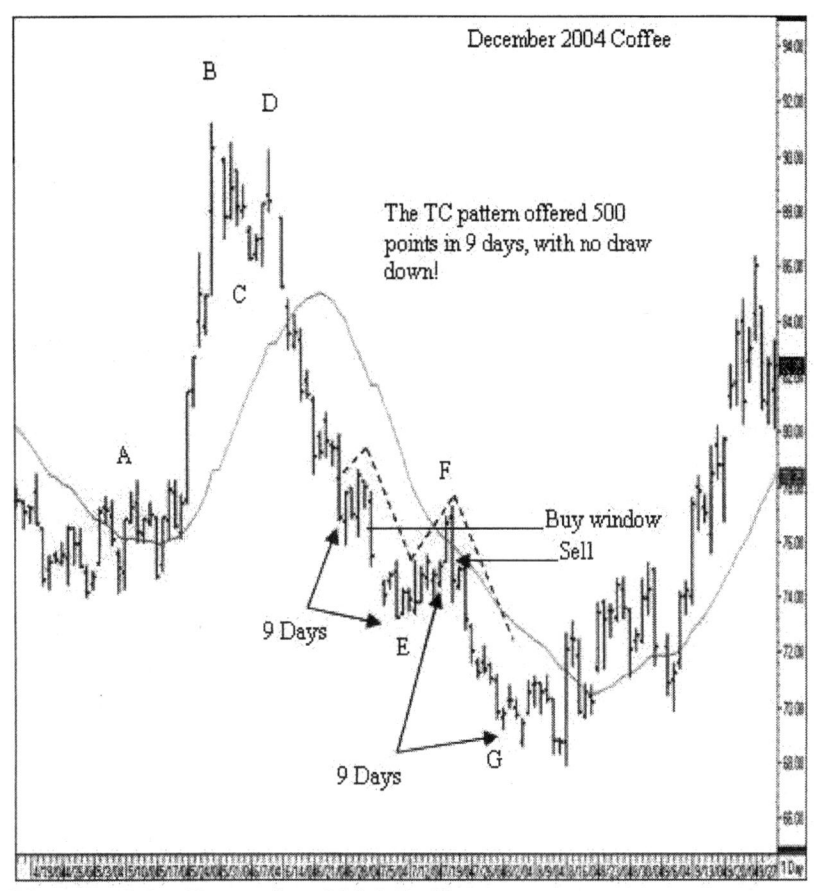

Figure # 3.2 – December 2004 Coffee

The market reversed on the following day, crossed below the 20-day SMA and traded through the sell stop to trigger the signal for a short position. After the signal was confirmed the procedure for the TC pattern is identical to the TR patterns. In other words, it is time to do a reverse/forward count and project the future Reversal date and the end of the cycle. The reverse count will start on the first price bar to the left of the beginning of the Reaction swing marked (E) and proceed back to the low of the previous Reaction swing. The previous low was 76.90 on June 25, so the reverse count equaled 9 days. Counting forward 9 days from the end of the Reaction swing –marked (F) – projected a future Reversal date of August 2 marked as (G). After the short position was triggered the Coffee continued the downward trend over the next 9 days and closed at 69.80 on August 2 (G). The short position was never behind and could have been closed for a very nice gain near the major low of the long-term trend. Using the Action/Reaction methods and the signals from the TR and TC patterns a trader could have captured most of the overall downward trend and exited near the major low.

June British Pound

Figure # 3.3 - In this example, the TR-1 pattern triggered a buy signal at 1.7430 and projected a Reversal date for April 19. The June 2006 British pound posted a high of 1.7951 on April 19 and closed at 1.7936.

The British pound formed a three-day Reaction swing between April 24 (E) and April 26 (D). The TR-1 signal finished with excellent gain and the TC-pattern was confirmed on April 27 when the British pound surged passed the 1.7960 trigger price and closed at 1.8042. At this point, the protective stop should be placed underneath the low pivot bar at (F) and a reverse/forward count done on the TC-2-pattern that formed between (E) and (F). The reverse count from (E) back to the high of the previous Reaction swing - April 4 – equaled 14 days. The forward count from (F) projected a future Reversal date of May 16—marked (G)—and forecasted higher prices over the next two weeks. Two days before the May 16 Reversal date, the June British pound peaked at 1.8934

Chapter 3 - Trend Continuation Patterns 93

and closed at 1.8897 on May 16. This was another excellent trading opportunity with very little drawdown. *(The action/reaction method and Reversal date Indicator predicted the end of a two-month trend, weeks in advance!)*

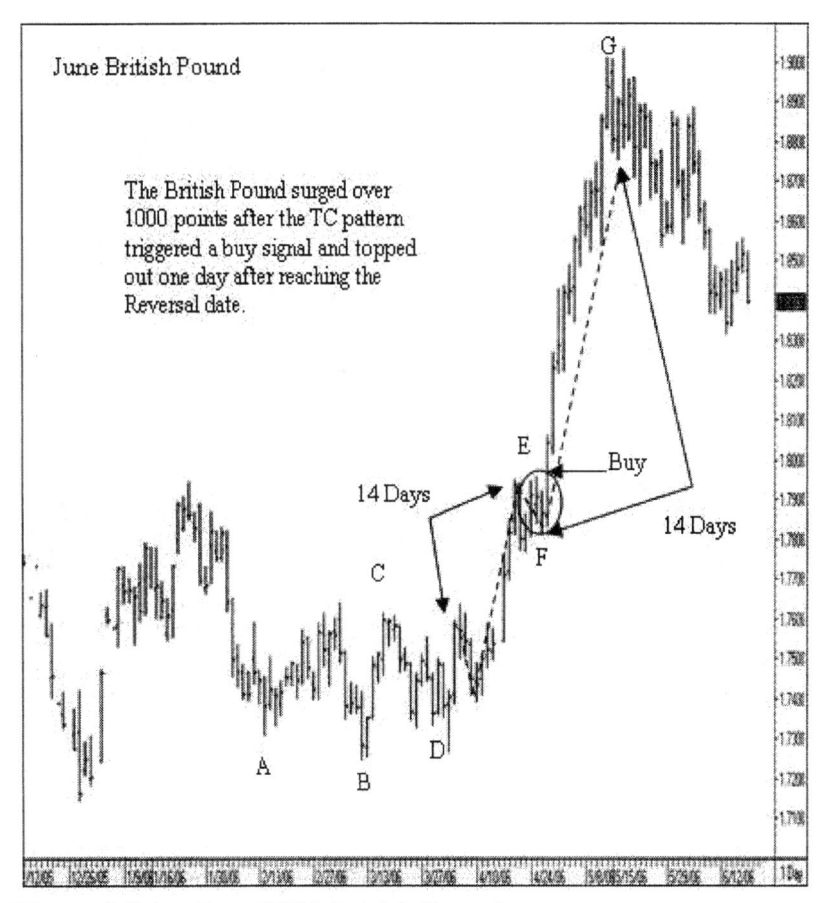

Figure # 3.3 – June 2006 British Pound

September T-Bonds

Figure # 3.4 - Let's take a look at another TC pattern in action. The September 2003 T-Bonds offered a classic example of the TC pattern. In *Figure #2.13*, the T-Bonds had been trending lower for over two weeks when the market closed at a low of 110-00 on July 21, marked (E). The next two trading sessions closed higher, reaching 111-12 and confirmed (E) as a low pivot and the beginning of a bearish Reaction swing. Three days after confirming the low pivot, T-Bonds traded below the low at (E), confirmed the Reaction swing and resumed the dominant downward trend. This price action triggered a new sell signal at 109-30. As soon as the short position was initiated it was time to do the reverse/forward count. The reverse count began on the first price bar to the left of the lowest closing price at (E), and counted in reverse to the low of the previous Reaction swing. The reverse count equaled 9 days.

The forward count started one day after the July 23rd high and counted forward 9 days. The forward count projected a future Reversal date due on August 5 (G). After breaking below the pivot low of 110-00 point (E), the T-Bonds continued the downward trend, finally posting a low close of 105-09 on the projected Reversal date of August 5. At this point the T-Bonds bounced higher and moved into a sideways trading range. However, the most important thing you want to notice in this example is the major price move that occurred between the Reaction swing and the projected Reversal date. Only after the T-Bonds posted the low close on the Reversal date of August 8, did the market begin to consolidate and move into a trading range.

Trident Microsystems Inc. (TRID)

Figure # 3.5 - After hitting a low of 24.81 and closing at 25.14 on May 11 (E) - the Reversal date forecasted from the TR-1 pattern - (*see Figure #2.15),* TRID entered into a six-day corrective rally that peaked at 28.07 on May 19 (F). The high was just above the 20-day SMA. The price action had formed the beginning of a new Reaction swing and set up a possible selling opportunity that suggested a continuation of the trend.

Chapter 3 - Trend Continuation Patterns 95

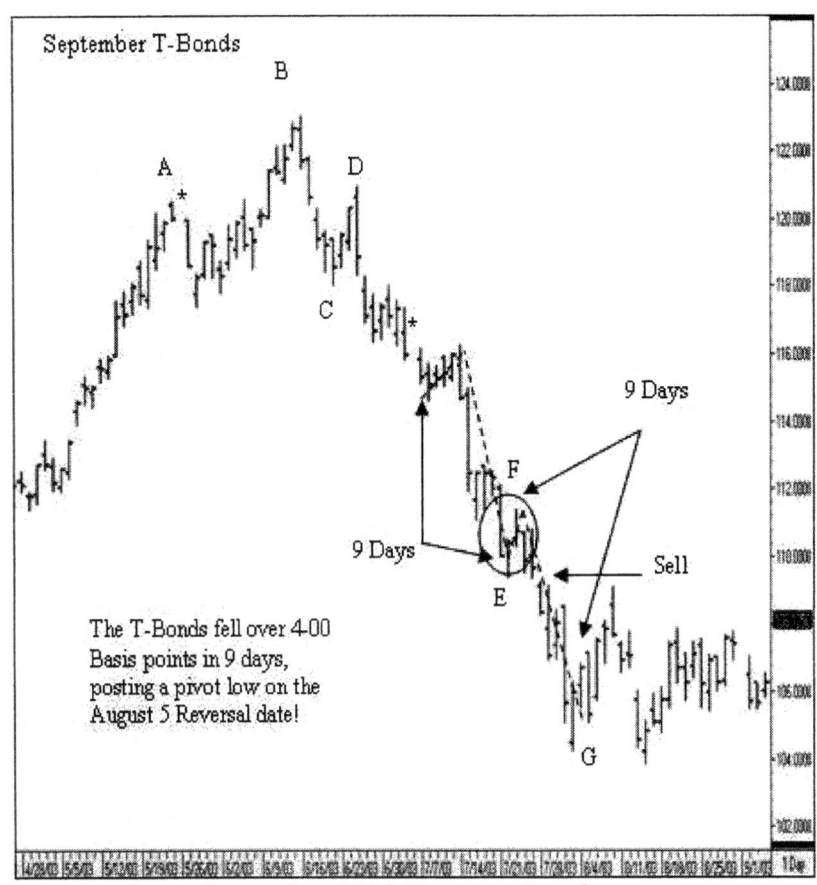

Figure # 3.4 – September 2003 Treasury Bonds

Since the rally broke through the 20-day SMA on May 19, it became the Signal bar and identified the trigger price as 26.60. It really didn't matter where the sell stop was placed because the market opened sharply lower on the following day and began trading at 23.80, and triggered the sell signal at the open.

The reverse count begins on the first day to the left of the day with the lowest closing price of the Reaction swing, marked as (E). In this example the lowest closing price of 24.99 actually occurred on May 15. So the reverse count will begin on May 12, the first price bar to the left of May 15 (E). The reverse count from (E) back to (C) was 16 days. The forward count forecasted a future Reversal date of June 12. Sixteen days after triggering the sell signal at 23.80, TRID reached a low of 18.35...a drop of $5.45 with only a two-day pause in the middle of the move. Following the Reversal date TRID moved into another corrective phase.

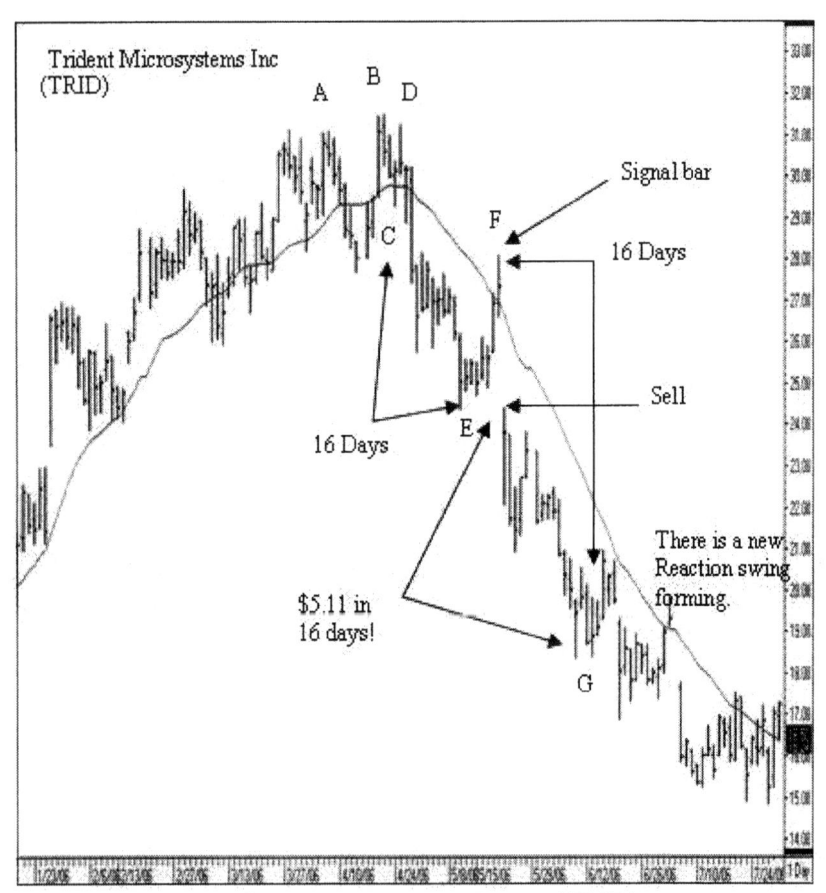

Figure # 3.5 – Trident Microsystems Inc. – (TRID)

June 2004 Japanese Yen

Figure # 3.6 - The June Japanese yen reached .9243 on May 5 - marked as (F) on the chart -just three trading days after posting a low of .9044 on the May 3 Reversal date (E), projected from the April 8 (C) to April 12 (D) Reaction swing. See *Figure # 2.25*. The

Chapter 3 - Trend Continuation Patterns 97

three-day rally was more than 60% of the previous downswing from April 26 to April 30 and slightly above the 20-day SMA. This means a new Reaction swing had formed and set up a sell signal and a possible TC- pattern. The trigger price to confirm the sell signal and the Reaction swing would be at .9135, just underneath the low of the price bar that entered the sell window (F). The market fell during the following day and traded through the trigger price and closed at .9118. The sell stop had been elected and the TR-1 pattern confirmed. The reverse count, from (E) back to the previous low (April 22), equaled 6 days. Projecting forward 6 days from the pivot high (May 5) forecast May 13 as the next Reversal date. Six days after hitting the trigger price of .9130, the Japanese yen closed at 8740...390 points lower! This date proved to be a major low and the beginning of a major rally!

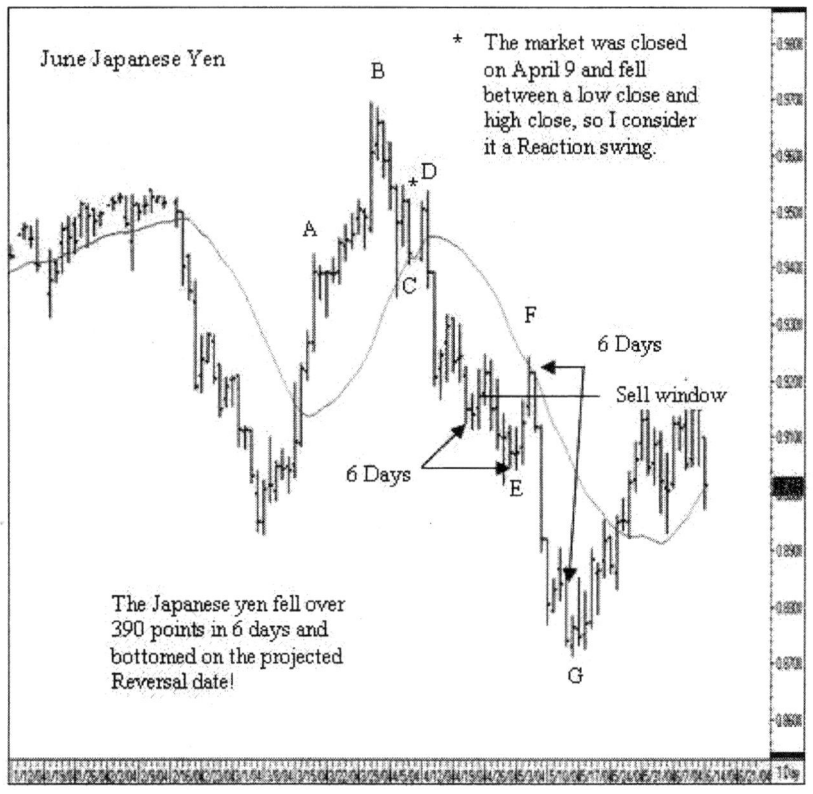

Figure # 3.6 – June 2004 Japanese Yen

December 2005 Cattle

Figure # 3.7 - On September 15, 2005, (E) December Cattle had reached the Reversal date projected from the preceding TR-1 pattern and promptly traded lower over the next four days and formed a new Reaction swing and possible TC pattern in the process (F). On the fifth day, December Cattle turned higher, ended the correction and set up a possible bullish Reaction swing. Since the retracement ended well above 60% of the previous market swing, the buy stop was placed at 89.10, above the beginning of the Reaction swing (E). It took three days for the market to trade above the trigger price and elect the buy stop, but it was worth the wait. The reverse count, from the beginning of the Reaction swing at (E) back to the previous Reaction swing marked (C) equaled 13 days. The forward count projected a future Reversal date of October 10. Over the next eleven days, Cattle continued to climb and finally closed at 91.40 on October 10, ending a nice trade signal that offered a potential gain of 230 points without any draw down along the way.

This chart brings me to a very important point. I will usually only trade one TC pattern following a TR pattern. There are times when a trending market will offer more patterns to trade, but I have found the majority of time the trend is beginning to mature after the first TC pattern is complete. This chart is a great illustration of what I mean. After the current TC pattern reached a climax on October 10, it formed a new Reaction swing and another buy set up. The market traded above the high pivot and triggered a new buy signal on October 13. However, the market failed to carry through and reversed the following day and closed sharply lower. This reiterates the need for good money management even with a trading method you have great confidence in and caution when entering a new trade after the first TC pattern is complete. There can be as many as three or four Reaction swings in the trend, but the risk increases as the number rises.

Chapter 3 - Trend Continuation Patterns 99

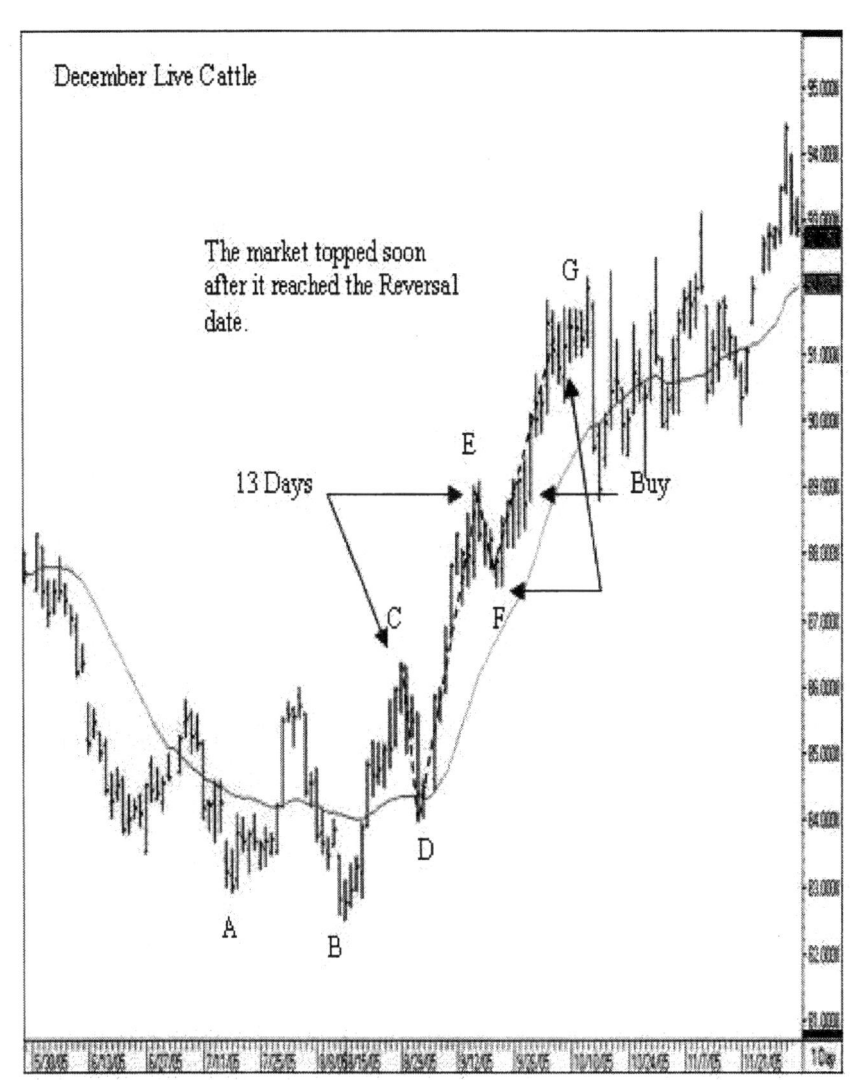

Figure # 3.7 – December Live Cattle

September Eurocurrency

Figure # 3.8 – May 26 was the Reversal date predicted by the TR pattern. However, the Reaction swing had formed between May 20 (E) and May 25 (F) with a trigger price at 1.2560. The Reaction

Chapter 3 - Trend Continuation Patterns

swing was confirmed on May 26, when Eurocurrency dropped through the trigger price and closed at 1.2541.

The reverse count from (E) back to the low of the previous Reaction swing (C) equaled 14 days and projected a future reversal day on June 14, marked as (G). The Eurocurrency fell sharply over the next five days before it hit support and formed a five-day consolidation. On the tenth day, Eurocurrency resumed the downward slide and continued lower into June 14 (G) where it closed at 1.2074.... 486 points below the trigger price! The following day marked the beginning of a 255-point three-day rally. Even though the market formed a new Reaction swing, the trend was losing momentum, therefore the risk increased if any new positions were initiated.

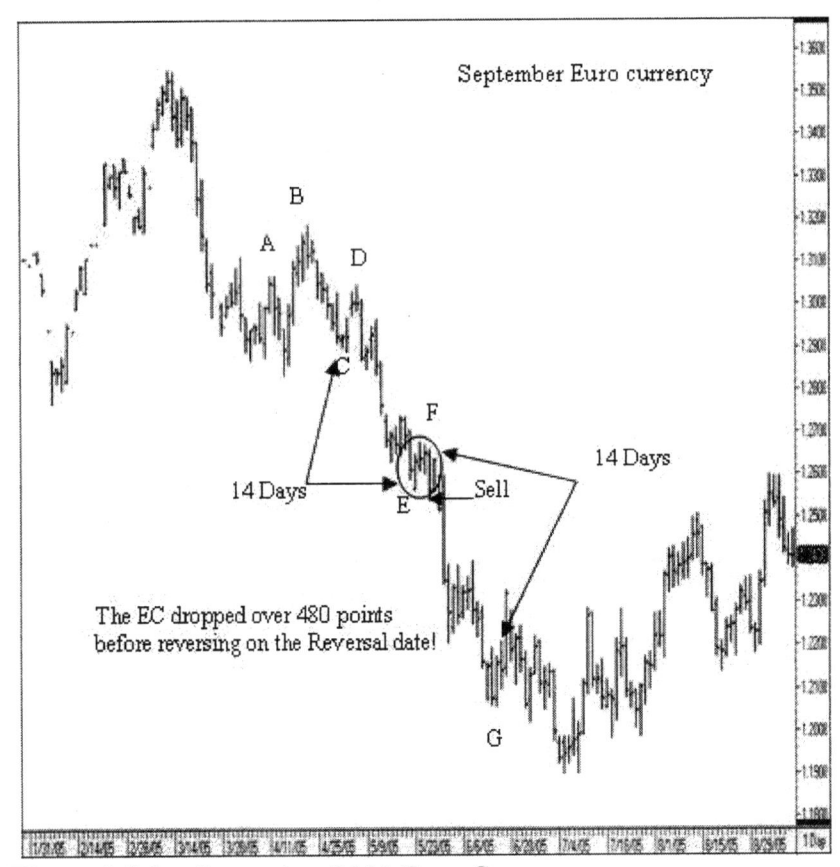

Figure # 3.8 – September 2005 Euro Currency

Billiton (BHP)

Figure # 3.9 - BHP closed at 43.50 after it peaked at 44.00 on the April 6 Reversal date (E). See *Figure # 2.27*. The market closed lower the following day and set up a Reaction swing and potential bullish TC-pattern at (F). Since the pullback was not at least 60% of the previous market swing the buy stop should be placed at 44.05, just above the pivot high, which was also the beginning of the Reaction swing. On April 11, BHP reached a high of 44.30, where it elected the buy stop and confirmed the pattern. The reverse count for (E) back to the high of the previous Reaction swing (C) equaled 14 days. The forward count projected the next Reversal date for April 27. BHP reached 47.19 on April 19, but pulled back to close at 44.36 on April 27 (H). The lower close – on the Reversal date – suggested the trend could continue.

Extending the Count

This is a technique I haven't discussed yet, although I have talked about how a market that trades higher into a Reversal date it will typically turn lower. On the other hand, when a market trades lower into a Reversal date it will typically turn higher. When this happens, as it did in BHP, the lower close on the reverse date is telling me the market will likely turn higher and continue into the next Reversal date. To get the new Reversal date, I will continue the reverse count back to the major low, in this case (B) or to a major high in a downward trending market. I will use this new information to continue the forward count. The count back to (B) equaled 20 days and projected a future Reversal date of May 5. BHP reached 48.27 on May 5 (I) and continued to a high of 50.74 four days later. Although, this TC pattern did not offer a large gain on the first Reversal date, it did give the trader more than one opportunity to profit and even closed with a slight gain on the April 27 Reversal date. However, the second Reversal date did offer a nice opportunity.

102   Chapter 3 - Trend Continuation Patterns

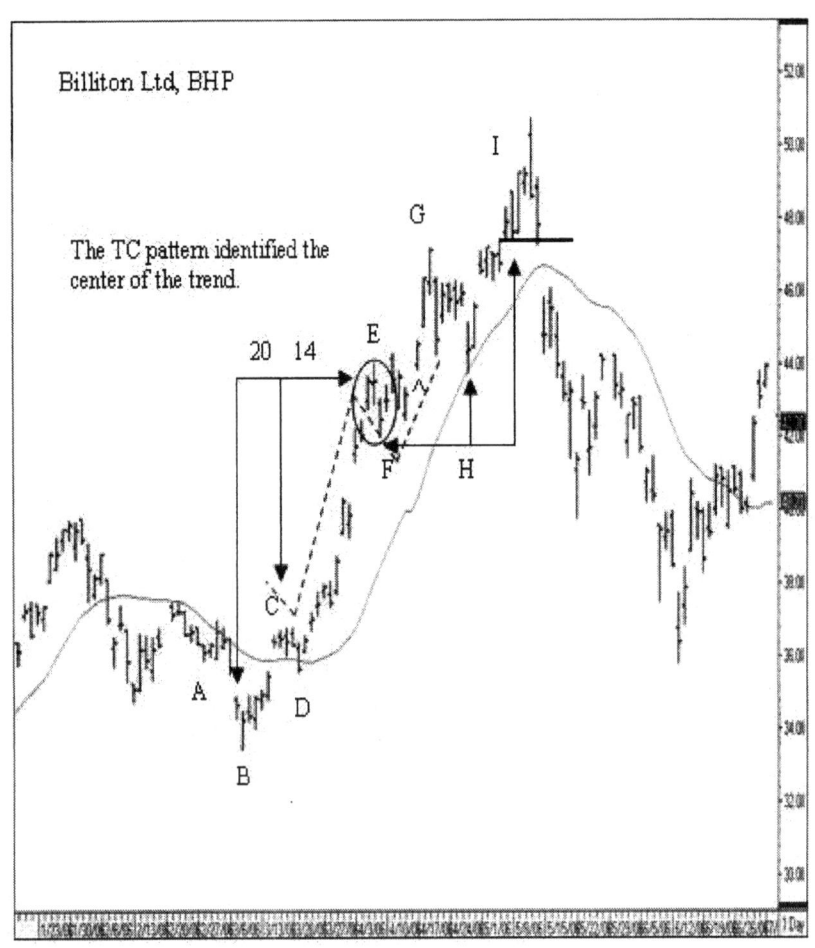

Figure # 3.9 – Billiton Ltd – (BHP)

Baker Hughes Inc. (BHI)

Figure # 3.10 - BHI reached a high of 78.46 one day before the April 24 Reversal date (E) projected from the March 30 (C) and April 3 (D) Reaction swing. See *Figure # 2.31*. The Reversal date closed slightly lower followed by another lower close on April 25 (F). The two lower closes confirmed a high pivot (E) and the beginning of a new Reaction swing and possible TC pattern. The

Chapter 3 - Trend Continuation Patterns 103

trigger price for a long entry was 78.50, just above the pivot high at (E). April 26, began trading at 78.36, but quickly breeched the 78.50 trigger price and reached a high of 81.10. The protective stop should be placed at 74.50, underneath the end of the Reaction swing, marked (F). The protective stop was tested on April 27 when the market dropped back to 75.88, but the market found support closed at 79.11. The reverse count from (E) back to the high of the previous Reaction swing (April 10) equaled 9 days and projected a future Reversal date of May 8. Nine days after confirming the buy signal at 78.50, BHI closed at 87.87. Two days later, BHI began a significant correction.

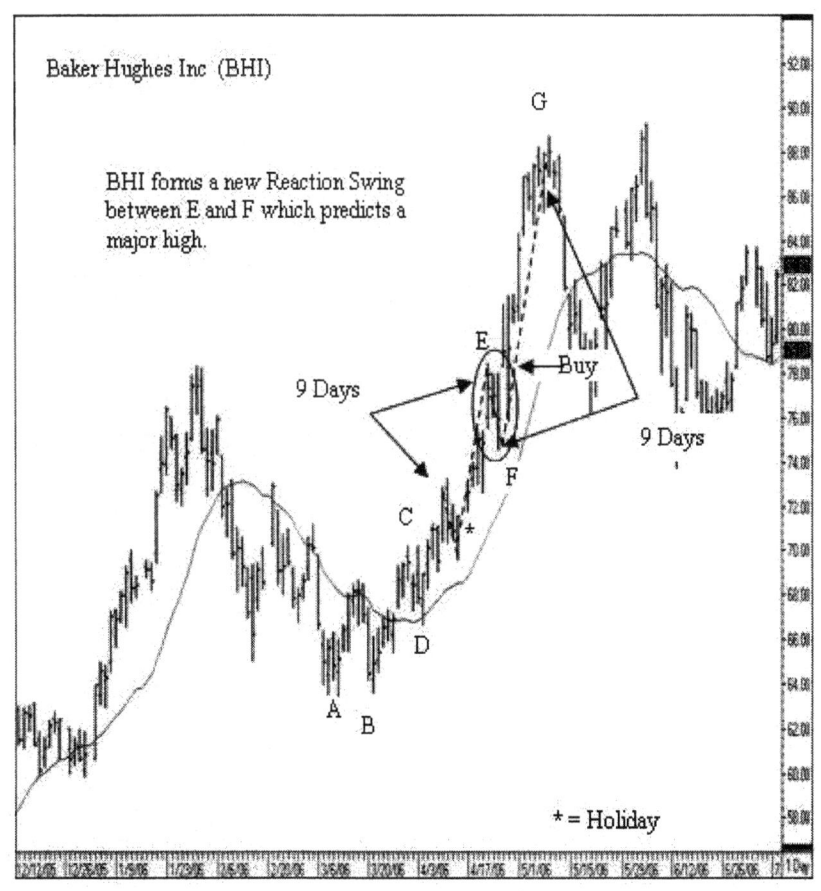

Figure # 3.10 – Baker Hughes Inc – (BHI)

Learning how to spot and trade the TR pattern and the TC pattern will give you the opportunity to enter the market at nearly every significant turning point and capture a major portion of the following price move.

The setups I have illustrated in this article appear often in every commodity and timeframe. However, you simply need to learn to understand the market behavior and be patient while you wait for the market to setup properly. The predictive behavior of the market can be a powerful tool when determining future market movements. Traders are always looking for an edge when it comes to entering or exiting positions. Little do they know the market itself has the answer when you know where to look. It's all about learning to understand market behavior and interpret the charts.

Chapter 4

"Because it's where the money is."
Willie Sutton – Famous Bank Robber

Price

Although using the Reaction swing to project Time can be a very powerful trading tool, it is still a one-dimensional trading approach. Through the years of working with many different traders, I have found most are focused on Price alone. They enter when the market breaks through a predetermined price level and then they look for an exit based on a price. I think this puts them at a disadvantage because—as I have shown in the previous chapter—Time can run out before the market meets its price projections. Without this foresight, a trader can give up a lot of the profit potential before they realize the move is over. Remember, it's not about entering at the very beginning and exiting at the very top—although that is good to do once in while—it's really about making consistent gains with as little stress and risk as possible. You aren't going to get rich on one trade; success is built over the long-term. I truly believe that by combining Time and Price together, any trader can improve their entry and exit of trade positions and help improve their bottom line.

Both the TR pattern and TC pattern can not only help determine how long a market should continue in the current trend, but also how much to expect out of the move or where the market will likely lose its momentum before reversing or moving into a sideways pattern. The more you know about a trade signal the more confident you will be about stepping into the market. The more confidence you have in your trading methodology the more likely you are to trade the signal properly and not exit too early or too late.

Action/Reaction is not an exact science and falls more in line with Fractal laws. Which means I am not looking for perfection in the trading signals, but I am looking for consistent performance. I have never forgotten a statement made by an experienced and successful trader. He said to me, "Amateurs look for perfection, but professionals look for performance, that is what separates the two." Fractal perfection allows for some variance in the projections of Time and Price. In other words, there are times when Price will accelerate and exceed Time. This means the Price projections are reached before the Time projections are met. On the other hand, there will also be trade signals where Time runs out before the Price projections are met. Either way, you will know in advance when it is time to take action.

In the early 1960s, one of Roger Babson's close friends and students, Dr. Alan Andrews, began to provide a study course based on the theory of the "Law of Action/Reaction." One of the techniques he taught was called the "Median Line Study." This technique employed a set of chart lines that were drawn from a significant low or high through the center of the following Reaction swing. Lines were also drawn parallel to the center line, from the high and low of the Reaction swing. When completed, these three lines resembled a pitchfork. Eventually, it became known as the "Andrews Pitchfork" and can be found on many charting programs today.

I have found the combination of Roger Babson's Action/Reaction theory and Dr. Alan Andrews Pitchfork is a powerful indicator of future price action. It seems that I have combined the two in a rather unusual way; yet it has proved to be an uncanny combination for price projection. *I call these price projection lines Action/Reaction lines.*

Price Projections using Action/Reaction lines.

Action/Reaction lines are the foundation to making price projections. They are simple to identify and very powerful when

Chapter 4 - Price

combined with the Time projections from both the TR (Trend Reversal) patterns and TC (Trend Continuation) patterns. Here are the rules for drawing the Action/Reaction lines from a Trend Reversal pattern (TR) in a downward trending market. The rules are reversed in an upward trending market. The first step is locating and drawing the center line. See *Figure # 4.1*.

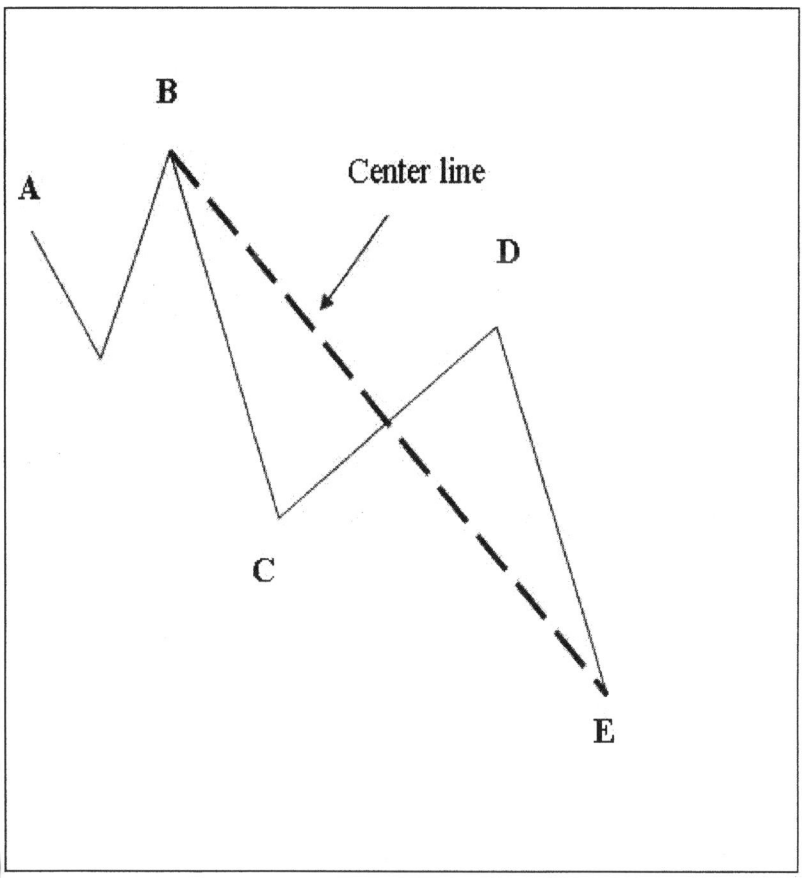

Figure # 4.1 – Find the Center line.

Rules for Finding the Center line.

1-Find the exact center of the (C) to (D) Reaction swing. This can be done by subtracting the low price from the high price and dividing by two. Add the sum to the low or subtract the sum from the high. Either way, you will get the exact center.

2-Now draw a line from the high at (B) through the exact center of the Reaction swing (C) to (D) and continue the line forward to the end of the chart. This line divides the cycle in the exact center and separates the *Action* segment from the *Reaction* segment of the market and is called the *center line*. See *Figure # 4.2*.

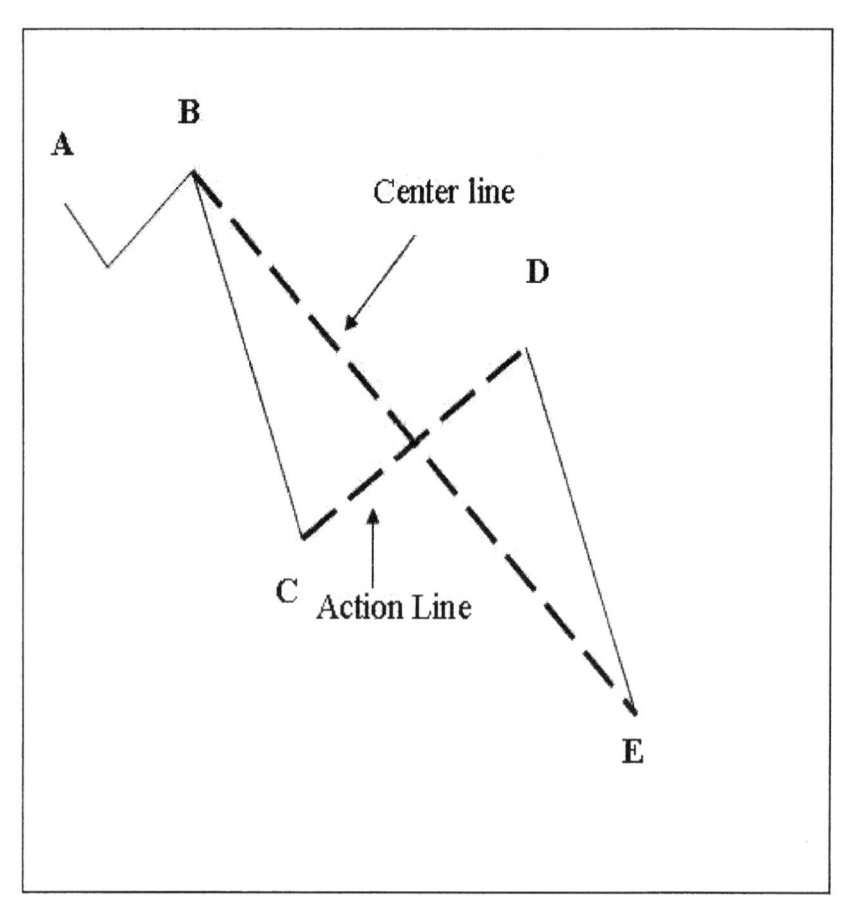

Figure # 4.2 – Draw the Action line

3-Draw a line from the low of the price bar with the lowest closing price at (C) to the high of the price bar with the highest closing price at (D). This line is called the *Action line.*

Chapter 4 - Price 109

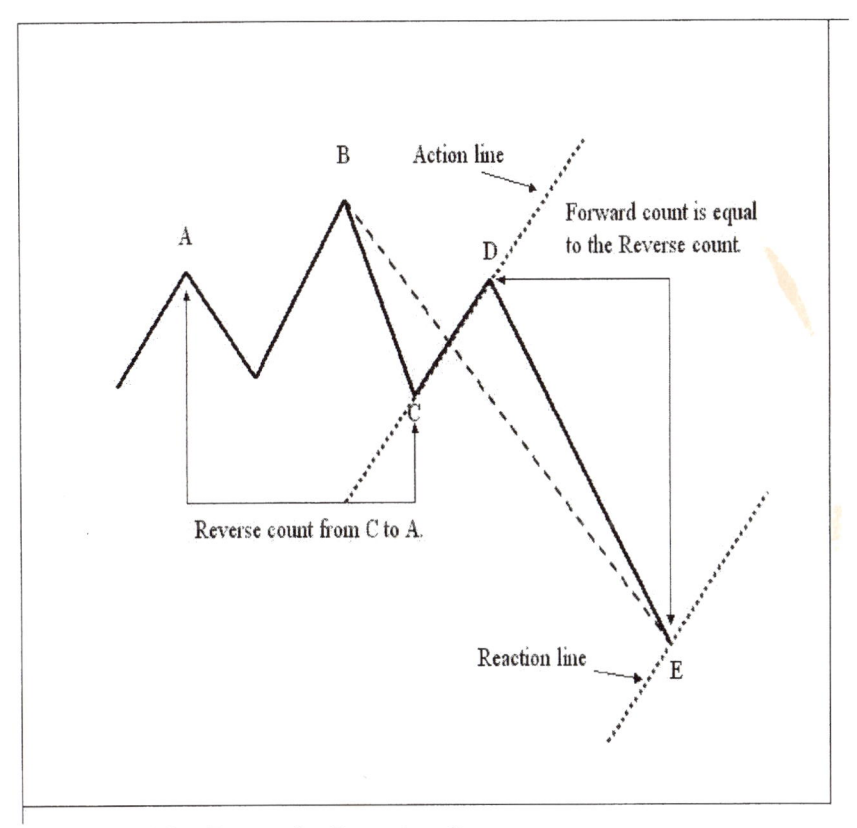

Figure # 4.3 – Draw the Reaction line

4-The next step is to do a reverse/forward count the same way it is done with the TR pattern and the TC pattern. The future Reversal date, determined by the reverse/forward count, is marked on the center line.

5-At the spot marked on the center line, draw a line parallel to the action line. This is known as the *Reaction line* and becomes the price objective. See *Figure # 4.3*.

(I use the Andrews Pitchfork function on my charting software to do this for me. The software will calculate the exact center of the Reaction swing and draw the Action line and center line for you. Most technical charting software packages include this function.)

To illustrate this concept I am going to use several of the same markets I used in the previous chapters. This way you can see how Time and Price work together.

March 2006 Crude oil

Figure # 4.4 - In *Figure # 2.10*, I made a Time projection for the March Crude. Now it is time to add another dimension to that chart. As soon as the high pivot point was confirmed at (D), I drew the Action line. Beginning at the low of (C), I drew a line to the high at (D). This gave me the Action line. Using the Andrews Pitchfork function of my charting software, I clicked on the high at (B), and then clicked on the lowest low of the pivot at (C) followed by the highest high at (D). This function drew a line through the center of the (C) to (D) Reaction swing and divided the Action segment of the cycle from the Reaction segment of the cycle. The center line became the first price objective. Alan Andrews states in his course that the market will reach the center line 80% of the time. I have found this statement to be very close to correct and very helpful in my market analysis. I have also made some of my own observations about the center line and put them to use in the trading rules I am about to illustrate.

The next step was to do the reverse/forward count, just as I did when projecting future Reversal dates using the TR pattern. The reverse count from (C) back to (A) equaled 13 price bars. The forward count of 13 price bars from (D) projected out to February 16. I located February 16 on the chart and marked this date on the center line. At the spot I marked on the center line, I drew a line parallel to the Action line. This is called the Reaction line or Target line and gave me a price objective to go along with the Time projections. In other words, if everything plays out as it should, I can expect the market to reach this line on or before the projected Reversal date.

I consider the price level where the reaction line crosses the center line as the primary price objective. This means the price objective of the short position in the March Crude oil was 58.65.

Chapter 4 - Price

Since the trigger price to enter the short position was 67.20, I anticipated the Crude oil to fall to 58.65 within the next 13 days. The Crude oil will either reach the Reaction line or run out of time; either way, I know in advance when the market is due to lose momentum and it is no longer advantageous to stay in the trade. That information is invaluable to a trader!

Crude oil reached the Reaction line on February 15—one day before the February 16 Reversal date—where it posted a low of 57.60 before bouncing back to 58.46 on the February 16. In this case, the market pushed past the projected price to reach the Reaction line early; either way, the market did exactly what the Reversal date Indicator had suggested.

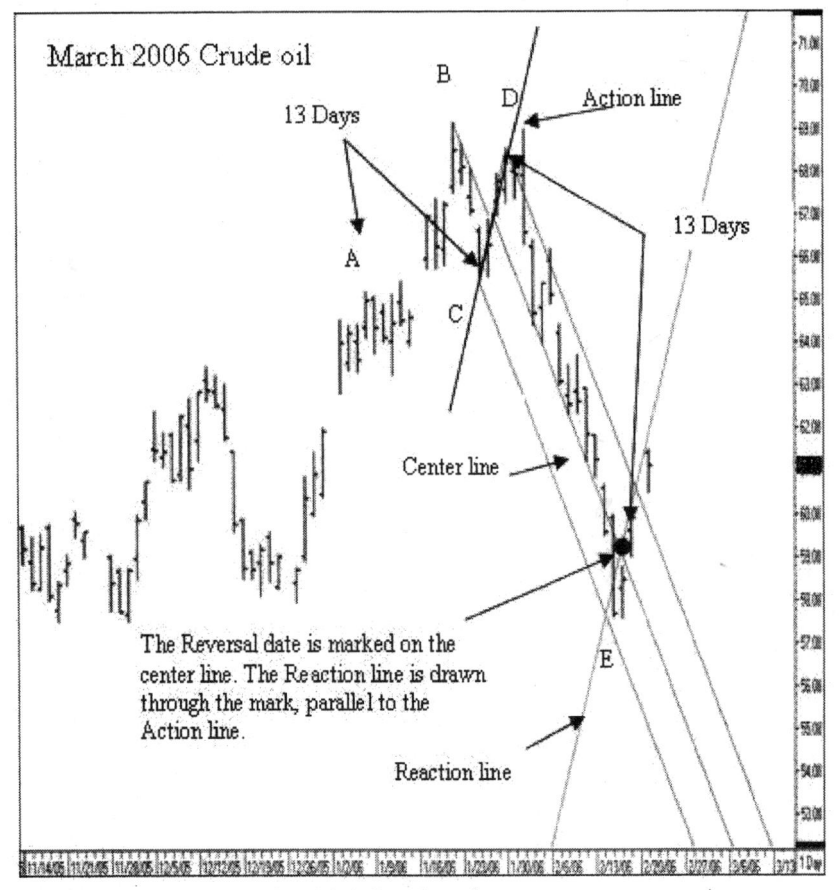

Figure # 4.4 – March 2006 Crude oil

The Sloping Reaction Line

The Reaction line is not a stagnant target. The line slopes away from the trend. This means in a downward trending market the bottom of the Reaction line is farther away from the entry price than the upper part of the Reaction line. The slope coincides with the strength or weakness of the trend. For example, in a downward trending market, the weaker the market, the farther down on the reaction line the market will go. On the other hand, the stronger the trend, the higher the market will be when it reaches the Reaction line.

This also holds true for which side of the center line the market is trading. In a downward trending market, the farther below the center line, the weaker the market. In an upward trend, the stronger the trend, the farther above the center line the market will trade. This is a very easy way to identify the momentum of the trend.

December 2004 Lean Hogs

Figure # 4.5 - After triggering the buy signal on September 9, the reverse/forward count projected a future Reversal date of September 23. Since I knew the potential duration of the new upward price swing, the next step is to determine what kind of price potential the trade has to offer. To answer that question, I started at the same place as I did when I made the Time projection – at the Reaction swing marked (C) to (D). I drew a line from the high of the price bar with the highest closing price at (C) to the low of the price bar with the lowest closing price at (D) to make the Action line. The next step was to identify the center of the (C) to (D) Reaction swing.

The high at (C) was 64.40 and the low at (D) was 61.90. Subtracting 64.40 from 61.90 equaled 250 points. Divide 250 in half and the total was 125. I can either add 125 to the low (61.90 + 125 = 63.15) or subtract 125 for the high (64.40 – 125 = 63.15) to find the exact center of the Reaction swing. The next step was to

Chapter 4 - Price 113

draw the center line from the low at (B) through 63.15 and continue it forward to project slope of the new trend. Next came the reverse/forward count. This was done the same way as the reverse/forward count used for projecting future Reversal dates. Beginning with the first price bar to the left of the highest closing price bar at (C), I counted back to the lowest close at (A). The reverse count equaled 11 days. Beginning with the first price bar to the right of the price bar with lowest closing price at (D), I counted forward 11 days and marked the center line. At the spot marked on the center line, I drew a line parallel to the Action line to make the Reaction line.

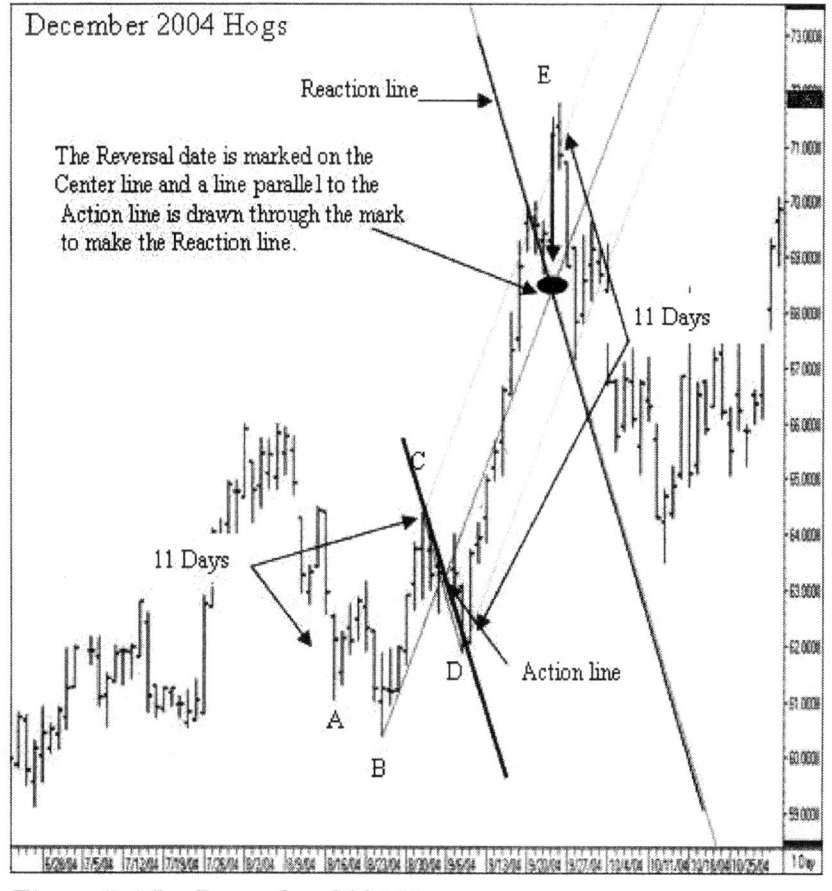

Figure # 4.5 – December 2004 Hogs

The Reaction line crossed the center line at 69.00, suggesting the December Hogs were projected to reach 69.00 or higher on or before the September 23 Reversal date. In other words, I could expect the December Hogs to rally 550 to 600 points within the next 11 days. That looked like a pretty good trade!

As expected, December Hogs reached the projected target price on September 20, three days before the Reversal date was due. Whether I was trading with just the Time portion and exited on the September 23 Reversal date or using the Price portion, both forecasted a successful trade with minimal risk. In fact, after entry, this trade would have never been negative!

Exceeding Price Targets

One thing you may have noticed in the last two examples, both markets exceeded their projected price targets. Typically, the TR pattern is the beginning of a fairly strong price move and the trend can accelerate quickly. A strong trend has a tendency to reach the center line quickly and move beyond the line. For example, March Crude oil—*Figure #4.4*—traded along the upper side of the center line until it approached the Reversal date. Just before the Reversal date, the market dropped through the center line and pushed to 57.65, slightly beyond the target price. The December Hogs—*Figure #4.5*—are another good example. The Hogs crossed above the center line mid-way through the cycle and reached the reaction line at 70.00, three days before the Reversal date was due. When a market crosses the center line, it suggests a strong price move is about to occur and the stronger the price move, the higher it will go before reaching the Reaction line. I always keep this in mind when considering a target price because targets are dynamic, just like the markets.

December 2005 Dow Jones

Figure # 4.6 - On October 24, 2005, the December Dow Jones traded above 10,335 to trigger the buy signal and confirm the Reaction swing marked (C) and (D). The reverse count from (C) to (A) equaled 20 days. The count forward from (D) identified the future Reversal date as November 18. I had all the information needed to make the price projection.

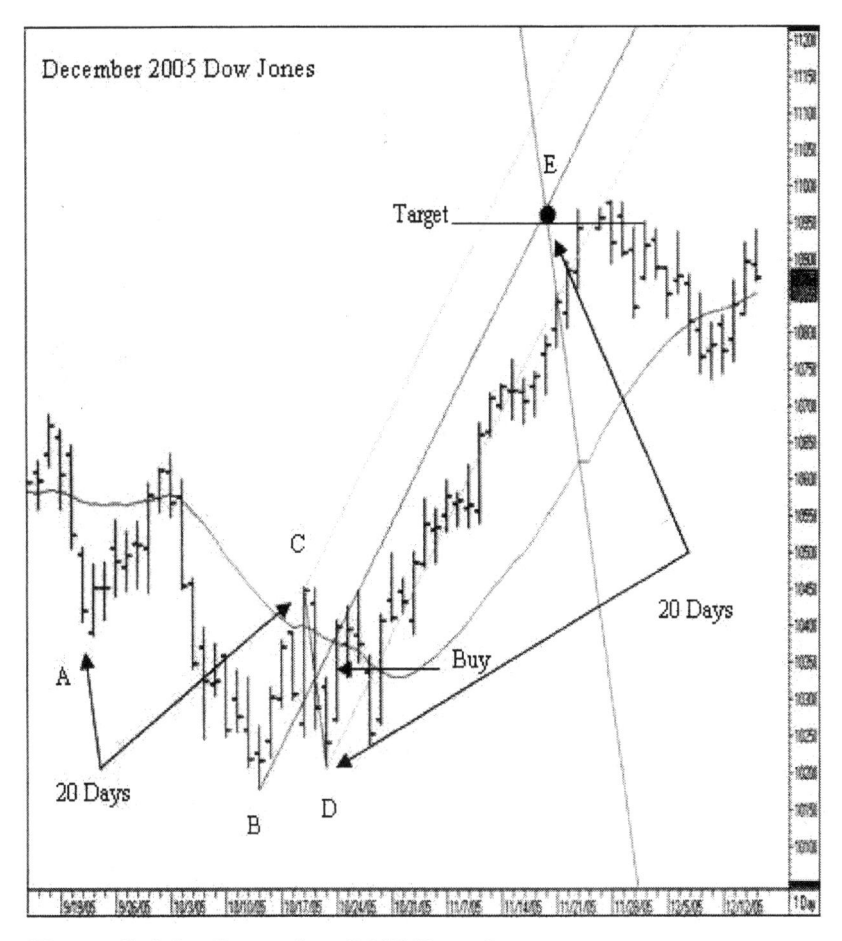

Figure # 4.6 – December 2005 Dow Jones

116   *Chapter 4 - Price*

I drew the Action line from the low at (C) to the high at (D), followed by the center line through the center of the (C) to (D) Reaction swing and extended it to the end of the chart. I then marked November 18, on the center line before drawing the Reaction line parallel to the Action line. The Reaction line crossed the center line and identified 10,930 as the first price target for the long position. If everything unfolded according to plan, the December Dow Jones would reach 10,930 on or before the November 18 Reversal date. In that case the buy signal suggested the potential price move of 590 points within the next 20 days!

Soon after the entry signal was triggered the Dow Jones experienced a two-day pullback before it began a steady climb over the next 20 days, but it was never able to break above the center line. Time ran out for the trade when the Dow Jones reached the November 18th Reversal date before it was able to reach the target price of 10,930. However, the Dow traded as high as 10,795 before closing at 10,782 on November 18. Eventually, the market did pass through the Reaction line and reached 10,968 on November 23...three days after the Reversal date. Although the Dow Jones was able to hit the ultimate target price, the early exit still would have captured over 60% of the entire price move.

September 2003 Treasury Bonds

Figure # 4.7, the (C) to (D) Reaction swing was confirmed on June 25 and triggered a sell signal when the T-Bonds fell below the 119-03 low at (C). As soon as the pattern was confirmed, I went through the steps to draw the Action line and center line, followed by a reverse/forward count. The reverse count from (C) back to (A) equaled 20 days. The count forward, from (D), identified July 22 as the Reversal date. I marked July 22 on the center line and drew the Reaction line parallel to the Action line. The initial target was identified as 107-10, where the Reaction line crossed the center line. I now had a price target of 107-10 to go along with the target date of July 22. If everything went according to plan, the T-Bonds

Chapter 4 - Price 117

should fall over 11-basis points during the next 20 days! That was a big move.

Over the next four weeks, T-Bonds continued the downward trend with only one three-day pause midway through the downward cycle, before it posted a low at 109-12 and a closed at 110-16, on the July 22 Reversal date. Even though time ran out before the market reached the price objective of 107-10, it still offered a potential gain of $8,500 over a three-week period with only a couple of pauses midway through the trade. Either way, it was a great trade signal!

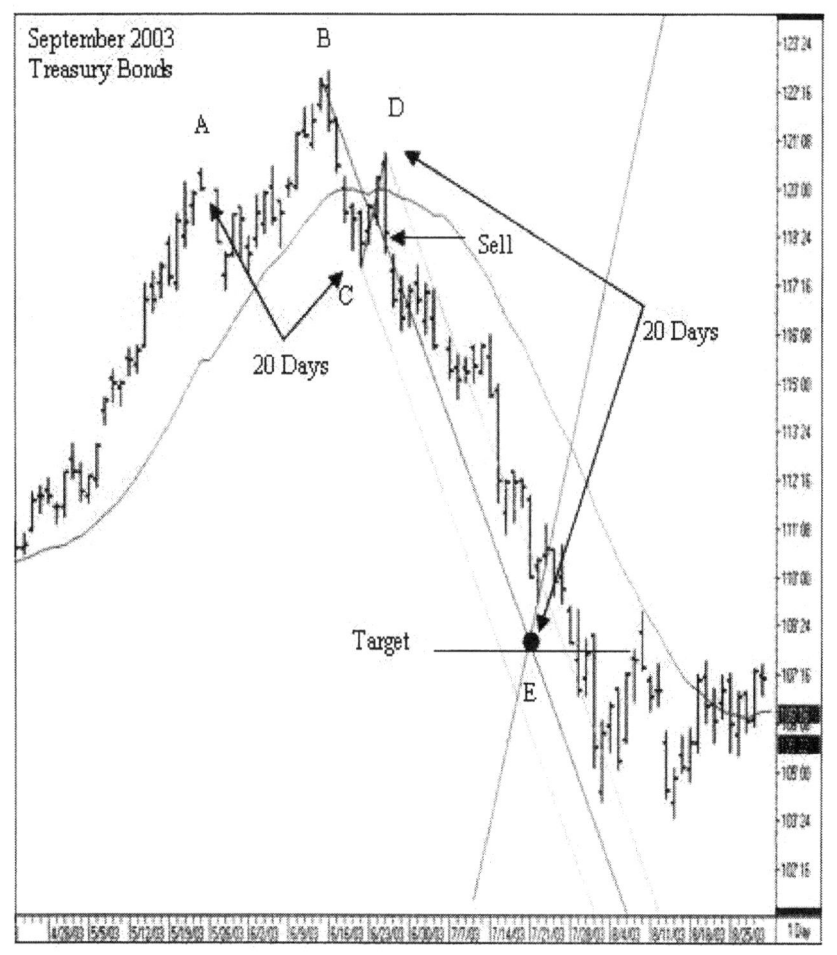

Figure # 4.7 – September 2003 Treasury Bonds

118   Chapter 4 - Price

Continuing the Trend – Projecting Price.

In the previous chapter, I introduced the Trend Continuation pattern and illustrated how to use it to project forward from a Reaction swing that falls inside the trend. The same rules for the Trend Continuation (TC pattern) apply when making price projections inside a trending market. I will use the following examples to illustrate how the TC pattern can also project future support and resistance levels or turning points.

September 2003 T-Bonds

Figure # 4.8 - September T-Bonds didn't reach the Reaction line target, but they did bounce after the July 21 Reversal day (E) and posted two consecutive higher closes on July 22 and July 23 (F). The two-day correction set up another possible Reaction swing and TC pattern. When the T-Bonds dropped below the pivot low (E) on July 25, they confirmed the Reaction swing and triggered the sell signal at 109-10. I have already illustrated, in *Figure # 3.4*, the reverse count from (E) back to the low of the previous swing pattern on July 8—marked as (P-1)—equaled 9 days. When I projected forward 9 days from (F) I identified August 5 as the next Reversal date.

However, drawing the center line is a little different when dealing with a TC pattern. *The center line begins at the end of the previous Reaction swing.* For example, the reverse count ended at the pivot low on July 8, marked as (P-1). This was the beginning of a swing pattern that ended with a high pivot on July 11, marked as (P-2). The center line began from the pivot high of July 11 (P-2) and extended downward through the center of the (E) to (F) Reaction swing and continued on to the end of the chart.

I marked August 5 on the center line, added the Action/Reaction lines and projected the initial target price as 103-06. Either the T-Bonds will reach 103-06 on or before August 5th or the market will run out of time and end the cycle. In this case

Chapter 4 - Price   119

the T-Bonds ran out of time when the market closed at 105-09 on August 5. T-Bonds failed to reach the target price, but they still offered huge potential as they traveled from 109-10 to 105-09 in 9 days!

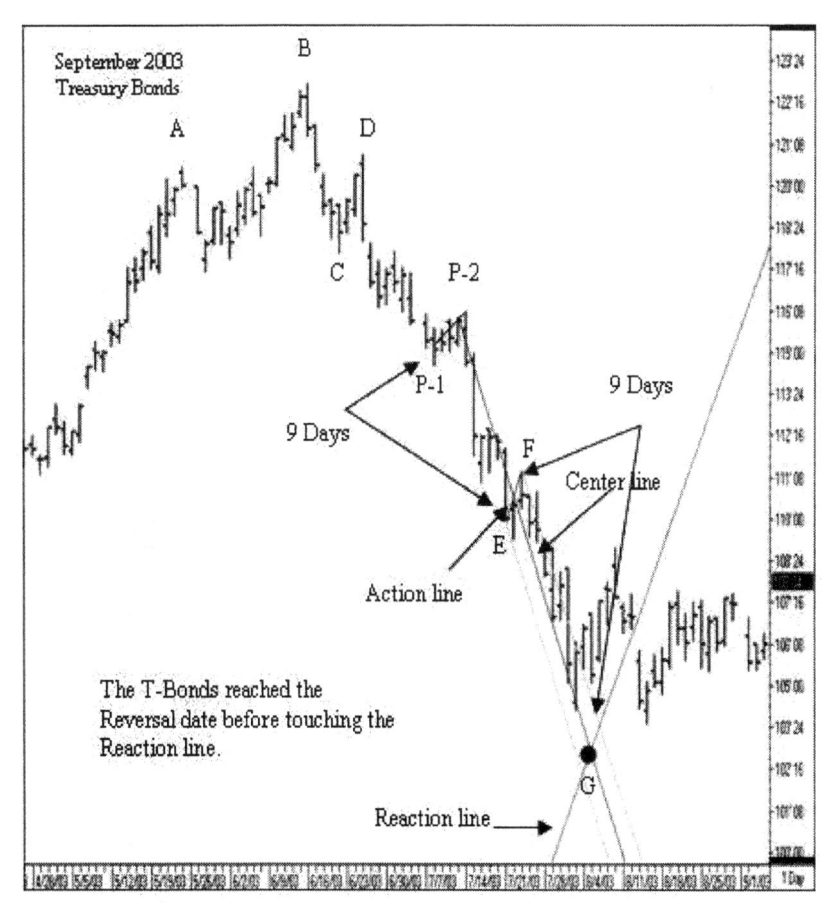

Figure # 4.8 – September 2003 Treasury Bonds

December 2004 Coffee

Figure # 4.9 - A sell signal was confirmed on June 14, when the December Coffee opened below the pivot low at (C) and began trading at 87.75. The reverse/forward count equaled 19 days, which in turn projected forward to July 8 as the future Reversal date. July 8 was marked on the center line and the Action/Reaction lines were drawn to project an initial target price at 78.00, the price level where the reaction line crossed the center line.

December Coffee quickly passed through the center line and stayed below the line throughout the course of the trade. Since the market was below the center line I anticipated the market would surpass the target price before it would reach the Reaction line. Sure enough, the selling pressure continued and the market fell past the initial target, settling at 75.45 on July 2...well below the initial target of 78.00, but still above the reaction line. The market was closed on Monday July 5, because of the July 4th holiday. July 6 opened with a gap lower and began trading at 74.50. This put the market below the reaction line and indicated it was time to exit the trade—a potential gain of 1,325 points in 17 days—because the market was overdue for a major low or correction. Two days later, the market turned higher and began the correction as anticipated. But it is not over!

December 2004 Coffee – TC pattern

Figure # 4.10 - The July 8 Reversal date (E) was the low pivot point before the market entered an eight-day correction that ended with a high close of 76.65 on July 20 (F). The following day began with a higher opening, but the market failed to find any willing buyers and began to fall. A sell signal was triggered at 75.20 when Coffee dropped below the low of the highest price bar at (F). Coffee continued to fall and dropped below the low pivot point at (E) and confirmed the Reaction swing. The next step was to make the price projection.

I began the reverse count at the low marked (E) and counted back to the previous pivot low on June 25, marked (P-1). The count equaled 9 days. The forward count of 9 days from (F) suggested August 2 as the future Reversal date. The center line

Chapter 4 - Price 121

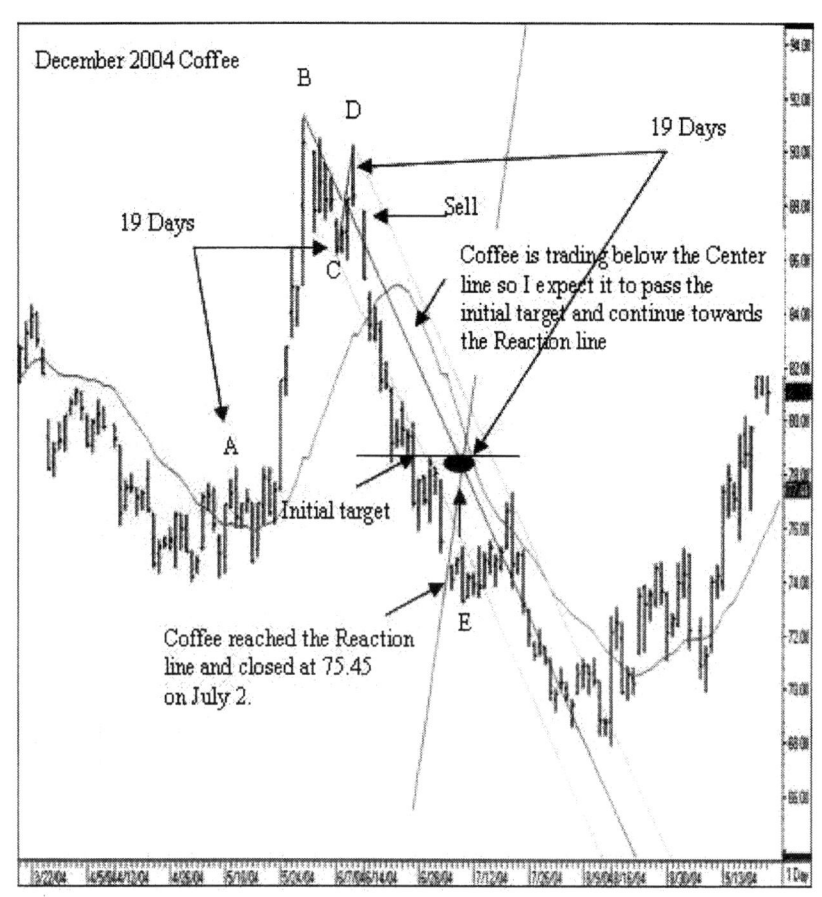

Figure # 4.9 – December 2004 Coffee

began at the pivot high on June 30—marked (P-2)—and extended downward through the center of the (E) – (F) Reaction swing and continued forward where August 2 was marked on the center line. As soon as the Action/Reaction lines were drawn, 70.25 was identified as the initial target price. The 70.25 target price was reached on Friday, July 30 as the market passed through the target and closed at 69.85. The following Monday—August 2—Coffee reached a low of 69.20 before the market moved into a bullish TR pattern and turned higher.

122   Chapter 4 - Price

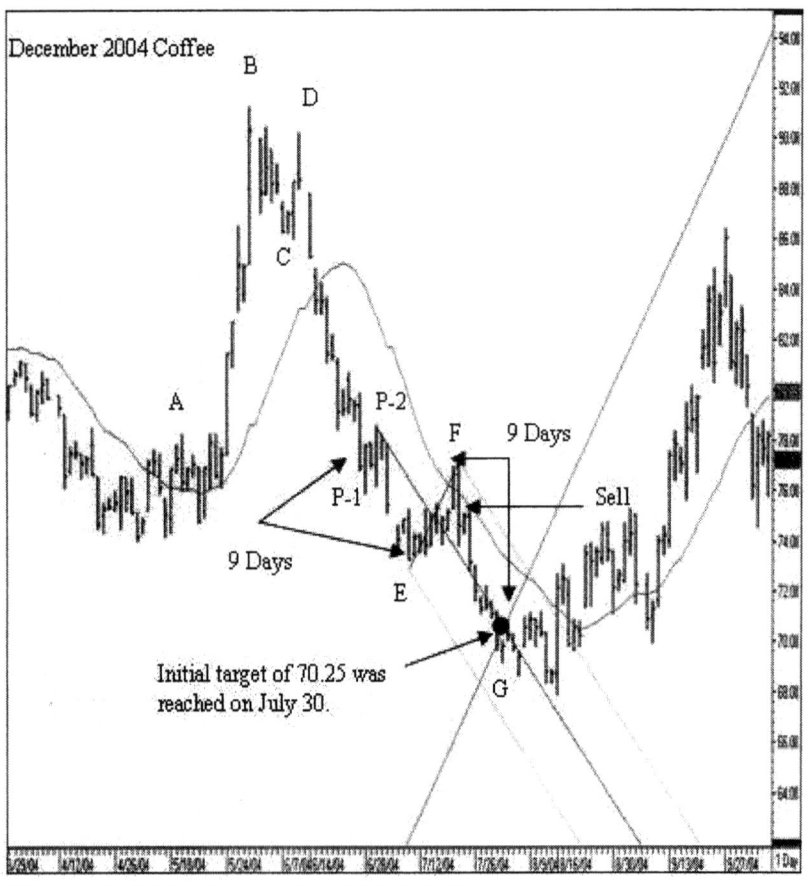

Figure # 4.10 – December 2004 Coffee

Trident Microsystems Inc. (TRID)

Figure # 4.11 - After the sell signal was triggered at 30.14, on April 26—*Figure # 2.15*—the market dropped quickly through the center line and stayed below the line until May 15. The reverse count from (C) to (A) was 12 days, which in turn projected May 11 as the future Reversal date. I marked May 11 on the center line and drew the Action/Reaction lines to identify the initial target price of 26.40.

TRID traded below the center line throughout the trend so Price was in control; therefore, the market was more likely to pass the

Chapter 4 - Price 123

target price and converge on the Reaction line on or before May 11. This scenario proved to be true as TRID reached the 27.00 target price on the third day of the trade where it moved into a consolidation pattern over the next six days. The market broke support on the seventh day and closed at 26.04 on May 9. This was just shy of the Reaction line, but the market continued lower during the following trading session and broke through the Reaction line, finally touching 24.38 on May 10. TRID immediately entered into a corrective rally into May 19, forming a new Reaction swing and a possible TC pattern, setting up the next potential sell signal.

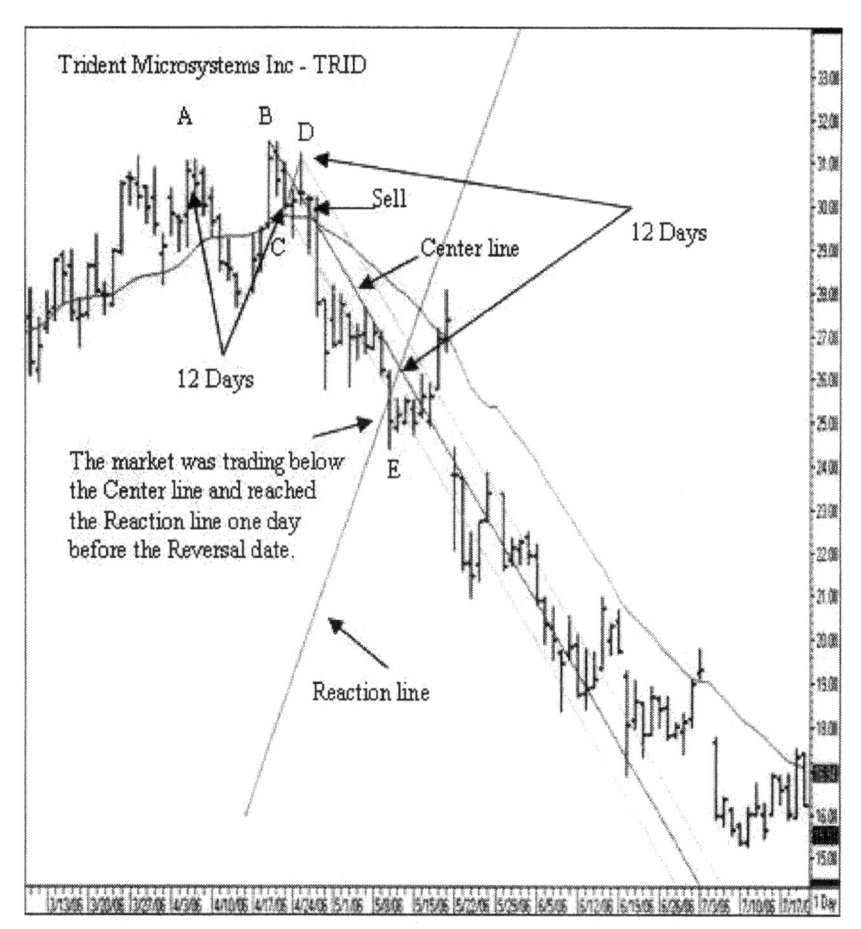

Figure # 4.11 – Trident Microsystems Inc. (TRID)

Managing the Trade

It can be debated which way it is best to trade this signal. Some traders think is best to wait for the market to reach the Reaction line before exiting because the market is below the center line and showing weakness. On the other hand, there are other traders who feel it is best to grab the quick gains when the market makes a parabolic move and wait for a corrective rally and another signal. That's up to the individual trader to decide.

Trident Microsystems Inc, TRID - TC pattern

Figure # 4.12 - After the May 11, Reversal day, TRID began a short-term rally and formed a new Reaction swing. However, the beginning of the Reaction swing was considered May 15 (E), because this date had the lowest closing price before the rally into May 19 (F). After the sell signal was triggered at 23.80—*see Figure # 3.5*—I drew the center line from the high at (D) downward through the center of the (E) to (F) Reaction swing and carried it forward. The reverse count from (E) to (C) is 16 days, which projected out to June 12 as the future Reversal date. I marked this date on the center line and drew the Action/Reaction lines to project a target price of 19.75.

The market dropped below the center line and remained below the line as it approached the Reaction line target. The target was reached on June 7, but the market was still above the Reaction line until June 8 when it dropped to a low of 18.35 before closing at 19.44. After a one-day bounce the market traded lower on the June 12 Reversal date and closed at 18.72. The price projected over two weeks earlier was reached before the scheduled Reversal date!

Microsoft Corp (MSFT)

Figure # 4.13 - As soon as MSFT triggered the sell signal at 27.01 on September 2—*Figure # 2.16*—I drew the center line through the (C) to (D) Reaction swing. The reverse count from (C) to (A)

Chapter 4 - Price 125

equaled 21 days. This put the Reversal date due on September 29. I marked the date on the center line and drew the Action/Reaction lines to project an initial target price at 25.42.

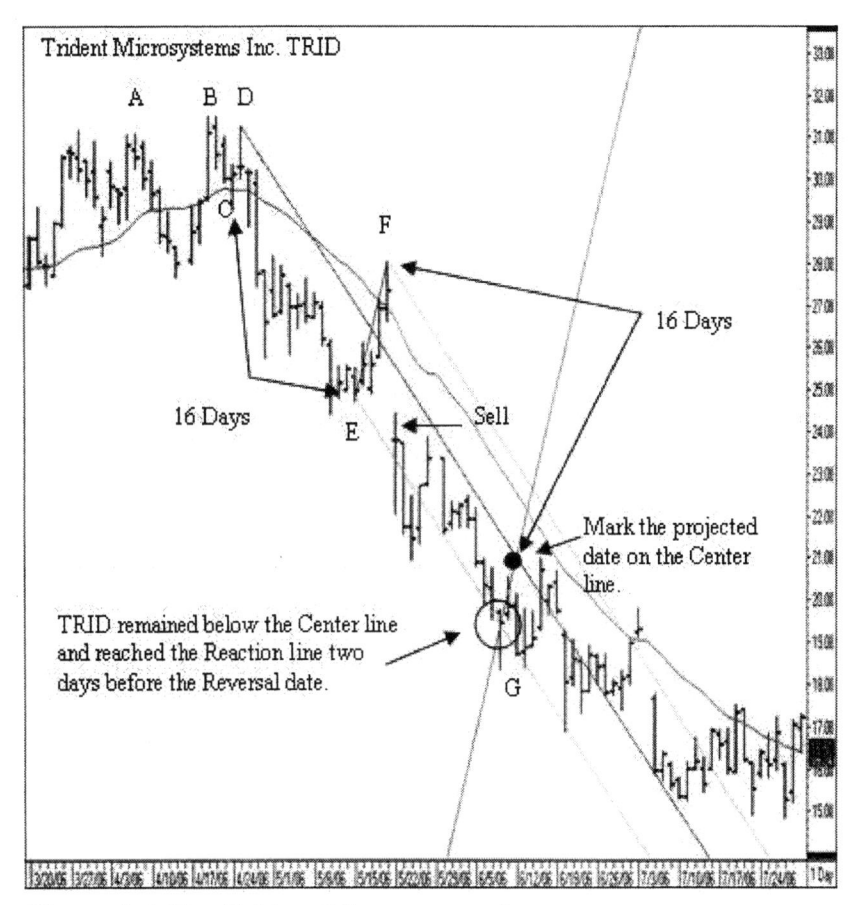

Figure # 4.12 – Trident Microsystems Inc.

MSFT traded along the center line until it broke through on September 16, where the downward slide began to accelerate towards the Reaction line. On September 22, (E) the market passed through the target—25.42—and touched the Reaction line at 25.15 before closing at 25.34 ... six days before the Reversal date is due. This is a classic case of the Price outpacing Time. The market reached the target price and the reaction line on the same day, so I expected to see a rebound from this reaction point and I got it!

The market bounced off the reaction line and traded higher into the September 29 Reversal date (F), forming a new Reaction swing and setting the stage for another sell signal. *(Note: When the market trades higher into a Reversal date the market will typically turn lower. A lower trade into the Reversal date will typically turn the market higher. Also worth noting is how the market stops at the 20-day SMA on the Reversal date.)*

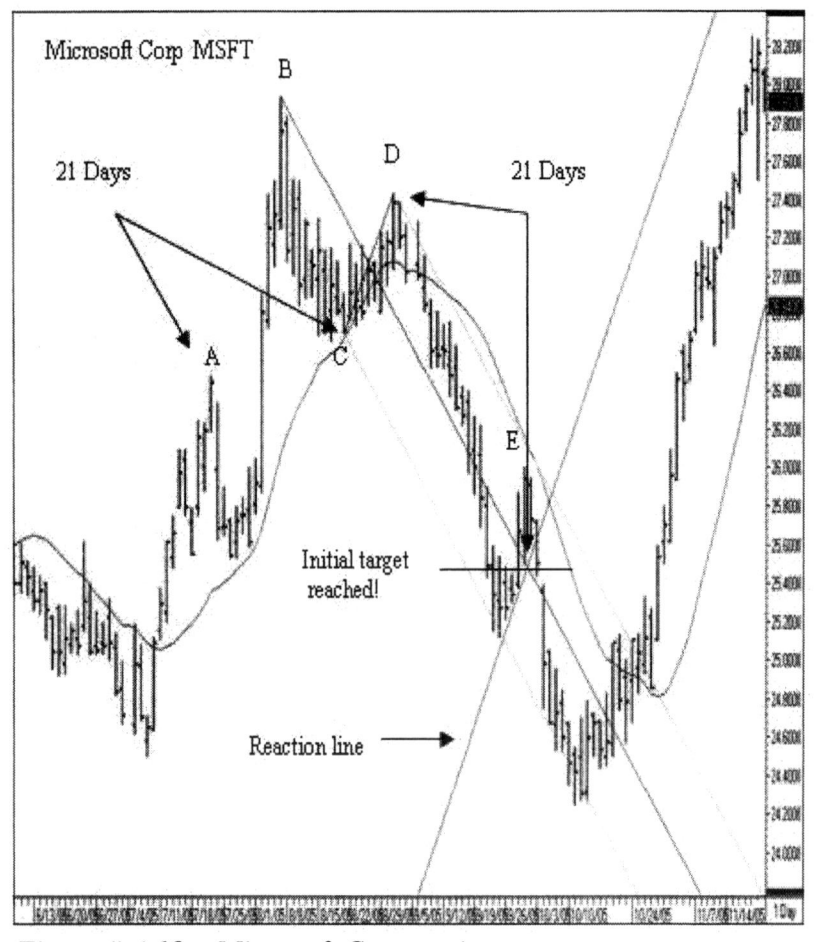

Figure # 4.13 – Microsoft Corporation

Chapter 4 - Price 127

Microsoft Corp – New Trend Reversal

Figure # 4.14 - MSFT peaked on the September 29 Reversal date and turned lower. On October 4, the market broke below the previous pivot low (E) and triggered a sell signal that also confirmed the Reaction swing. The center line began at the end of the previous Reaction swing (D) and continued downward through the center of the (E) – (F) Reaction swing on to the end of the chart. The reverse count for (E) to (C) equaled 25 days. After counting forward 25 days from (F), I marked November 3 on the center line and projected 22.80 as the target price.

On October 10, the market bottomed at 24.70 (BB) and turned higher. Five days later—on October 19—the market crossed the 20-day SMA before it peaked at 25.09 (CC), posting a new pivot high that was followed by two consecutive lower closes on October 21 and October 22 (DD). A new Reaction swing formed and signaled the end of the downward trend. The market shifted from a downward trending market to a an upward trending market.

The bullish TR pattern was completed on October 24, confirming the major reversal that and ended the downward trend and signaled the new buy at 25.02. This should have also closed the short position shy of the projected target price and the November 3 Reversal date.

It is important to remember, if a market forms a new TR pattern that contradicts the existing position, the new TR pattern will prevail.

Microsoft Corp. (MSFT) the Buy

Figure # 4.15 - The buy signal at 25.02 was triggered on October 24 and MSFT jumped out of the box quickly and began to trend sharply higher. The reverse count from (C) to (A) equaled 18 days and projected the future Reversal date for November 16 and a target price of 26.40. It did not take long for the market to trade above the center line and continue the steep upward trend. The trend remained

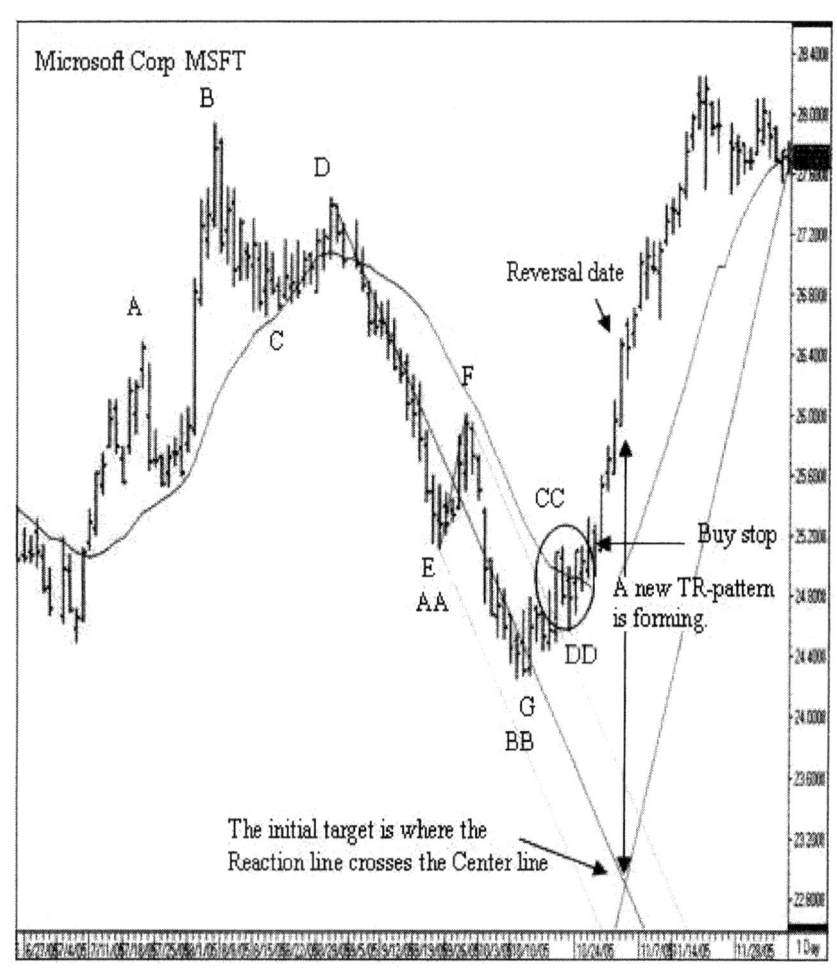

Figure # 4.14 – Microsoft Corporation

strong and the market was still below the reaction line when MSFT reached 26.40 on November 2. Since there was still 10 trading days left before the Reversal date was due and the reaction line was still considerably above the current market price, I expected there was more upside potential. The market reached the Reaction line on November 11 when the market gapped above the Reaction line and began trading at 27.15 and closed at 27.28.

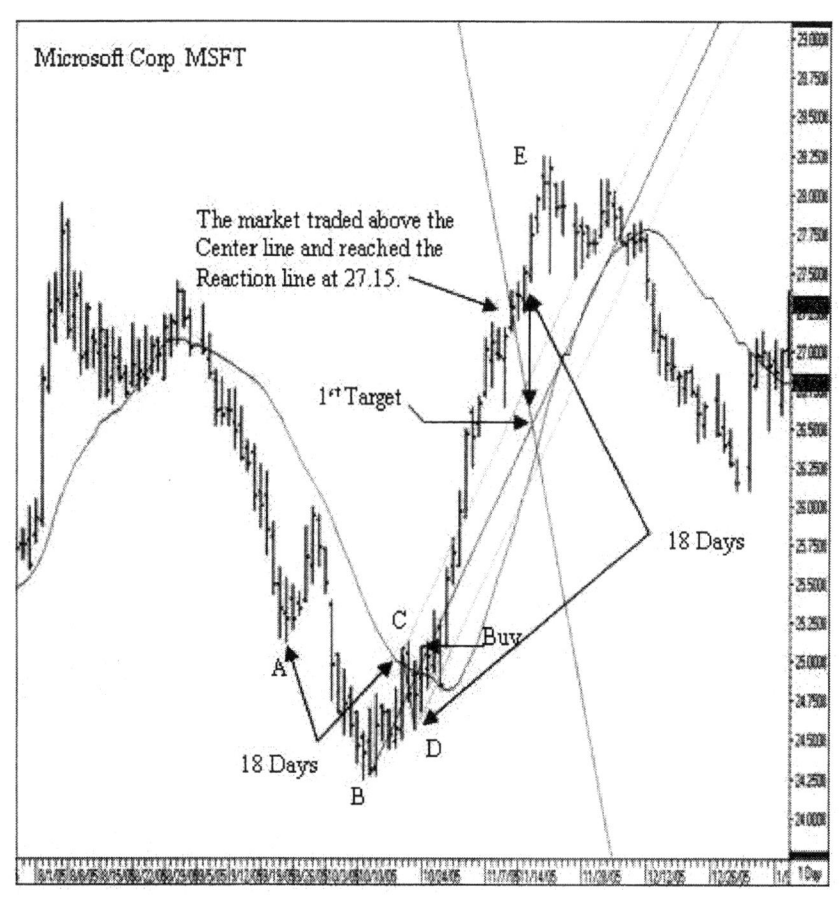

Figure # 4.15 – Microsoft Corporation

Managing the Trade

The market reached the preliminary target but still was considerably above the center line, suggesting a strong potential to continue the trend into the reaction line. Again, this is up to the individual trader as to whether to exit at the target price or elect to move the protective stop underneath the November 2nd low of 25.93 and hold until the market reached the Reaction line or the protective stop order had been breeched. Either way, the signal offered a great trading opportunity with little or no draw down.

May 2005 Soybeans

Figure # 4.16 - A signal to go long the May Soybeans was triggered on February 28 when the market gapped above the trigger price (C) and began trading at $5.41 ¼. The center line and the Action line were drawn. The reverse count from (C) back to the low at (A) equaled 20 days, which in turn projected a future Reversal date of March 16. I drew the Reaction line and identified $6.21 as the initial target price.

The market remained in a steep trend and broke above the center line, suggesting the market should surpass the preliminary target of $6.21 and continue to push towards the sloping Reaction line. On March 2, May Soybeans reached a high of $6.33, before moving into a sideways consolidation pattern. The buy signal offered a potential gain .79-cents without any draw down!

Six days later, the market broke through the Reaction line at $6.38 and raced to a high of $6.91 ½ on the March 16th Reversal date.

August 2005 Gold

Figure # 4.17 - On June 10, August Gold rallied past the $430.00 trigger price and confirmed the Reaction swing and the longer-term TR pattern. I determined June 23 as the future Reversal date in conjunction with a target price of $450.00. Ten days after the entry signal was triggered, August Gold peaked at $444.20 on the June 23 Reversal date. This is an example of a market reaching the Reversal date before the projected target price. In other words, Time ran out before the price objective was achieved. Still, the signal would have offered a potential of a $14.00 gain.

Chapter 4 - Price 131

Figure # 4.16 – May 2005 Soybeans

December 2005 Gold

Figure # 4.18 - On the morning of November 16, December Gold opened sharply higher and triggered the buy signal at the opening price of $473.70. As soon as the buy signal was confirmed, I took the steps to project the future Reversal date as December 9. I marked the date on the center line and drew the Action/Reaction lines to identify the initial target price of $505.00.

After the higher opening on November 16, December Gold continued to surge higher and remained above the center line throughout the remainder of the trade. It only took 13 days for the

132   *Chapter 4 - Price*

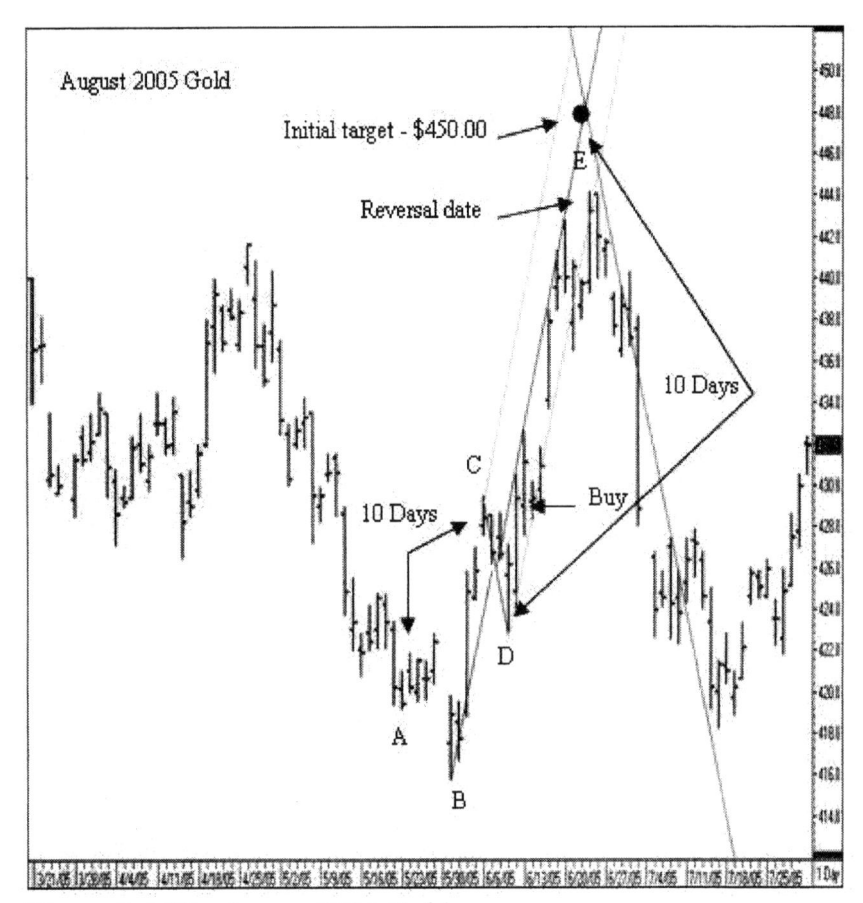

Figure # 4.17 – August 2005 Gold

market to rally over $31.00 and reach the $505.00 target, but it wasn't finished. Gold continued to make new daily highs over the next seven days before finally reaching a peak at $538.50 on Monday, December 12…three days after the predicted Reversal date!

September 2006 Wheat

Figure # 4.19 - The (C) to (D) Reaction swing confirmed a buy signal on May 5. The market gapped above the 20-day SMA and began trading at $3.81 and never looked back. The reverse count from (C) to (A) was 11 days and I used it to project forward to the next Reversal date of May 19. I marked the date on the center line and drew the Action/Reaction lines, which identified $4.15 as the target price.

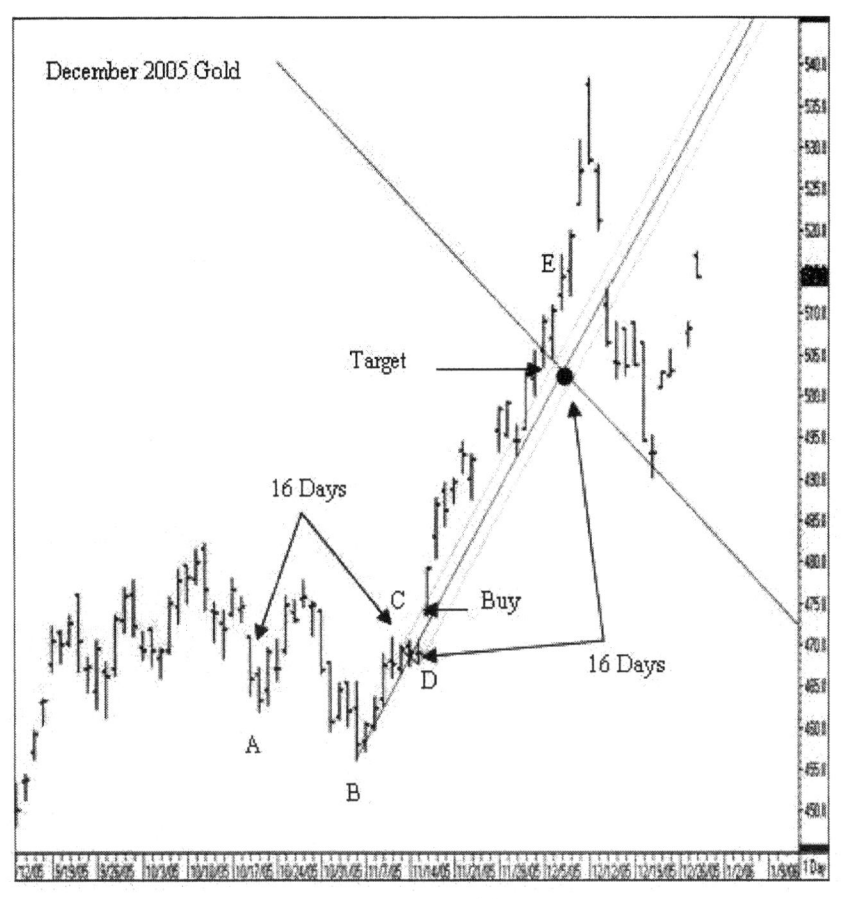

Figure # 4.18 – December 2005 Gold

The September Wheat was expected to rally at least .34 cents within the next eleven days. It didn't take the full eleven days as September Wheat continued the strong upward climb and reached the $4.15 target price on the eighth day. As predicted, the price target was reached well within the eleven-day time period.

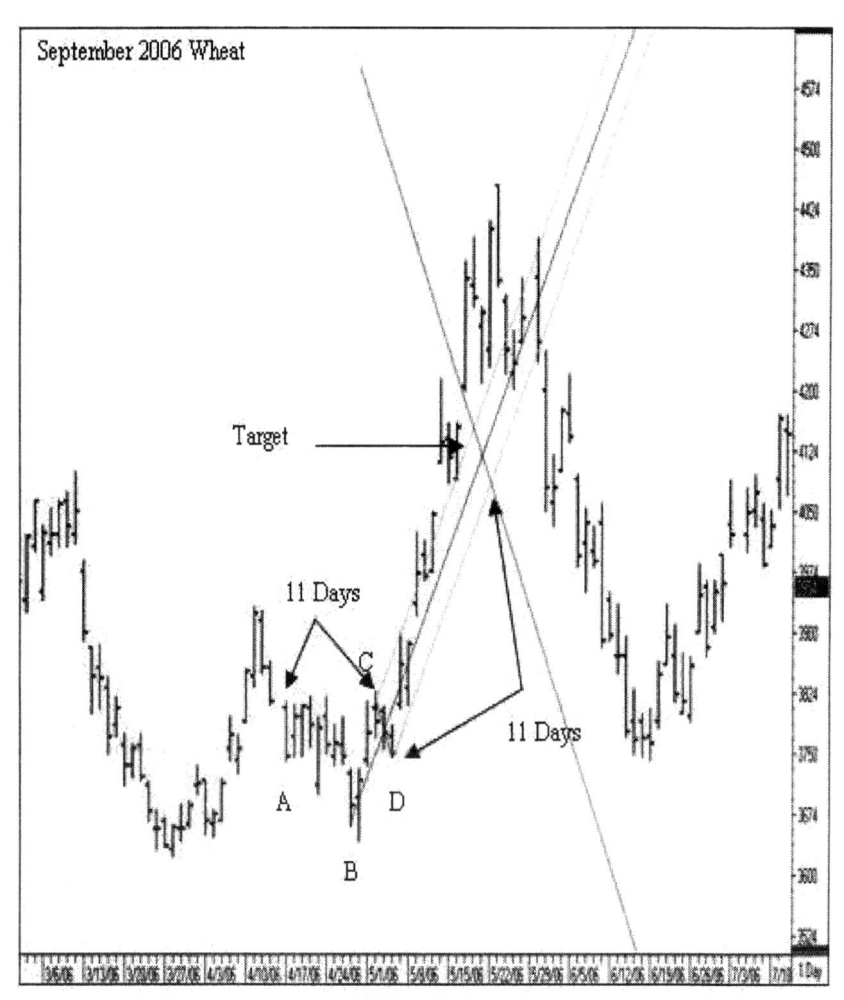

Figure # 4.19 – September 2006 Wheat

September 2006 Cocoa

Figure # 4.20 - A small swing pattern between June 16 and June 20—marked (C) to (D)— was confirmed as a bullish Reaction swing on June 26, when unrest broke out in the Ivory Coast and caused Cocoa prices to explode higher and triggered a buy signal at 1560. The reverse count of 14 days predicted the future Reversal

Chapter 4 - Price

date of July 10. The steep rally continued as September Cocoa raced towards the future Reversal date. As with any runaway market, it's hard to predict when or where the end will come; however, the Action/Reaction lines came very close. I marked July 10th on the center line and used the Action/Reaction lines to forecast an initial target price of 1680... one hundred and twenty points above the entry!

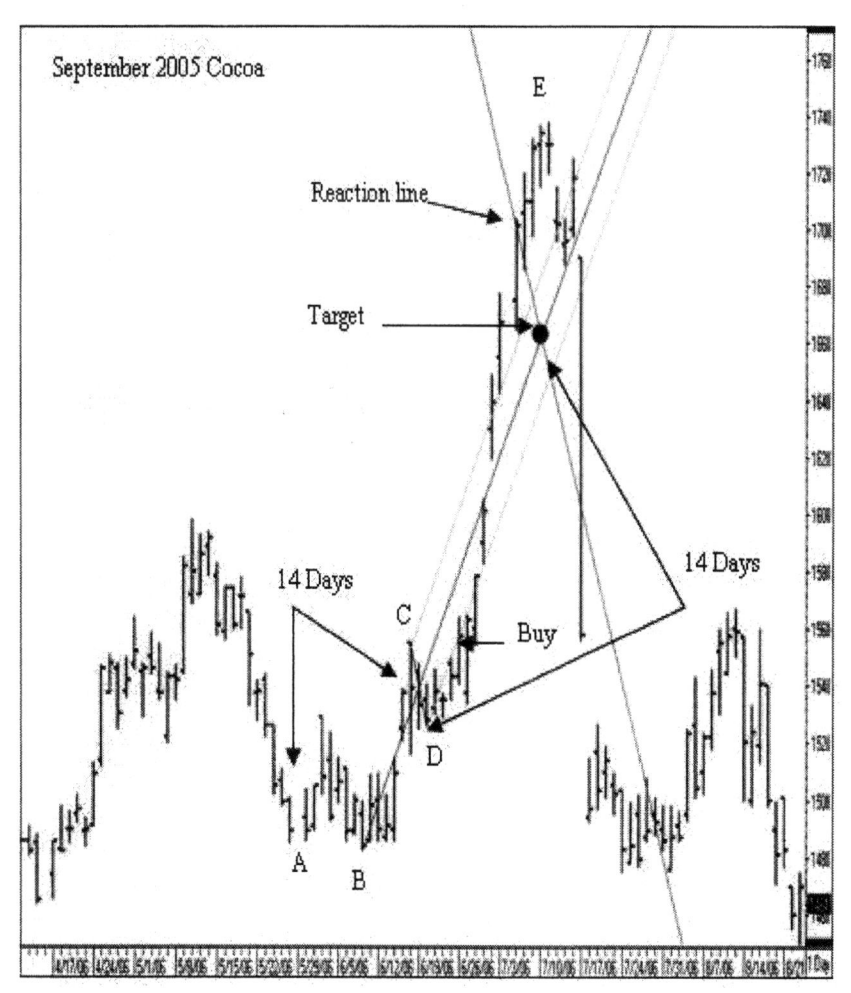

Figure # 4.20 – September 2005 Cocoa

136 Chapter 4 - Price

September Cocoa reached the initial target price seven days after the entry signal, but continued higher until it reached 1737 on the July 10 Reversal date (E). This date proved to be a pivotal date as the market collapsed soon after, giving back all the gains in only five days. Without the foreknowledge of the pending Reversal date and price projection, the long position could have turned disastrous very quickly!

July 2004 Silver

Figure # 4.21 - After a substantial sell-off between April 6 and April 14, July Silver paused long enough to form a bearish Reaction swing, marked (C) to (D) on chart. However, the Silver didn't rest long as the market quickly dropped through the pivot low (C) and began trading at $6.50 on April 21.

The center line began at the high (B) and sloped downward through the center of the (C) – (D) Reaction swing and continued lower to the end of the chart. The reverse count of 16 days was used to project forward to the May 11 Reversal date where I marked it on the center line. The Action/Reaction lines predicted an initial target price of $4.00. The July Silver continued lower over the next three weeks, but ran out of time before the target price was reached. Silver bottomed at $5.50 on May 11, the predicted Reversal date.

June 2004 Japanese Yen

Figure # 4.22 - The June Japanese yen is a good example of a TR pattern followed by a TC pattern. The initial sell signal occurred when the market traded below the low pivot at (C) and triggered a sell at .9410.

Chapter 4 - Price 137

Figure # 4.21 – July 2004 Silver

I drew the center line from the high marked (B), continued lower through the center of the (C) to (D) Reaction swing and extended the line to the end of the chart. The reverse count from (C) back to (A) was 15 days and projected out to a future Reversal date of May 3rd where I marked it on the center line. Next, I drew the Action/Reaction lines and used them to forecast the primary target at 8866. The price objective was not reached because the market ran out of Time. However, the short position did close at .9073 on the May 3 Reversal date, even though the market did not reach its goal. The trade signal offered a potential gain of over 330 points in 15 days!

138   Chapter 4 - Price

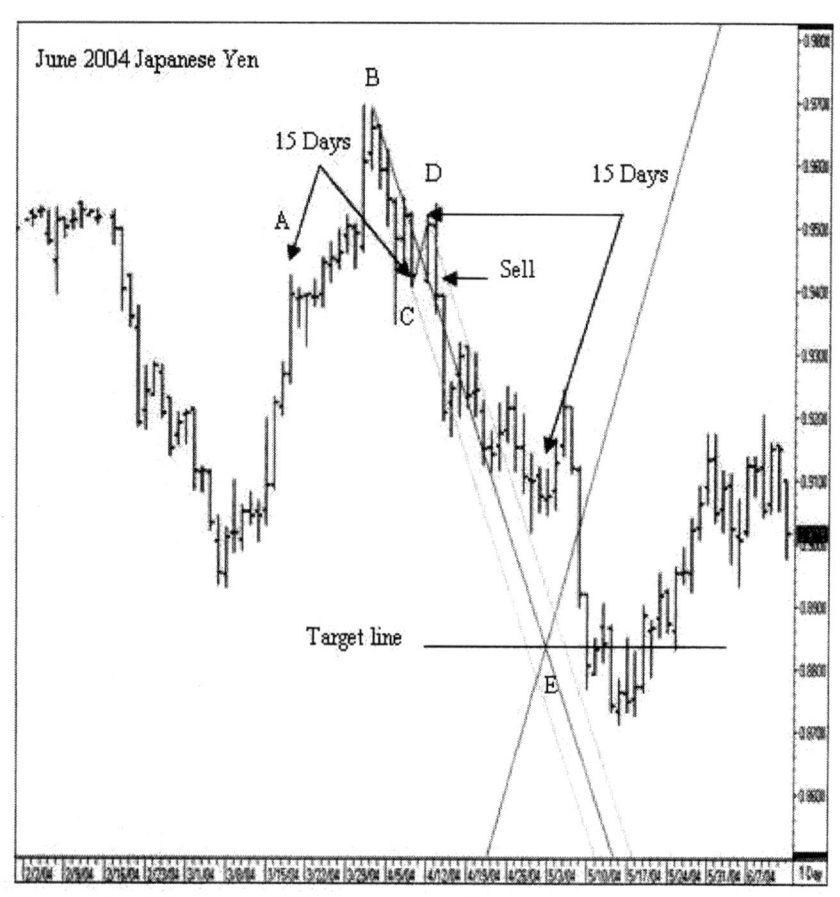

Figure # 4.22 – June 2004 Japanese Yen

June 2004 Japanese Yen continued.

Figure # 4.23 - As soon as the June Japanese yen reached the May 3rd Reversal date it began to form another Reaction swing above the Reaction line. The TC pattern was completed on May 6 and another sell signal triggered at .9130. The Japanese yen was off and running again. Since this was a TC pattern signal, I began the reverse count at (E) and stopped at the pivot low of the previous swing pattern, marked (P-1). The count equaled 6 days and was used to project forward from the high pivot at (F) to identify May 13 as the future Reversal date.

The beginning of center line was at the pivot high, marked (P-2) because it is the first high pivot point following the (P-1) low. The center line was extended lower through the center of the (E) to (F) Reaction swing and I marked May 13 on the line and drew the Action/Reaction lines. When all steps were completed, .8970 was identified as the initial target price.

Figure # 4.23 – June 2004 Japanese Yen

The rapid decline dropped through the center line and reached the target price on the second day, but it was still way above the

Reaction line. Since the market was below the center line the downward momentum continued to push the market lower and reached the Reaction line on the third day. The Japanese yen touched the Reaction line at .8870, a full point below the initial target price of .8970. Once again, it is up to the individual trader as to whether to take the quick gain at the initial target or wait for the bigger reward at the Reaction line. Either way, the trade signal was correct!

Billiton Ltd – BHP

Figure # 4.24 & Figure # 4.25 - As soon as the buy signal was triggered at 36.90, it was time to make the price projection. The reverse count from (C) back to (A) equaled 12 days and projected forward to a Reversal date of April 6. I marked this date on the center line and drew the Action/Reaction lines to project 42.00 as the initial target price. The target price was reached with ease, but the trend was not over. BHP formed a new Reaction swing around the April 6th Reversal date, just above the Reaction line. It wasn't long before the next buy signal was triggered at 44.10 on April 11. Once again, I was looking at a TC pattern so I began the reverse count at (E) and ended at the high of the previous Reaction swing; in this case the high is marked (C). *(Note: The market is trending higher so the reverse count ends on a pivot high.)* The reverse count equaled 14 days and 20 days. *(Remember in Figure # 3.9, the initial Reversal date closed lower, which implied a continuation of the upward trend, so the reverse count continued on to the major low marked as (B).)* The forward count of 14 and 20 projected future Reversal dates of April 27 and May 5. I marked both dates on the center line and drew two Reaction lines. The initial target was identified at 52.10 and a secondary target of 55.80 was also forecast.

The trend began to weaken right after the April 7th Reversal date when the market dropped below the center line. BHP did manage to reach a high of 47.19 on April 19 before falling back into the April 27th Reversal date. The market found support at the 20-day SMA and made another run at the Reaction line where it

Chapter 4 - Price

finally touched the 1st Reaction line at 47.60 on the secondary Reversal date of May 5.

This is an example of how a market reacts when it drifts away from the weak side of the center line. The market is losing momentum and cannot continue along the center line. It is debatable whether it is a good idea to hang on to a trade in this scenario.

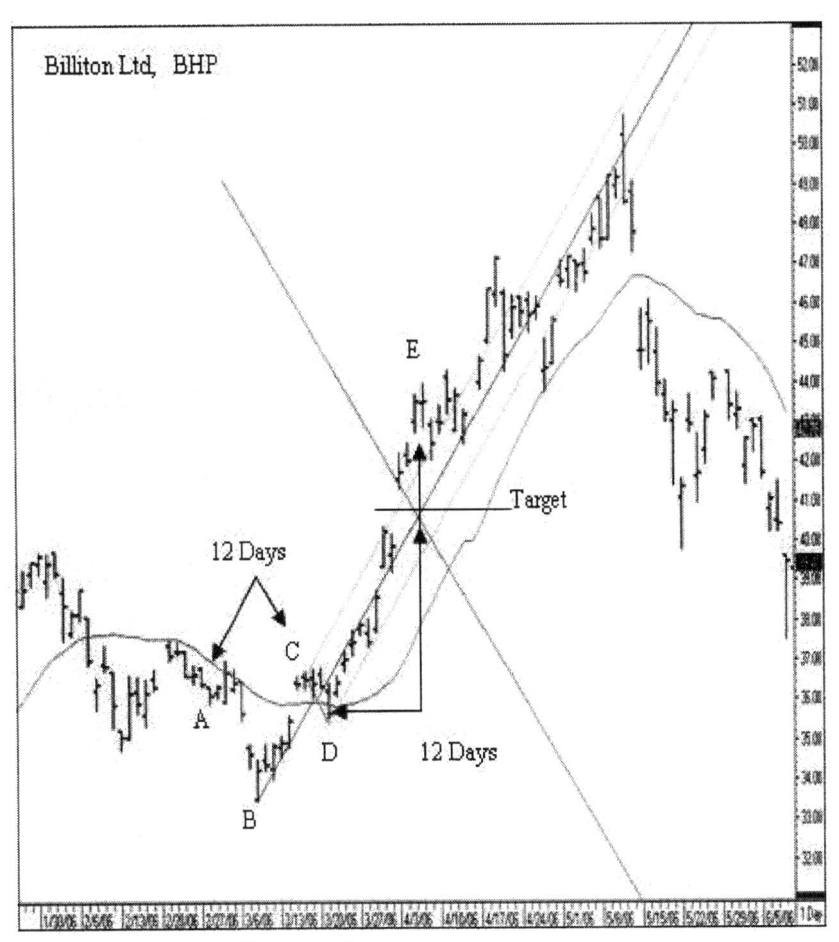

Figure # 4.24 – Billiton Ltd

142   Chapter 4 - Price

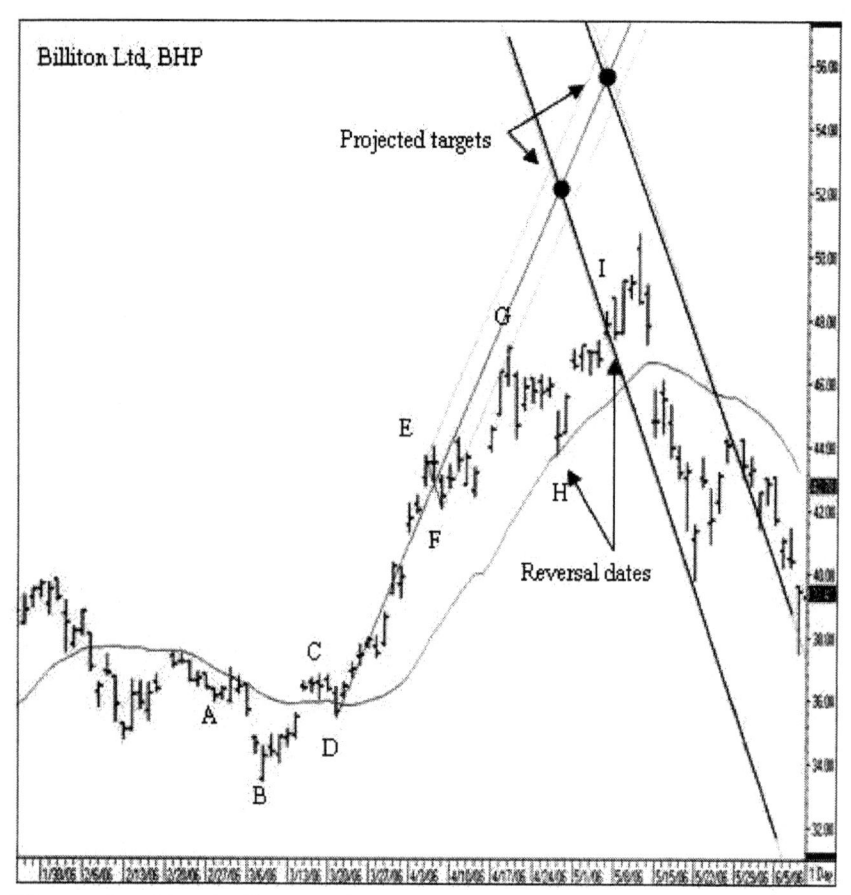

Figure # 4.25 – Billiton Ltd.

Dell Inc. DELL

Figure # 4.26 - The initial buy signal was triggered on May 13 when the market opened sharply higher and began trading at 37.87. The reverse count from (C) back to (A) equaled 14 days and projected out to May 30 as the next Reversal date. I began the center line at (B) and continued it upward through the center of the (C) – (D) Reaction swing to the end of the chart. Here, I marked May 30 on the center line and drew the Action/Reaction lines and used them to project the initial target price of 40.40.

Chapter 4 - Price

The market reached the target with very little effort and peaked at 40.56 on May 26. After reaching the target price, DELL moved into a sideways trading market and remained locked in the pattern for several weeks.

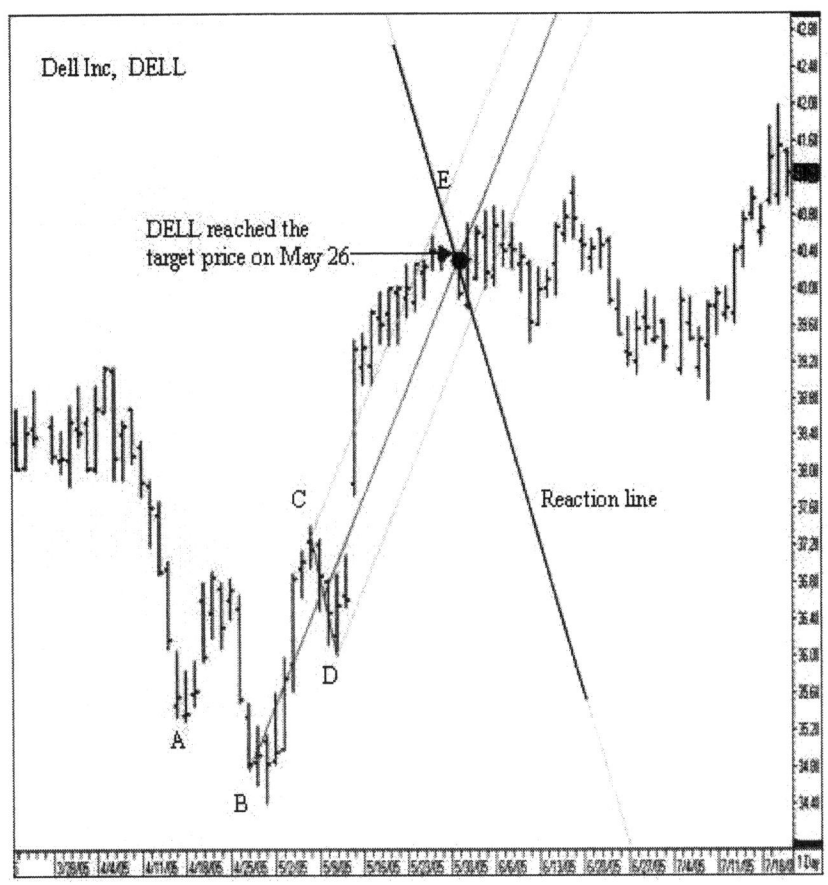

Figure # 4.26 – Dell Inc.

Amazon.com (AMZN)

Figure # 4.27 - After the buy signal was triggered at 34.48, on July 8, AMZN continued to climb higher, but really exploded on the 12th day of the cycle. Normally, a radical price move makes it

Chapter 4 - Price

difficult to make a price projection, but the Action/Reaction lines were right on target!

The reverse count from (C) to (A) was 15 days and projected a future Reversal date of July 28. I marked this date on the center line and drew the Action/Reaction lines to pinpoint 45.00 as the initial target. AMZN reached the 45.00 target price on July 28... the same date predicted 15 days earlier!

Figure # 4.27 – Amazon.com

Baker Hughes Inc. (BHI)

Figure # 4.28 & Figure # 4.29 - A buy signal was triggered on April 5th when the market passed through the entry price of 70.22. Since I had already predicted the future Reversal date as April 24 – see *Figure # 2.30* – I marked the date on the center line and drew the Action/Reaction lines to predict 77.00 as the initial target price. The target was reached on Friday, April 21 (E) where the market immediately began to form a new Reaction swing around the April 24 Reversal date when BHI closed lower on April 24 and April 25 (F).

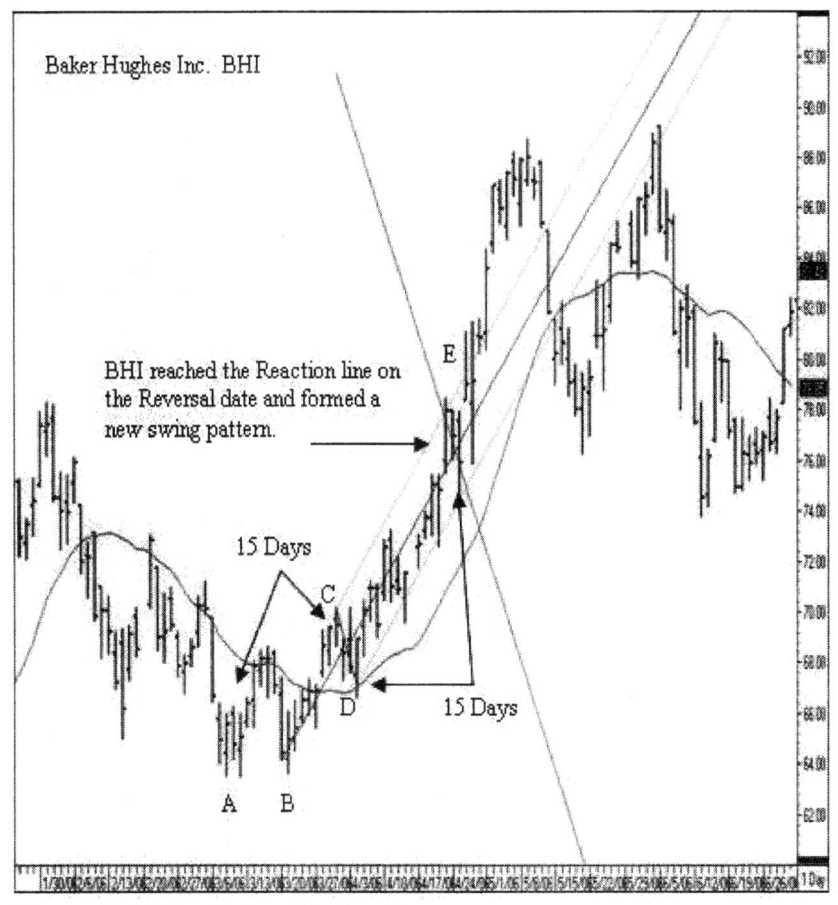

Figure # 4.28 – Baker Hughes Inc.

The following day began with the market opening sharply higher with the opening price of 78.36 and closed above the April 21 pivot high of 78.46 (E). This was enough to trigger the new buy signal at 78.50 for a new long position and complete the TC pattern. The TC pattern should also identify this swing pattern as the center of the cycle and the beginning of another bullish leg in the market.

Figure # 4.29 – Baker Hughes Inc.

The reverse count from (E) back to the previous high pivot, marked at (P-1), equaled 9 days. The forward count from (F) forward 9 days projected the future Reversal date as May 8.

Chapter 4 - Price 147

I drew the center line from the first low pivot following (P-1) and extended it forward through the center of the (E) to (F) Reaction swing and continued to the end of the chart. I then marked May 8th on the center line and drew the Action/Reaction lines to forecast the initial target price of 83.95. Seven days after the entry signal and two days before the projected Reversal date, BHI reached the target price!

December 2006 - E-mini – S&P 500

Figure # 4.30 - As soon as the December E-mini S&P triggered the buy signal at 1339.00, the center line and Action/Reaction lines were drawn. The reverse count of 12-10-minute price bars was used to project forward 120 minutes in the future and mark the center line. The Reaction line identified a target price at 1345.00.

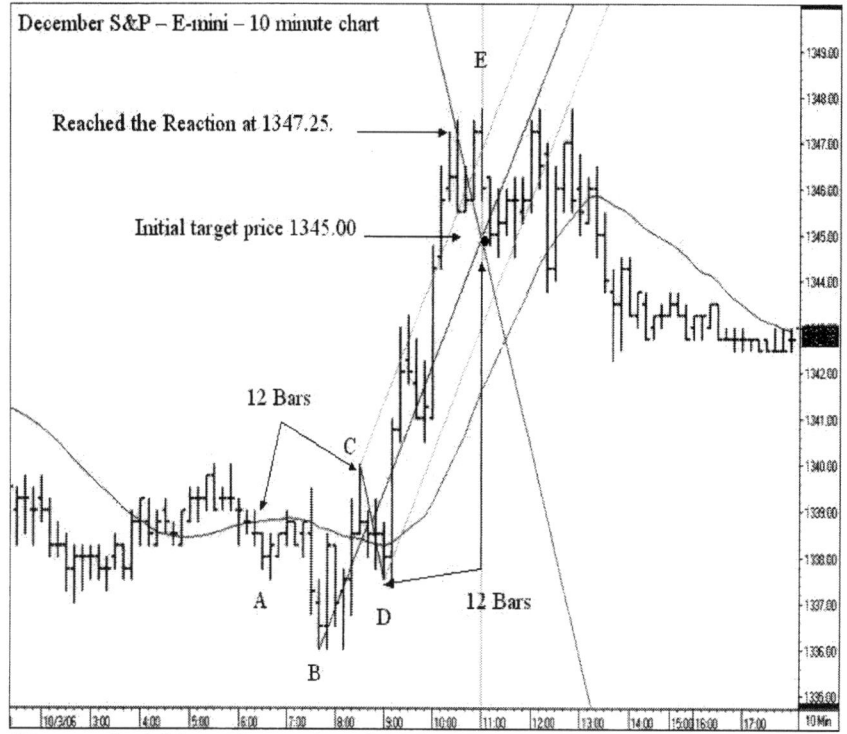

Figure # 4.30 – December 2006 – E-mini S&P 500 – 10-minute chart

After a short-term pause the S&P passed through the center line and surged higher. The target price at 1345.00, was reached in less than one hour after the entry signal was triggered. However, the market was well above the center line and continued higher until it reached the reaction line at 1347.25. The trade signal lasted less that 90 minutes and ended near the high of the entire price move!

The Three Things That Can Happen.

Each signal generated by the Reversal date Indicator can end in one of three different ways. First, the signal can be wrong and the protective stop is hit very quickly and the trade is over so you can move on to the next signal. Second, the market will reach the Price objective on or before the predicted date, or third, the market will run out of Time and the trade is closed on the Reversal date. Two out of three isn't bad!

Chapter 5

"He who could foresee affairs three days in advance would be rich for thousands of years" - Chinese proverb

Connecting patterns

After looking at all the charts in the previous chapters I am sure there is one question that comes to mind. "How do you know if the trend is ending at the Reversal date or will a TC pattern develop and trigger another buy signal?" The good new is, there is an identifiable pattern that can give a "heads up" to a possible trend continuation.

Three to Seven day swing patterns.

The first thing I watch for is how many days it takes to form the new Reaction swing. Strong trending markets will not pause or correct for a long period of time. The strongest continuation swing patterns will typically retrace between three to seven days from the pivot high or pivot low. However, I don't consider the three to seven days correction as a hard and fast rule, it is more of a "rule of thumb". There are always exceptions to the rule, such as the December Coffee—*Figure # 3.2* and Microsoft Corporation—*Figure # 2.16* where the correction extended to eight days, but still offered excellent trading opportunities. Anything longer will characteristically form a longer-term zigzag corrective pattern. This type of corrective pattern is also called an A-B-C pattern and is a key component of the Elliott Wave Theory. While I will not get into an in depth discussion about the Elliott Wave Theory at this point, it may be helpful to explain that the Elliott Wave Theory suggests that a market trend should unfold in five identifiable waves. Each price move, in the direction of the dominant trend, is followed by a price retracement or correction. Once the market has completed the fifth wave and final wave, the market will either experience a substantial correction that consists of three waves – also known as an A-B-C correction - or begin a new trend consisting of five waves. Zigzag or A-B-C patterns usually connect two longer-term reaction cycles. In other words, there is frequently a TR pattern at the beginning of the correction and another TR pattern at the end of the correction. Although, the zigzag pattern is usually short-term, it can still offer some good trading opportunities.

The second clue to watch for is where the corrective swing pattern ends. For example, a strong upward trending market will make shallow corrections with the pivot low bottoming above the high of the previous swing pattern. Once the pivot low has been established the market will normally break above the previous high within the same number of days as the correction. In other words, if the current correction has lasted three days, once the market moves off the pivot low it should reach or break above the pivot high within the next three days.

A weak market will typically drop below the high of the previous Reaction swing and correct 60% or more of the previous price wave. Although this is still a good trading market, it will take longer for the correction to end and will typically form the zigzag pattern in the process.

Once again, to illustrate this point I am going to refer back the some of the same markets used in the previous chapters.

September 2003 Treasury Bonds

Figure # 5.1 - After trending lower for over three weeks, the September 2004 T-Bonds closed at 109-31 on July 20. The close was near the bottom of the daily trading range and one day before the projected July 21 Reversal date, marked as (E). The following day dipped to a low of 109-12 before it closed at 109-31. The next

Chapter 5 – Connecting Patterns

day—July 23—T-Bonds pushed to a high of 111-12 and closed at 110-23, (F) where it completed a three-day corrective swing pattern. Based on this formation, a possible short-term continuation pattern had formed and the market was poised to turn and continue the downward trend. The Reaction swing consisted of three trading days, counting the low close on July 20 and the high close on July 23.

However, that is not the only clue that suggested we're dealing with a strong trending market. The low of previous Reaction swing (C) was 114-19 on July 8, well above the July 23rd high of 111-12.

In the previous chapter I talked about entry signals for the TC pattern, but just for review, a sell stop should be placed below the low of the Reaction swing to enter a short position as soon as the pattern is confirmed.

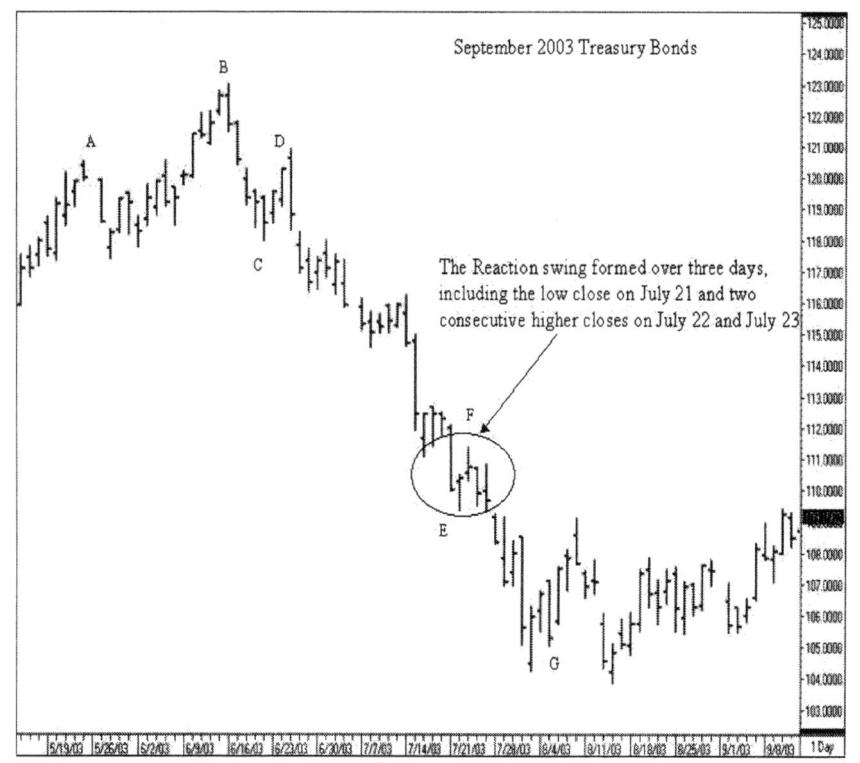

Figure # 5.1- September 2003 Treasury Bonds

June 2006 British Pound

Figure # 5.2 - After a three-day rally into April 19, (E) the June 2006 British pound entered into a sideways consolidation pattern. Three days later—April 24—the British pound closed at 1.7908, followed by two consecutive lower closes of 1.7903 and 1.7864 on April 25 and April 26, marked as (F). The low of the swing pattern – 1.7814 – was well above the high of the previous swing pattern of 1.7630 that occurred on April 5 and above the 20-day SMA. This pattern had all the earmarks of a bullish Reaction swing and suggested the trend was still strong and poised to continue higher.

April 27 opened trading at 1.7860, but quickly surged higher and traded above the April 25 pivot high of 1.7957 (F) and closed at 1.8402. The TC pattern was confirmed and the market continued to trend higher over the next two weeks.

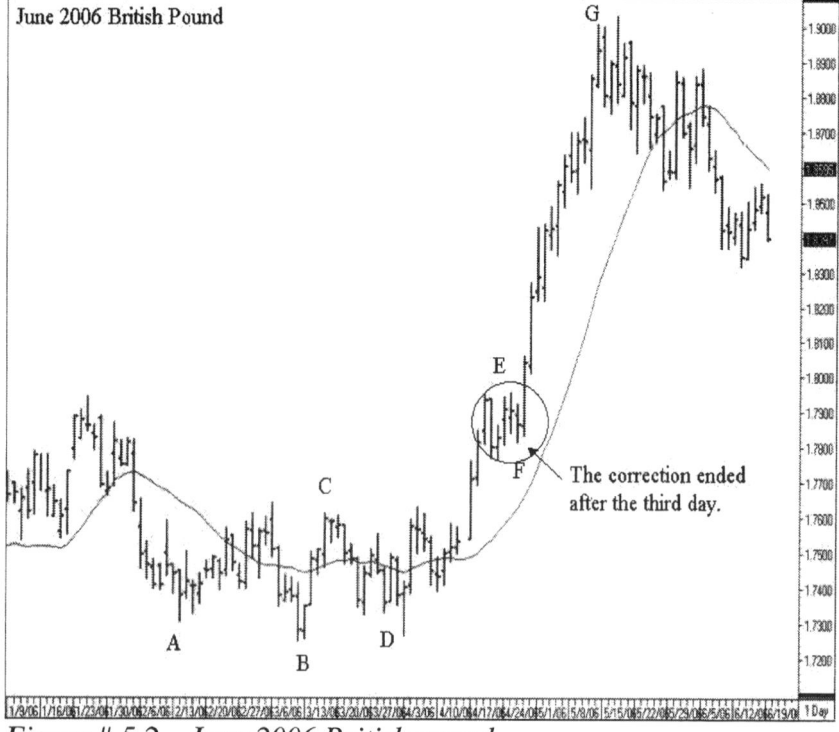

Figure # 5.2 – June 2006 British pound

Chapter 5 – Connecting Patterns

Trident Microsystems Inc. (TRID)

Figure # 5.3 - On May 15, TRID closed at 24.99, (E), near the bottom of the trading range. This marked the beginning of a four-day corrective rally that peaked at 28.07 on May 19, (F), where it formed a bearish Reaction swing. The high of the swing pattern was well below the low of the previous swing pattern (C) and the 28.07 high was slightly above the 20-day SMA.

The following day opened sharply lower and began trading at 23.79, well below the low pivot low at (E) and below the 20-day SMA. The Reaction swing was confirmed and the market continued lower into the June 16 Reversal date, marked as (G), where another four-day swing pattern suggested more downside potential.

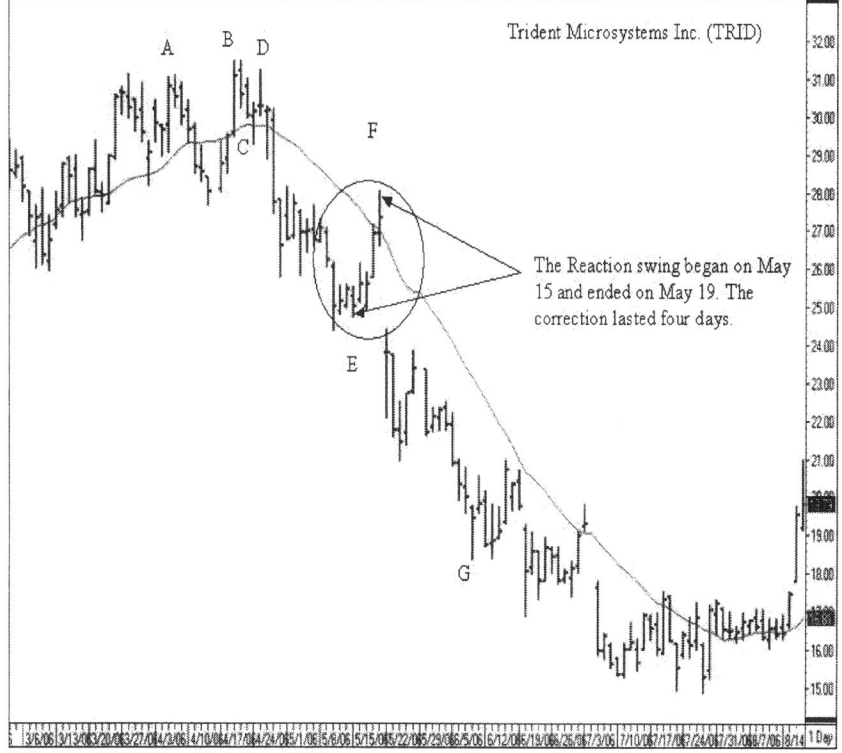

Figure # 5.3 – Trident Microsystems Inc. – (TRID)

Microsoft Corporation

Figure # 5.4 - After trending lower for three weeks, MSFT posted two identical closes of 25.27 on Friday, September 23 and Monday, September 26, marked as (E). The market was oversold and overdue for a correction. The stock did climb higher over the next three days and closed at 25.94, (F), just below the 20-day SMA. The next day opened lower and continued the dominant downward trend for another nine days. The Reaction swing consisted of five trading days, including the two low closes at the beginning of the swing pattern and the high close at the end of the swing pattern. Once again the Reaction swing pattern identified a short-term pause in the trend.

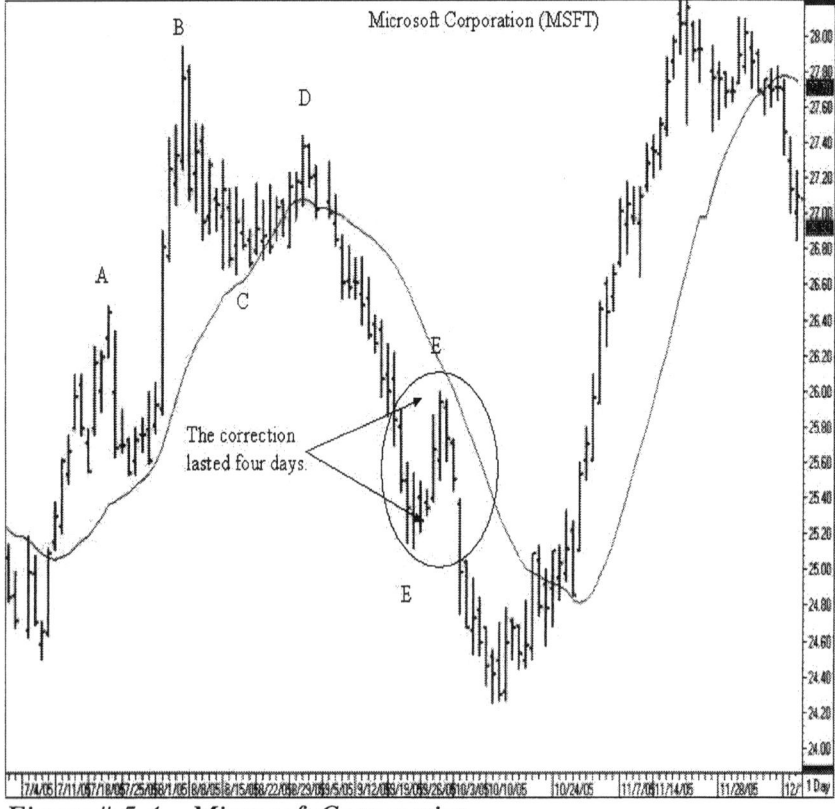

Figure # 5.4 – Microsoft Corporation

Chapter 5 – Connecting Patterns

June 2004 Japanese Yen

Figure # 5.5 - After a three week slide June Japanese yen posted a low close on the May 3 (E) Reversal date and began to trade higher. Two days later, the Japanese yen reached the 20-day SMA at .9243 on May 5, (F), before it turned lower the following day, effectively ending the corrective rally and resuming the downward trend. The Reaction swing consisted of three trading days, including the low close and the high close.

Figure # 5.5 – June 2004 Japanese Yen

After testing the 20-day SMA, on the third day of the correction, the market turned lower and plunged over the next three days until it posted a low close of .8805 on May 10. The next two trading sessions ended with two consecutive higher closes and formed another swing pattern and possible continuation pattern. However, based on the projections from the TR pattern and TC pattern I considered the trend near the end of the cycle therefore, the risk increased significantly if a trade was entered based on the swing pattern following a TC pattern. This was illustrated very clearly by the Japanese yen. The market broke support and closed at a new low on May 13 (G). This was a trap because the market opened lower on the following day, reversed and never looked back. A swing pattern failure can lead to a dramatic move in the opposite direction; this is a classic price pattern and can be a very powerful signal.

Baker Hughes Inc.

Figure # 5.6 - A three-week rally peaked at 78.46 on the Friday 21, (E), one trading session before the projected Reversal date. Monday's session was quiet and finished as an inside day. The following day also closed lower and formed a three-day Reaction swing that ended at (F). The swing pattern proved to be a short-term pause before BHI surged higher over the next ten days.

Longer-term swing patterns

How do you know when the market correction is not going to be a short-term pause inside the longer-term trend or a significant correction or perhaps a major turn in the market? Actually, it is very simple. For example take a look at the December 2004 Hogs. See *Figure # 5.7*. Just before the market peaked on the September 23 Reversal date, the market had formed a small three-day swing pattern with a pivot low of 86.70 on September 22. Three days later December Hogs reached a high of 71.80 before they closed at 67.82. The market had just dropped below the previous pivot low.

Chapter 5 – Connecting Patterns

Figure # 5.6 – Baker Hughes Inc. – (BHI)

This is the first hint that the trend was changing. From this point, the Hogs formed a new bearish swing pattern and TR pattern that was confirmed on October 4. At this point the correction had lasted seven days, but the market continued to make lower lows and lower highs below the 20-day SMA, bottoming seven days later. Once the correction had surpassed the seven-day threshold, it can no longer be considered as a minor correction. Instead, it should be considered a major correction, which could last up to twelve days. Once the twelve-day threshold is surpassed, it is no longer considered a correction. Instead it is time to look for a TR pattern instead.

158   Chapter 5 – Connecting Patterns

[December 2004 Hogs chart. Annotations: "The correction unfolded as a 5-wave zigzag pattern spanning 13 days." Points labeled A, B, C, D, E with internal waves 1, 2, 3, 4, 5. "The market retraced over 60% of the price move from D to E."]

Figure # 5.7 – December 2004 Lean Hogs

The Zigzag Corrective Pattern

    A major correction will typically retrace at least 60% of the previous market swing and unfold as a three or five-wave zigzag pattern. This zigzag pattern is most commonly known as an A-B-C correction. When this pattern connects two Action/Reaction cycles it can be a powerful tool for long-term traders.
    A single zigzag pattern is a simple three-wave pattern labeled A-B-C whereby the top of wave B is noticeably lower than the start of wave A. Occasionally, zigzags will occur twice or even three times in succession, particularly when the first zigzag falls

short of the normal target, producing a five-wave pattern also a called a double zigzag.

Whether the zigzag pattern has three waves or five waves, it will most likely begin and end with a TR pattern and trigger another signal. However, do not get caught in the idea that every A-B-C corrective pattern will be followed with a new signal. There are many times a market will move into a consolidation pattern or continue to trade in a sideways or choppy trend that does not offer any new trading opportunities. When this happens look at another markets. Understanding market behavior opens up the possibility of using your knowledge on a wide variety of markets. There are plenty of opportunities in other markets and new opportunities are always being setup. *Always wait for the proper setup before entering a trade!*

Here are some examples of markets that did not continue the existing trend after a short-term swing pattern.

Microsoft

Figure # 5.8 - After MSFT posted the low close October 12, (B), the market began to trade higher over the next five days and closed above the 20-day SMA, (C). At this time the market pulled back and closed lower on two consecutive days, forming the beginning of a potential bullish Reaction swing at (D). Three days later—10 days after the October 12 low—the Reaction swing was confirmed and MSFT was off and running. The market never traded below the October 12 low, therefore, new swing pattern sell signal was never confirmed.

The same scenario unfolded after MSFT reached the November 16, (E), Reversal date signaled and ended the three-week rally. Three days after the predicted Reversal date, MSFT hit a new high and closed at 28.16 where it turned lower. Five days into the correction the market bounced off a low at (F) and closed higher for three consecutive days and ended with a pivot high on December 2, (G). A new swing pattern had formed inside the counter-trend move and suggested a longer-term A-B-C correction.

160   Chapter 5 – Connecting Patterns

MSFT dropped through the 20-day SMA and continued the downward slide. The correction lasted 27 days and retraced close to 60% of the price move between October 12 and November 21.

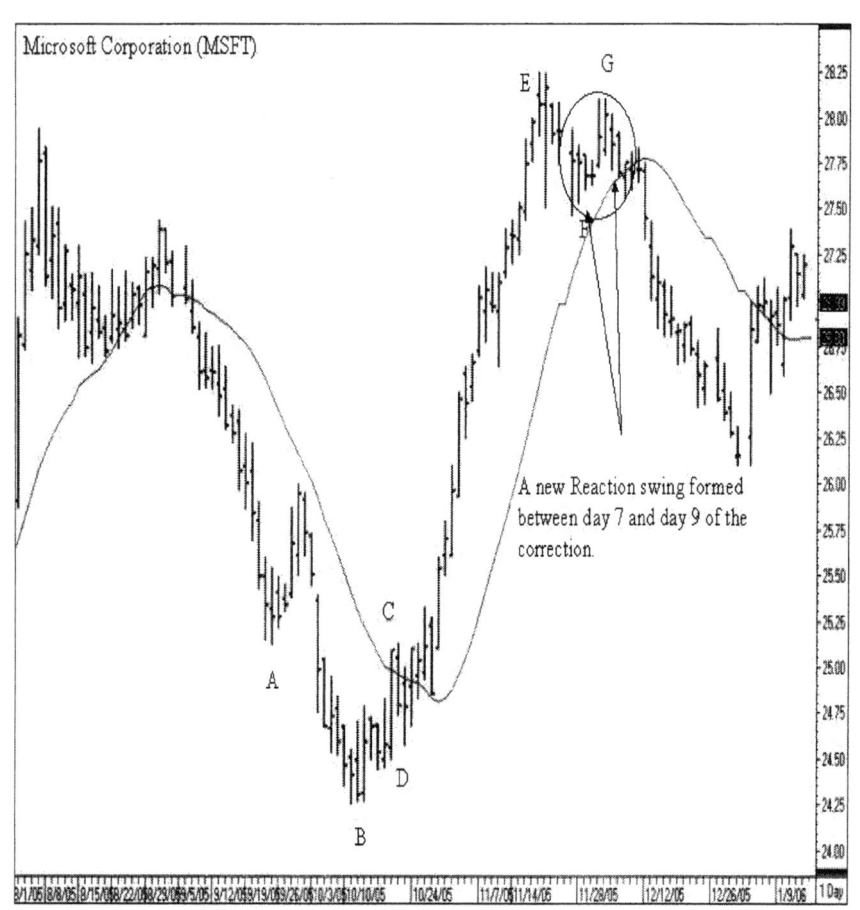

Figure # 5.8 – Microsoft Corporation

May 2005 Soybeans

Figure # 5.9 - After breaking out of a short-term consolidation May Soybeans surged to a high of $6.91 ½ before closing at $6.73 ½, (E). From this high point the Soybeans entered a correction phase that lasted ten days and retraced all the way back to the previous consolidation—(F)—area before staging a two-day bounce. Soybeans remained in a choppy sideways trend for several days and never offered another trading opportunity.

Figure # 5.9 – May 2005 Soybeans

August 2005 Gold

Figure # 5.10 - August Gold closed near its daily high on the June 23 Reversal date, (E). The following day marked the beginning of a market correction. Eight days into the correction the market paused, forming a short-term zigzag consolidation before dropping below the low of the (C) to (D) Reaction swing. After 15 days of falling prices Gold finally bottomed and ended the correction.

162   Chapter 5 – Connecting Patterns

Figure # 5.10 – August 2005 Gold

September 2006 Wheat

Figure # 5.11 - September Wheat reached a high of $4.40 on the May 22 Reversal date, (E). The following day the market closed lower and continued lower over the next three days before trading higher into May 30, (G). Six days into the correction the September Wheat had formed a new bearish Reaction swing that indicated the upward trend is over and a new trend had begun. The market continued lower for the next twenty-one days.

Chapter 5 – Connecting Patterns 163

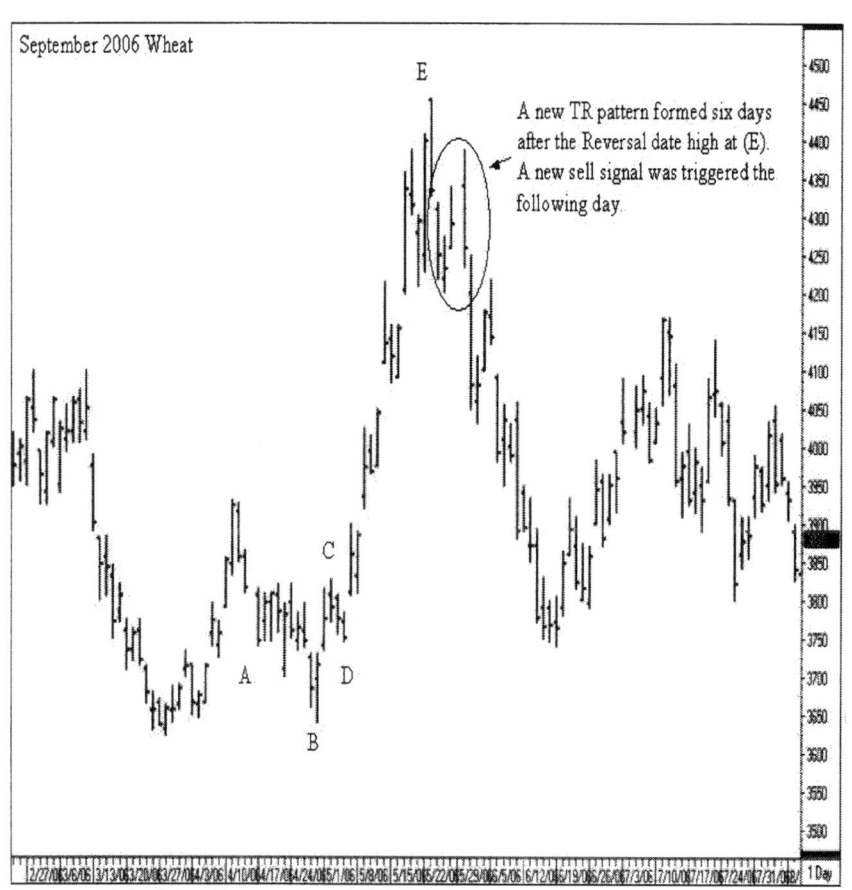

Figure # 5.11 – September 2006 Wheat

September 2006 Cocoa

Figure # 5.12 - September Cocoa staged a strong rally in early July, but the subsequent market collapse was even more dramatic. One day after peaking on the July 10 Reversal date, (E), Cocoa began to pull back for the high. Twelve days later the market traded below the (C) to (D) Reaction swing that started it all back on June 26. The market never threatened the July 10 high at (E).

164   *Chapter 5 – Connecting Patterns*

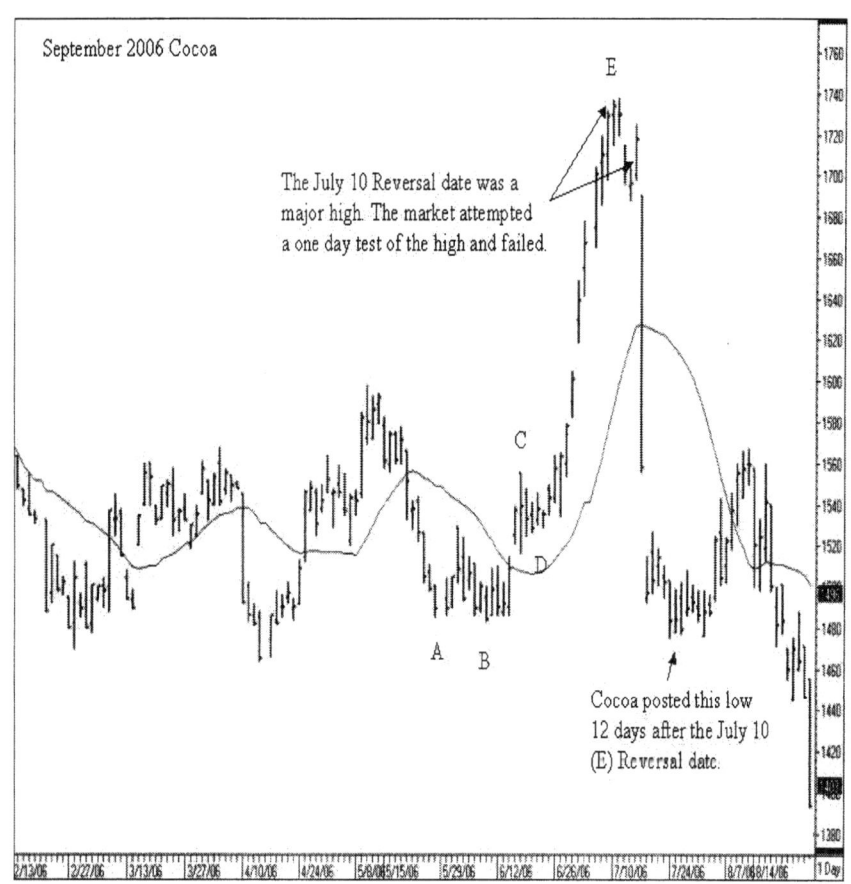

Figure # 5.12 – September 2006 Cocoa

Dell Inc. (DELL)

Figure # 5.13 - Dell Inc. closed at 40.40 on May 26, two days prior to the May 30 Reversal date, (E). The market traded lower on May 27 and May 31, (F), forming a potential bullish Reaction swing. The market traded to a high of 40.71 on June 1 and confirmed the Reaction swing buy signal. However, the market failed to follow through and dropped below the May 31 pivot low on June 10, where it continued to meander back and forth over the next few weeks.

Chapter 5 – Connecting Patterns

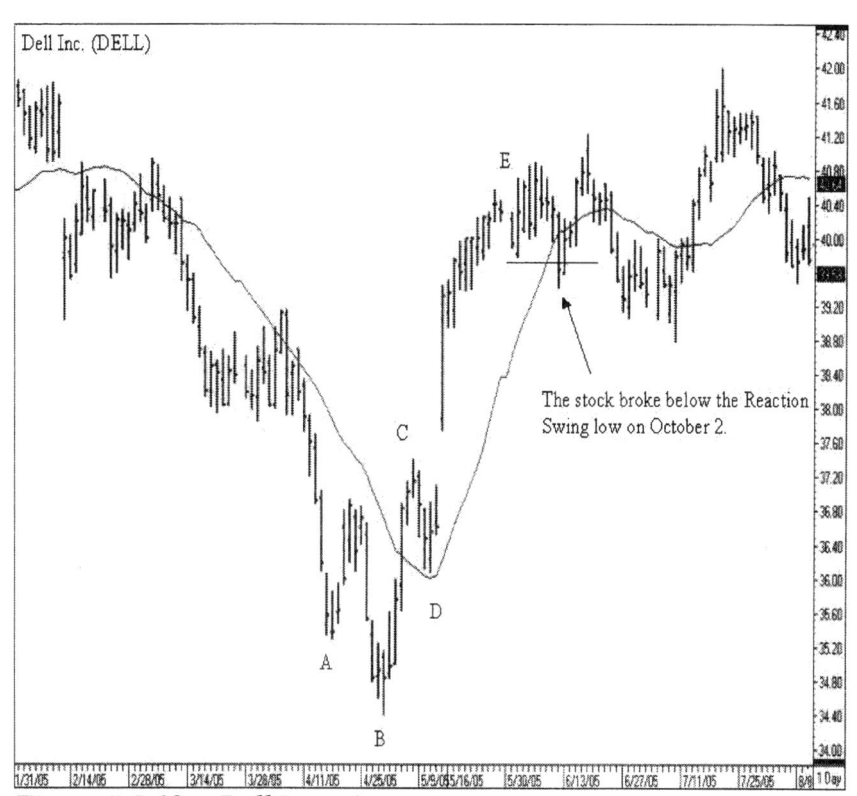

Figure # 5.13 - Dell Inc – (DELL)

Amazon.com (AMZN)

Figure # 5.14 - Amazon.com closed at the high of the daily trading range on the July 28 Reversal date, (E). The next day, July 29, closed lower followed by another lower close on August 1 that completed a potential Reaction swing at (F). The Reaction swing was confirmed on August 2 when AMZN traded to a new high and closed at 46.51.

That high was still standing three days later as the market pulled back to a pivot low of 45.17, (G), followed by two higher closes into (H). The market had formed a new bearish Reaction swing and

166   Chapter 5 – Connecting Patterns

Figure # 5.14 – Amazon.com (AMZN)

possible TR pattern that could not be ignored. The Reaction swing was confirmed the following day—August 10—when the market dropped below the pivot low. This should have closed out any existing long position with a small loss and entered a new short position in front of the market collapse.

Las Vegas Sands Corporation (LVS)

Figure # 5.15 - After the November 23 Reversal date high, (E), LVS began to trade lower. Once the correction surpassed seven days, the possibility of a quick turnaround diminished. In fact, the market formed a small zigzag or A-B-C pattern between December 5- marked as (P-1) - and December 8 – marked as (P-2), before resuming the downward correction. The entire counter-trend price

Chapter 5 – Connecting Patterns

move lasted seventeen days before it moved into a new bullish TR pattern. It is also worth noting that the swing pattern from December 5 to December 8 was the exact center of the correction. The reverse count from December 5 to the November 24 high was seven days and the forward count of seven days from the pivot high of December 8 projected out to December 19...the low of the correction.

The market moved into a correction phase, after the peak, and formed a three-wave zigzag pattern. The correction ended after 15 price bars *(B)* and went on to form a new TR pattern and trigger another buy signal. The reverse count equaled 14 price bars and the market topped on the projected reversal bar at *(E)*.

A zigzag or A-B-C pattern will typically appear in the center of a longer-term trend and connects two Reaction cycles. One of the key characteristics of this pattern is that it will begin with a TR pattern and end with a TR pattern.

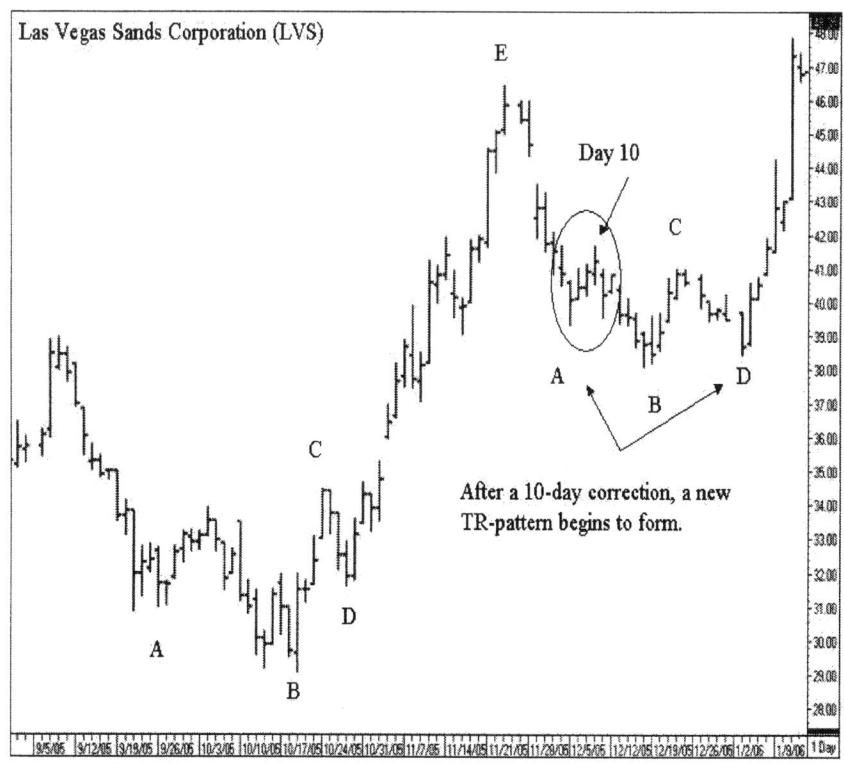

Figure # 5.15 – Las Vegas Sands Corporation (LVS)

168   *Chapter 5 – Connecting Patterns*

December 2006 S&P 500 –E-mini – 60 minute chart

Figure # 5.16 - The chart is a classic example of the three-wave zigzag pattern connecting two bullish trends. *(You may remember this chart from Chapter 2 as Figure # 2.33).* The December E-minis had formed a bullish TR pattern between Friday September 22 (B) and Monday September 25 (D). The 60% rule, the trigger price of 1160.50, was hit during Monday's session and the buy signal was confirmed.

The reverse count from (B) to (A) equaled 28 price bars or 28 hours. The E-mini continued higher, but began to consolidate mid way through the September 27 session, but managed to breakout and peak 2 hours after the projected Reversal bar marked (E).

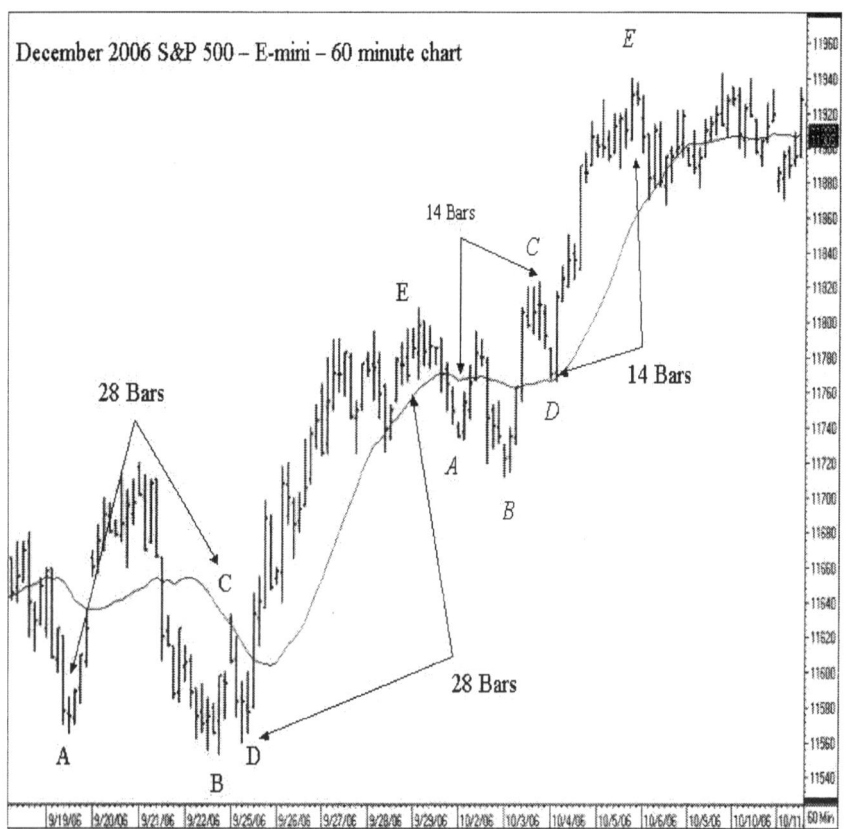

Figure #5.16 – December 2006 E-mini S&P 500 – 60 minute chart

Chapter 6

"Nothing happens until it happens"
Yogi Berra

Market Tells

An old time trader who was also an avid Poker player once told me that trading and poker are similar in many ways; but not in the way many people think. New poker players always learn the different hands (card combinations) and the odds of winning with each. They concentrate on betting strategies and the rules of the game. He insisted that even though all this knowledge is necessary and important, it is not the key to becoming a consistent winner. When I asked him what he meant by this statement, he said, "People; you have to learn to study people. Once you learn this, you can tell what they are about to do without them even knowing they have already tipped their hand." He went on to explain that veteran poker players study the other players at the table. Veteran players play very cautiously, at the beginning of a game, and do not play aggressively until they start to notice small, normally unnoticeable characteristics about their opponents. These can be such things as a player seeming more nervous when he's bluffing, or another who holds his cards differently when he thinks he has a winning hand. Whatever these characteristics are, they can give an edge to the player who is aware enough to identify these tendencies. In the poker world, these tendencies are known as **"Tells."**

The markets are similar to poker players in that the markets also exhibit "Tells" or certain characteristics that can give clues to future market price action. If you are aware of the Tells, they can forewarn you of a price move about to happen. There are probably enough "Tells" to fill an entire book, but in this chapter I will limit the "Market Tells" to the ones that are extremely useful when combined with Reversal dates and Action/Reaction trading method.

Patterns

There are some new traders who know very early in their trading career what type of trading approach is best for them. Whether they choose to be a day trader, a short-term swing trader or a long-term position trader, many will gravitate towards the technical side of analysis while others choose to use fundamental information to determine trading decisions. Either way, it is up to the individual trader to find his or her own way.

Many years ago, I decided to be a technical trader. After a short time of looking in other directions I decided I wanted to use the price charts to determine buy and sell signals. I made this decision when I became painfully aware that it was extremely difficult to know all the current fundamental information of all the markets and be able to interpret it as quickly and as expertly as the large commercial firms. I believe this is a problem for many traders. It is difficult to know if you have all the relevant news on a market and how the other major players in the market are going to react to the news. Therefore, I decided that I wanted the market to tell me what it was about to do. It is assumed that the market factors in all the current fundamental news and the traders' interpretations of that news. Therefore, current price action should reflect this information and that current price actions are revealed in market behavior and chart patterns. I realized, if I could learn to interpret chart patterns with some degree of accuracy, I would have a slight advantage in the market. To succeed, all you really need is a slight advantage - just ask the boys in Las Vegas!

Chapter 6 – Market Tells

The Breakout Bar

So far I have talked extensively about the Reaction swing and what to do after the trigger price is hit and the trade is entered. I have also explained the reverse/forward count process to project Time and Price with a high degree of accuracy. But, we all know not every confirmed Reaction swing pattern is going to carry through and offer a risk free trade. Nothing is 100% percent.

A Reaction swing is confirmed when the market trades through the previous high or low pivot price and reaches a new high or low. New highs and new lows are usually significant price junctures watched by day traders, swing traders and trend traders. The ability for the market to exceed a previous high or low is a powerful signal and can trigger a chain reaction of new buying or selling activity.

Of course, for a market to continue the breakout and establish a longer-term trend it must maintain momentum and continue to make new highs or new lows. The market behavior after the breakout is very important and can provide insight into future price action. However, I use a "Market Tell" as a secondary confirmation of the buy or sell signal. It is based on the market action that occurs after the Breakout bar. (The Breakout bar is the price bar that penetrates the pivot high or pivot low and triggers the entry signal.) Let's take a look at the rules for this "Market Tell" conformation of a bullish Reaction swing.

Once the market has traded above the Reaction swing high and triggered a buy signal (in an upward trending market) it should remain above the low of the Reaction swing and close above the pivot high by the third price bar. Therefore, after the entry the initial protective stop is placed underneath the low of the Reaction swing. After two consecutive closes above the pivot price the protective stop can be placed underneath the low of the Breakout bar. After the a third close above the pivot price the protective stop can be moved to the entry level. I have found a market that closes above the pivot price for three consecutive days has a high probability of continuing the current trend into the next projected Reversal date.

Once the protective stop is at the entry level, I will usually give the market room to fluctuate until it approaches the Reversal date. After the close of the Reversal date, I will place the protective stop underneath the Reversal date low and repeat the same procedure after each successive higher close until the stop is elected. Of course, this procedure can be modified to fit the risk tolerance of the individual trader. *Figure # 6.1* illustrates how the pattern should unfold.

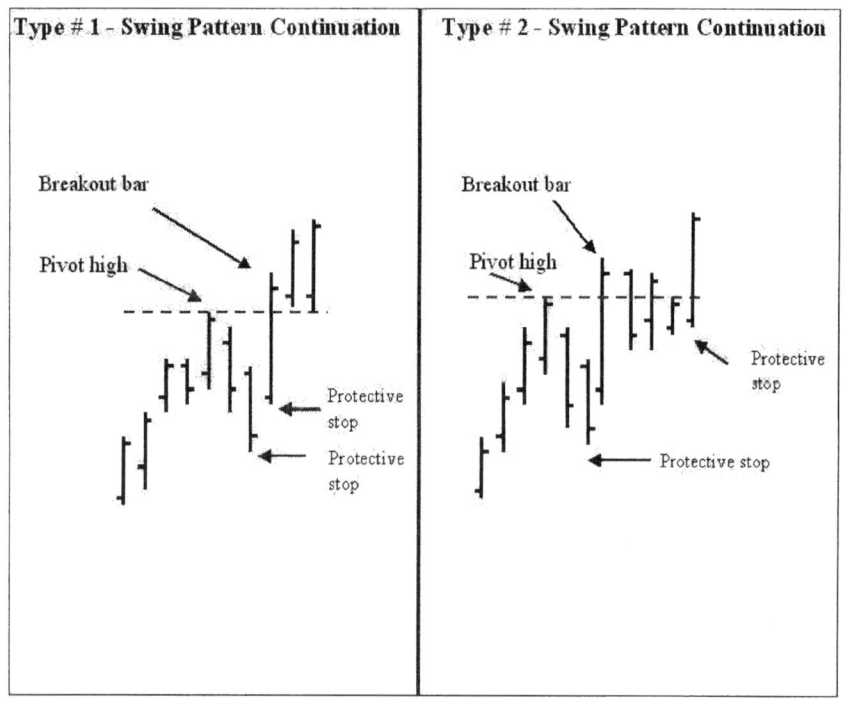

Figure # 6.1 – Breakout bar – Pattern confirmation

March 2006 Crude oil

Figure # 6.2 - The bearish Reaction swing formed between January 25 (C) and January 30 (D) in the March 2006 Crude oil. The sell signal was triggered on February 1, but the market did not trade below the pivot low of 65.45- (C) - until the following day.

1-Day one – February 2 - The Breakout Bar - Crude oil opened slightly lower and dropped through the 65.45 pivot support and finally closed at 64.68. The close was below the swing pivot low at (C).

2-Day two – The market pushed to a new low of 63.95 before closing at 65.37.

3-Day three – The market opened higher and tested the 20-day SMA at 66.20, but still remained below the high of the Breakout Bar.

4-Day four – The market gapped lower and began trading at 64.20 before it closed sharply lower. The downward trend was entrenched and continued lower into the projected Reversal date.

December 2004 Hogs

Figure # 6.3 - The Reaction swing formed between September 1 and September 8 marked as (C) and (D) on the chart. The high of the (C) pivot point was 64.40. The buy signal was confirmed on September 9, when the market passed through the trigger price and continued higher
1-Day one – September 9 - Breakout Bar – The market closed above the 64.40 pivot price (C).

2-Day two – September 12 - Another higher high and a higher close.

3-Day three – September 13 - Steady opening before the market tested the low of day two, but rallied into the end of the session and closed at 66.57...way beyond the (C) pivot high.

The upward trend remained strong into the September 23 Reversal date and the trade signal was never in danger of a failure.

174 Chapter 6 – Market Tells

Figure # 6.2 – March 2006 Crude oil

December 2005 Dow Jones

Figure # 6.4 - The high of the Reaction swing was 10,453 on October 19 (C) and the low of the swing pattern fell on October 21 (D). Using the 60% entry rule, the buy signal was triggered on October 24, but the Breakout bar did not occur until six days later. This is not a typical situation as the Dow Jones continued to trade in a choppy sideways trend for a week after the buy signal was confirmed, but it also stayed above the previous pivot low and the protective stop so the trade was still active when the market finally

Chapter 6 – Market Tells 175

broke above the 10,453 pivot high (C) on October 31. However, at the end of the day the Dow Jones closed at 10,410, below the 10,453 pivot high.

Figure # 6.3 – December 2004 Hog

The next two price bars were critical for this trade to remain active and not end as a swing pattern failure.

1-Day one – October 31 - Breakout Bar – After five days of sideways trading the Dow Jones broke above the 10,453 pivot high and reached as far as 10,500 before fading into the close. At the end of the day, the Dow Jones closed at 10,410, below the high pivot price, but remained above the low pivot and protective stop.

Chapter 6 – Market Tells

2-Day two – The market finished as an inside day, but managed to close 21 points higher than day one.

3-Day three – The Dow Jones opened below the low of day two—but remained above the Breakout bar low and closed well above the high of day two.

The trend is intact and the market continued higher with only minor pullback before it reached the Time and Price objective.

Figure # 6.4 – December 2005 Dow Jones

Chapter 6 – Market Tells

August 2005 Gold

Figure # 6.5 - A four-day Reaction swing formed between June 6 (C) and June 9 (D) with a pivot high at $429.50. Gold reacted quickly after the June 9 low and traded above $429.50 the next day.

1-Day one – June 10 – The Breakout bar - The market rallied off the low and traded above the pivot high trigger price $429.50 (C) to confirm the buy signal. However, the Gold closed at $429.30, slightly below the entry.

2-Day two – June 13 – The daily low was $427.60 and the close was $431.10, well above the pivot high.

3-Day three – June 14 – Gold had a quiet day with a small trading range and finished as an inside day and above the breakout point at (C).

After the one-day pause on June 14, Gold surged forward and continued the upward trend until it peaked at $444.20...$14.70 above the breakout price at (C).

Microsoft (MSFT)

Figure # 6.6 - The beginning of the bearish Reaction swing was August 19—marked as (C)—with the pivot low price at 26.70. After MSFT posted a high on August 31, the stock turned lower, but did not break the pivot support at (C) until September 8 when the market closed at 26.61...9 cents below the pivot low.

1-Day one – September 8 – Breakout bar – The stock traded through the pivot low support and closed lower.

178   Chapter 6 – Market Tells

Figure # 6.5 – August 2005 Gold

2-Day two – September 9 – The market finished as an inside day with a close slightly below the previous day's close.

3- Day three – September 12 – Another inside day and the market closed at 26.61...9 cents below the pivot low.

The next day MSFT dropped out of the small pennant formation that had developed between day one and day three and continued the downward trend for another two weeks.

Chapter 6 – Market Tells 179

Figure # 6.6 – Microsoft Corporation (MSFT)

Figure # 6.7 - A second Reaction swing formed after the market bottomed at *(B)*. The high of the swing pattern was on October 19 *(C)* followed by the subsequent low on October 21 *(D)*. The pivot high was 25.13.

1-Day one – October 26 – Breakout Bar – After testing the pivot high during the previous two trading sessions, MSFT broke the resistance and traded to a high of 25.33, but pulled back to close at 25.11.

2-Day two – October 27 – The market pulled back and closed below the previous day's low, but remained above the protective stop at 24.55.

180   *Chapter 6 – Market Tells*

3-Day three – October 28 – The stock began trading at 25.10 and pushed above the previous high where it closed at 25.70...well above the breakout point. The market continued higher into the projected reversal day without any substantial corrections.

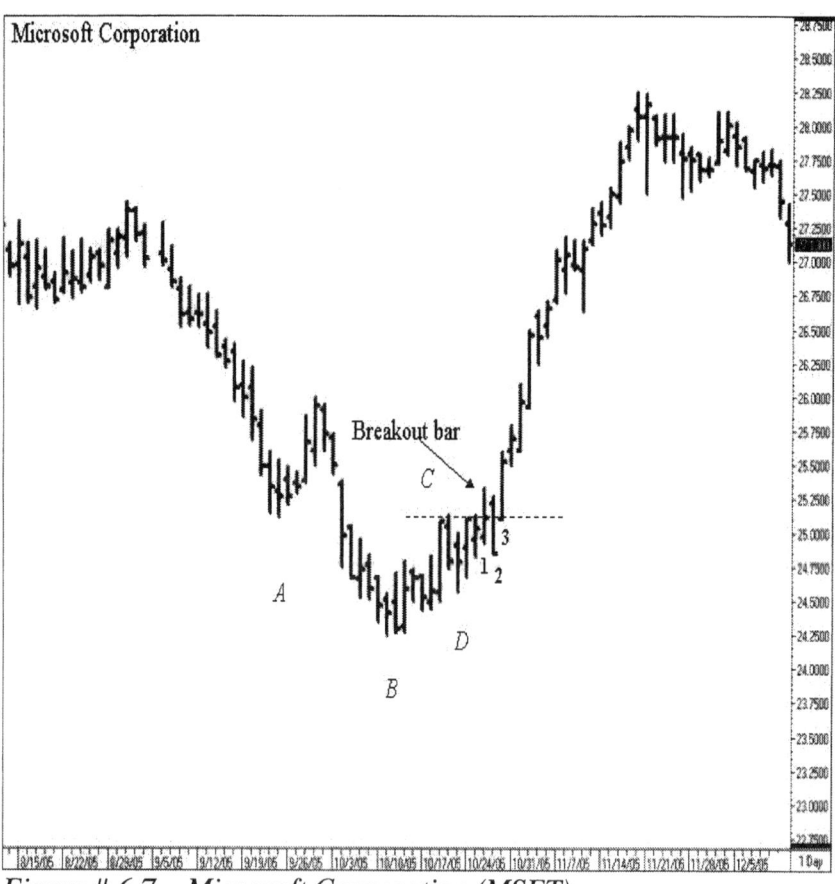

Figure # 6.7 – Microsoft Corporation (MSFT)

December 2004 Coffee

Figure # 6.8 - The low of the Reaction swing was 73.25 and occurred on July 8, marked as (C). The Reaction swing ended after a pivot high was confirmed on July 20 (D).

Chapter 6 – Market Tells

1-Day one – July 23 – Breakout Bar – Coffee broke below the pivot low support of 73.25 and closed at 73.15.

2-Day two – July 26 – Coffee continued the downward slide and closed at 72.00.

3-Day three – July 27 – The market was quiet and traded in a very small price range, but managed to close lower for the third day in a row.

The downward trend was solidly intact and continued lower into the projected date.

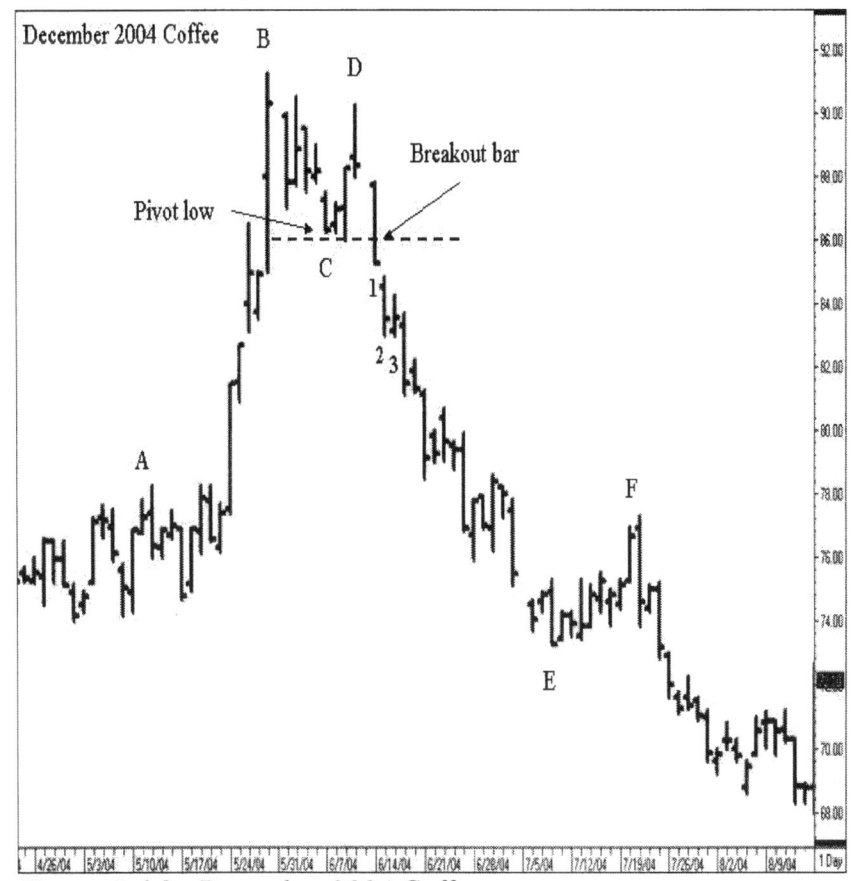

Figure # 6.8 - December 2004 Coffee

June 2006 British Pound

Figure # 6.9 - A small three-day Reaction swing formed at the end of a short-term consolidation pattern. The beginning of the Reaction swing was confirmed on April 24 (E) with a pivot high price of 1.7945. Two days later the British pound posted a low at 1.7814, (F), followed by a surge higher that broke through the 1.7945 pivot high.

1-Day one – April 27 – Breakout Bar – The market broke through the overhead resistance at (C) and closed sharply higher.

2-Day two – April 28 – Another strong trend day with the close near the high of the daily price range.

3-Day three – May 1 – The British pound pushed to a high of 1.8428 before fading into the close and finished the day at 1.8285.

The close was well above the breakout point and the trend was still valid.

September 2005 Eurocurrency

Figure # 6.10 - The low of the three-day Reaction swing was 1.2563 and occurred on May 23, one day after the low pivot at (E). The Reaction ended on May 25(F).

1-Day one – May 26 – Breakout Bar – The market dropped through the support and closed at 1.2561...slightly below the previous low of 1.2563.

2-Day two – May 27 – The market rebounded and closed at 1.2632, the high of the daily price range, but remained below the high of the Breakout Bar of 1.2659.

Chapter 6 – Market Tells 183

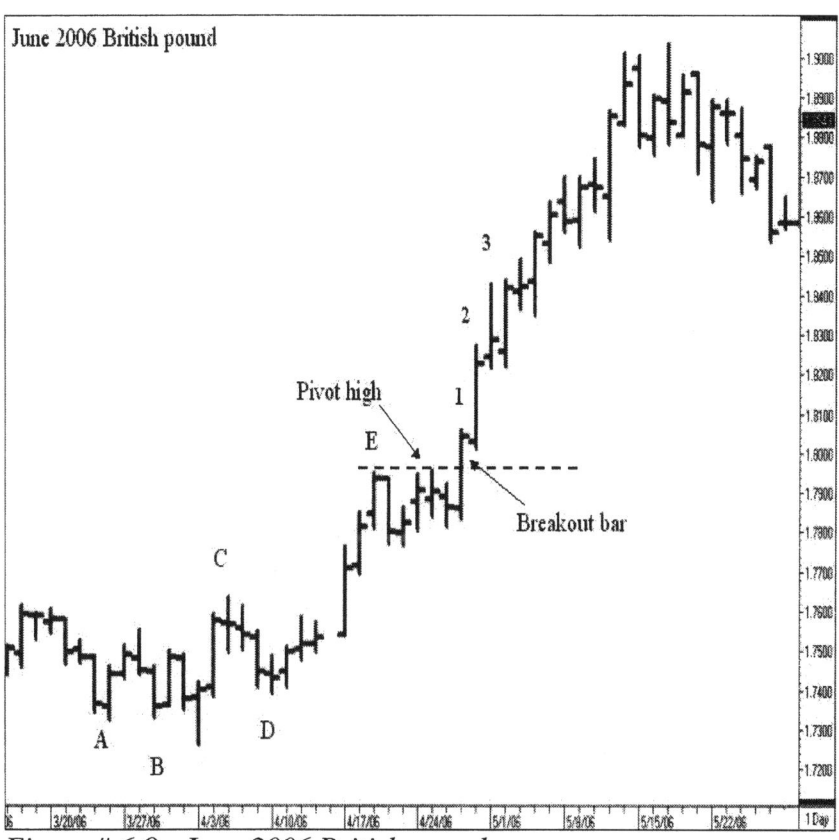

Figure # 6.9 - June 2006 British pound

3-Day three – May 30 – A lower opening triggered heavy selling and the market dropped below the previous low and continued to fall for the remainder of the day, finally closing at 1.2515.

The breakout was confirmed and the downward trend remained intact into the projected Reversal date.

Billiton (BHP)

Figure # 6.11 - The high of the Reaction swing was 44.00 and occurred on April 6 (E). The low of the Reaction swing was 42.03

and occurred on April 7 (F). Two days after the April 7 low, BHP traded through the resistance at 44.00.

1-Day one – April 11 – Breakout Bar – The market opened sharply higher and began trading at 44.30. This was above the (E) pivot high price of 44.00. However, the market faded into the close and finished the day at 43.55. The close was lower than the opening price and below the pivot price. BHP was in danger of a possible swing pattern failure. The protective stop was placed underneath the pivot low of 42.03.

2-Day two – April 12 – The market opened lower—42.77—but quickly recovered and closed at 43.65, higher than the opening price.

3-Day three – April 13 – Another lower opening, but the low—43.34—was still above the low pivot price of 42.03. The market closed higher than the opening price, but remained below the breakout price of 44.00. The trade signal was still in danger on the third day so the stop should be adjusted to 42.40, just below the low of day three.

The market was closed on April 14 due to a holiday, but opened higher on the following trading day, April 17. The stock opened at 43.97 and closed at 44.53 ... above the breakout price of 44.00.

Baker Hughes Inc (BHI)

Figure # 6.12 - The high of the (E) to (F) Reaction swing was 78.46 and occurred on April 21. The low was 74.60 on April 25. The swing pattern was confirmed the following day when the market opened sharply higher.

1-Day one – April 26 – Breakout Bar – BHI opened sharply higher and reached a high of 81.10 before settling back to 79.00.

Chapter 6 – Market Tells

2-Day two – April 27 - BHI traded in a wide trading range with a low of 75.88 and high of 81.50. The market appeared ready to break below the low pivot, but turned higher and never threatened the protective stop.

3-Day three – April 28 – The day began promising when the market opened $1.72 higher, but the excitement quickly faded. The stock remained in a tight trading range for the rest of the day and closed at 80.83. However, the close was above the high pivot price at (E) and the trend continued higher.

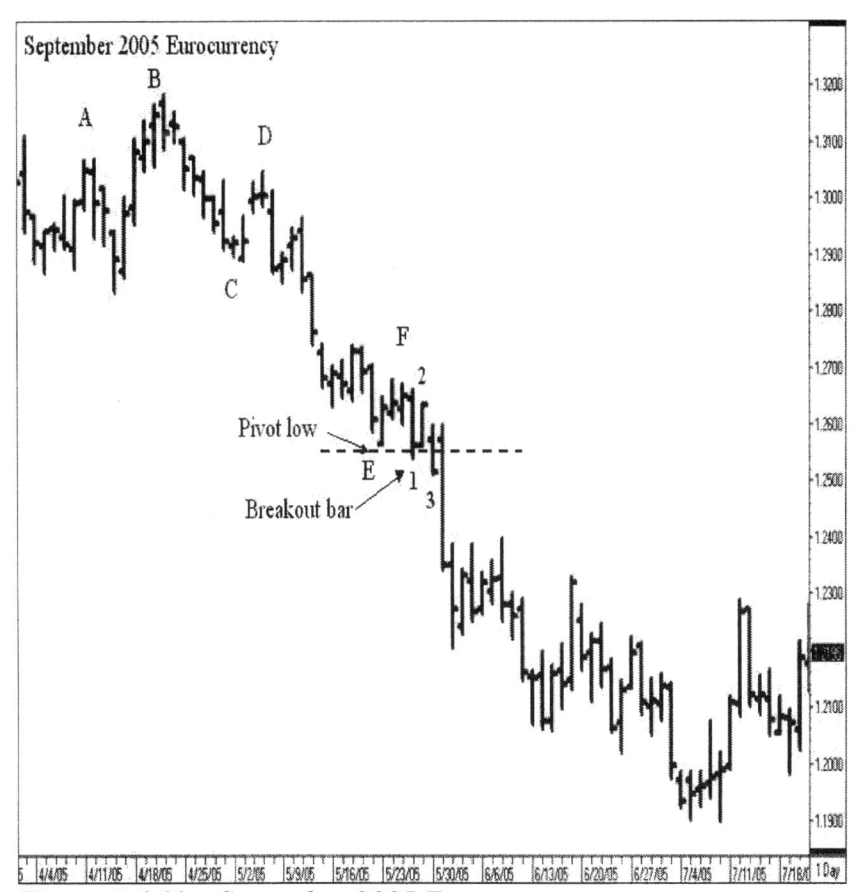

Figure # 6.10 – September 2005 Eurocurrency

186   *Chapter 6 – Market Tells*

Figure # 6.11 - Billiton (BHP)

December 2005 Cattle

Figure # 6.13 - The Reaction swing began at the high pivot price of 89.00 on September 15 (E) and ended on September 21 (F) with a low of 87.50.

1-Day one – September 26 – Breakout Bar – Three days after posting a pivot low of 87.50 on September 21 (F), December Cattle broke above the high at (E) and reached 89.10.

Chapter 6 – Market Tells

2-Day two – September 27 – The daily price range remained inside the price range of the previous day and closed at 8907.

3-Day three – September 28 – Cattle reached a high of 89.40 before turning lower and closed near the low of the daily price range. The closing price of 88.75 was below the pivot at (E), but above the low of the Breakout Bar. The market was in danger of reversing the trend and trading lower. Therefore, the protective stop should be placed below the September 28 low.

September 29 opened slightly higher and never looked back until it reached a high of 91.65 on the October 10 Reversal date.

Figure # 6.12 - Baker Hughes

188   Chapter 6 – Market Tells

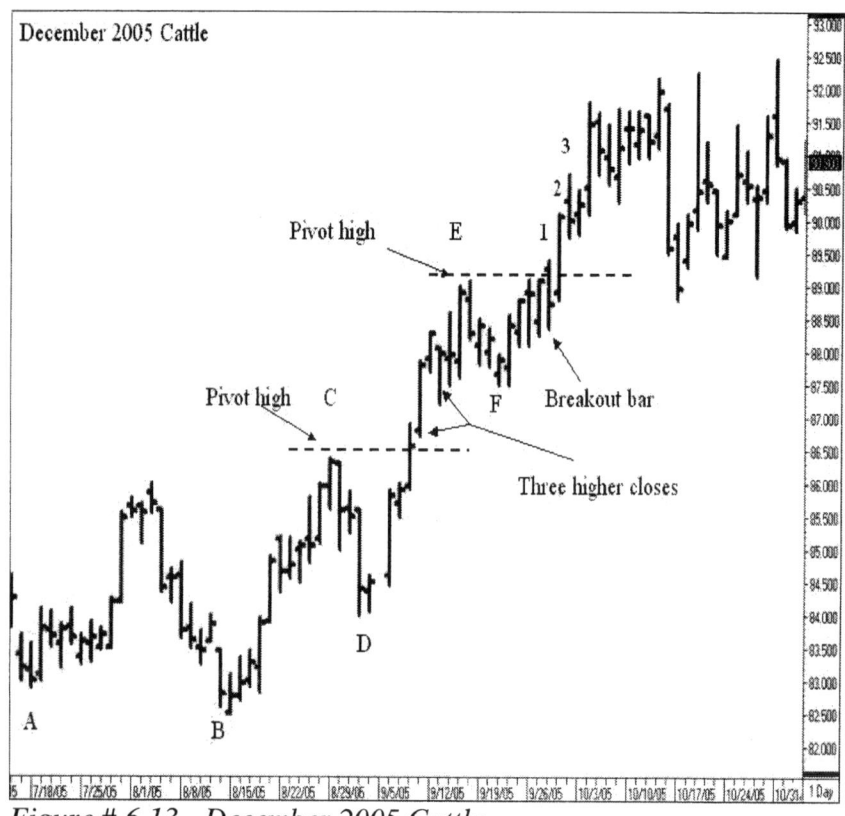

Figure # 6.13 - December 2005 Cattle

Reaction Swing Failure

We've all heard the old adage about "making lemonade out of lemons". This also holds true with a failed signal. Turning failure into success can be easy, if you know the "Tells" preceding a swing pattern failure. See *Figure # 6.14*.

When a market makes a run at a new high it can draw many traders into the market in anticipation of much higher prices. However, if the buying frenzy cannot sustain itself it can cause a price vacuum that leads to a subsequent collapse. Therein lies the opportunity for the experienced and knowledgeable trader to take advantage of the failed swing pattern and turn failure into success.

Chapter 6 – Market Tells

There are two different scenarios that lead to a swing pattern failure. The first occurs when the market trades above the high pivot—the beginning of the Reaction swing in an upward trending market—and closes above the pivot high. The next two price bars are critical. If either of the following two price bars trades below the low of the Breakout bar it is most likely a false breakout and a trap for unaware traders. When traders realize they have been duped, they run for the sidelines and the market accelerates to the downside.

Type # 1 Swing Pattern Failure
The market closes above the previous pivot high.

Type # 2 Swing Pattern Failure
The market trades above the previous pivot high and closed below breakout price.

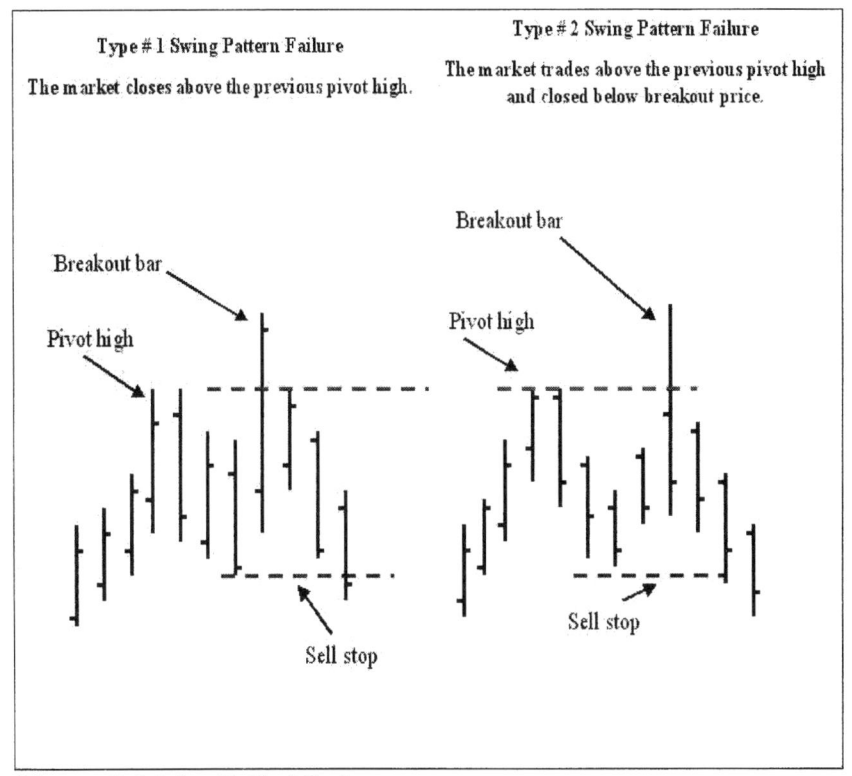

Figure # 6.14 – Failed Swing patterns

The second set-up occurs when the market trades above the pivot high and fails intra-day. In other words, the market cannot hold the early gains and closes below the pivot price. This is an early warning of a possible reversal. It is critical for the market to recover during the next two price bars and not trade below the pivot low. Aggressive traders can take advantage of this market situation by placing a reversing stop underneath the Reaction swing low and keep it in place until the first three price bars are completed. As I will illustrate in several examples, a failed signal can lead to a significant market move in the new direction.

End of the Cycle

The one thing most all failed swing patterns have in common is that they typically occur at the end of a cycle. For example, a TR pattern will usually unfold in a five-wave pattern sequence that consists of a thrust, pause, a second thrust, which is usually the most powerful price move of the trend, followed by another pause leading into the final thrust into completion of the cycle. The initial thrust begins from the major low marked as (B)—*see Figure # 6.15*—followed by a pause or correction, marked as (C) to (D). The second and usually most powerful market thrust is followed by another pause before the third and final thrust into (E). It is at this point that the likelihood of a swing pattern failure will occur. The same scenario follows the TC pattern with the likelihood of a failed swing pattern increasing after every Reaction swing that follows the completion of the TC pattern at (G).

After the completion of the TC pattern the trend is usually reaching maturity and losing momentum. Every new Reaction swing that forms after the TC pattern increases the risk of a major market reversal. Knowing this ahead of time can help you avoid major trading disasters and offer significant trading opportunities. The following examples illustrate the swing pattern failure in action.

December 2004 Hogs

Figure # 6.15 - On September 23, (E) the December Hogs surged pass the previous pivot high of the Reaction swing that formed

Chapter 6 – Market Tells

between September 20 and September 22 – marked as P-1 and P-2 on the chart. The high at the beginning of the Reaction swing was 69.97.

1-Day one – September 23 - Breakout bar – Hogs reached a new contract high and closed at 71.20, near the top of the daily trading range. This was the third thrust and the end of the TR pattern projection. The risk of a swing pattern failure is high.

2-Day two – September 24 – The market opened higher, topping out at 71.80 before it reversed trend and closed lower than the opening price. The market had closed above the high of the Reaction swing for the second day so the stop should be adjusted and placed under the low of the Breakout bar. The low was 69.10.

3-Day three – September 27 – The market traded sharply lower and closed at 68.82, below the low of the Breakout bar.

4-Day four – September 28 - The swing pattern was a confirmed failure and ended the two-week rally in the December Hogs on the September 23rd Reversal date. After a two-day bounce December Hogs continued to trade lower until they reached 63.50 on October 13.

Knowing the "Tells" of a possible swing pattern failure could have turned a potentially trading disaster into a good trading opportunity.

December 2004 Coffee

Figure # 6.16 - Soon after December Coffee reached the August 2 (G) Reversal date, projected from the (E) to (F) Reaction swing. Three days later, Coffee dipped to a new contract low on August 15, but rebounded the very next day. The reaction cycle, projected from the TC pattern, was complete therefore a possible reversal could come into play. The next four trading sessions were spent in

Chapter 6 – Market Tells

Figure # 6.15 – December 2004 Lean Hogs

a sideways trading pattern before falling to a new contract low of 68.30 on August 12, marked as Day # 1 on the chart. A bearish swing pattern was confirmed and Coffee was poised to continue the downward trend... or was it?

1-Day one – Breakout bar – August 12 - Coffee traded below the previous contract low at 68.60 established five days earlier. The new low was 68.30 and the close was 68.80.

2-Day two – August 13 - Coffee traded in a narrow price range and finished as an inside day.

Chapter 6 – Market Tells

3-Day three – August 16 - Coffee dipped to a new low early in the trading session, but quickly reversed and raced higher. The market closed at 72.10, above the previous pivot high of 71.20 posted on August 11.

The new low marked the end of the downward trend and the end of the reaction cycle. This example illustrates the increased risk from a new Reaction swing after the TC pattern projection is completed. As I mentioned earlier in this book, any new Reaction swing that forms after the TC pattern has reached its completion has increased risk because the trend is reaching maturity. Traders should always be aware of where the market is in the cycle and keep this in consideration before entering a trade at the end of a cycle.

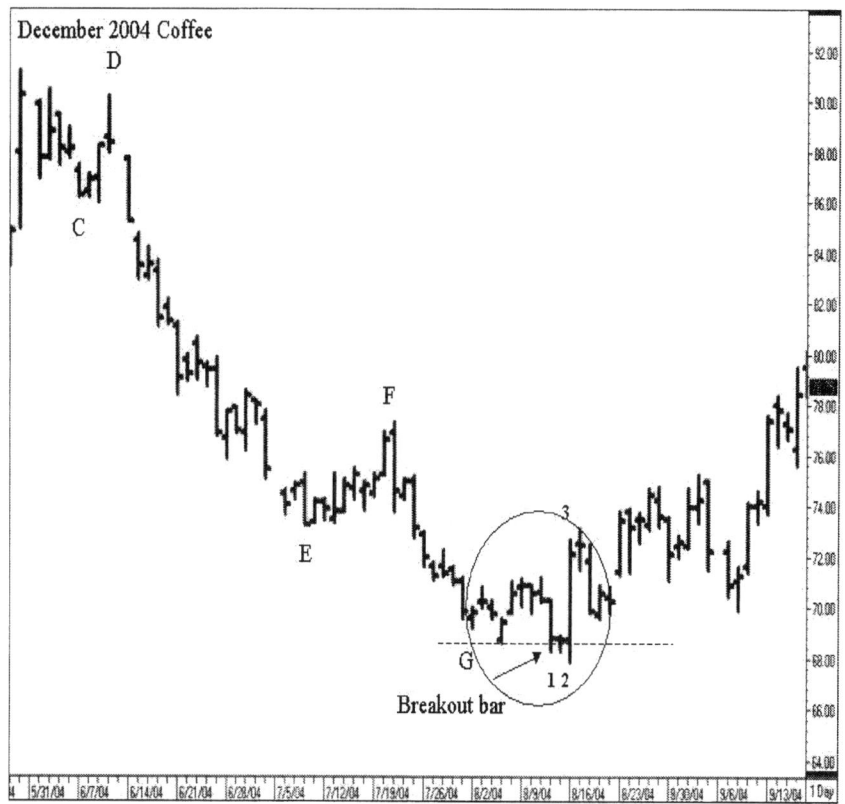

Figure # 6.16- December 2004 Coffee

August 2005 Gold

Figure # 6.17 - The June 9th low at $423.00 marked the beginning of a seventeen-day rally that ended at $444.20 on the June 23rd Reversal date. In Chapter 2, *(see Figure # 2.19)* I explained how the TR pattern and the (C) to (D) Reaction swing could be used to project the price move from (C) to the Reversal date at (E). However, what I didn't tell you was how a failed swing pattern on May 31st signaled a major change of trend before the (C) to (D) Reaction swing was formed.

August Gold created a low pivot at $419.20 on May 2 (A). Gold followed with a four-day correction before it gapped sharply lower and made a new 20-day contract low on May 31 at (B). The new contract low marked the end of a five-wave down trend.

1-Day one – May 31 - Breakout bar – After being closed for Memorial day, August Gold opened $4.90 lower. This put the market below the previous low of $419.20 at (A). Gold went on to hit a low price of $415.80 before regaining some of the lost ground and finally closed at $418.90. However, the close was still below the previous low at $419.20 (A).

2-Day two – June 1 – The trading session ended as an inside day with a close at $417.70, the second consecutive close below the previous pivot low.

3-Day three – June 2 - Gold began the day with a slightly higher open, but a flood of new buying caused the market to surge higher and break above the previous pivot high and close at $424.80. The close was well above the high of the Reaction swing and also above the 20-day SMA. The market had reversed and the trend shifted after the bearish swing pattern had failed to continue the downward trend.

Chapter 6 – Market Tells 195

Figure # 6.17 – August 2005 Gold

September 2005 Wheat

Figure # 6.18 - September Wheat had just reached a new contract high at $4.41 on the May 22 Reversal date, completing the TR pattern at (E). Under normal circumstances this would mark the end of the trade, but May 22 was also a Breakout bar from the newly formed three-day Reaction swing. If the signal was correct, the Wheat had set up for another run at higher prices, but the following day suggested there could be trouble with the signal.

1-Day one – May 22 – Breakout bar – Wheat surpassed the previous high established three days earlier and closed at the high of the daily trading range.

2-Day two – May 23 - The market reached a new high of $4.45 1/2, but reversed and closed below the opening price and below the previous day's closing price. The market looked a little negative, but the price was still above the pivot low of the Reaction swing.

3-Day three – May 24 – The market gapped lower at the open and never recovered.

4-Day four – May 25 - Wheat broke below the previous pivot low and triggered the protective stop.

The breakout had failed and the trend shifted from a strong upward trend to a new downward trend. The new trend was confirmed four days later when September Wheat completed a new bearish TR pattern.

June 2004 Japanese Yen

Figure # 6.19 - May 13 (G) was not only the Reversal date projected from the (E) to (F) Reaction swing, it was also a Breakout bar from the new Reaction swing that had just formed at the end of the cycle. This was the first reaction after the TC pattern, therefore the trend was reaching maturity and susceptible to a swing pattern failure.

1-Day one – May 13 – Breakout bar – The June Japanese yen dropped to a new contract low of .8731, after the two-day rally failed to continue. The close of .8740 was below the previous pivot low.

Chapter 6 – Market Tells 197

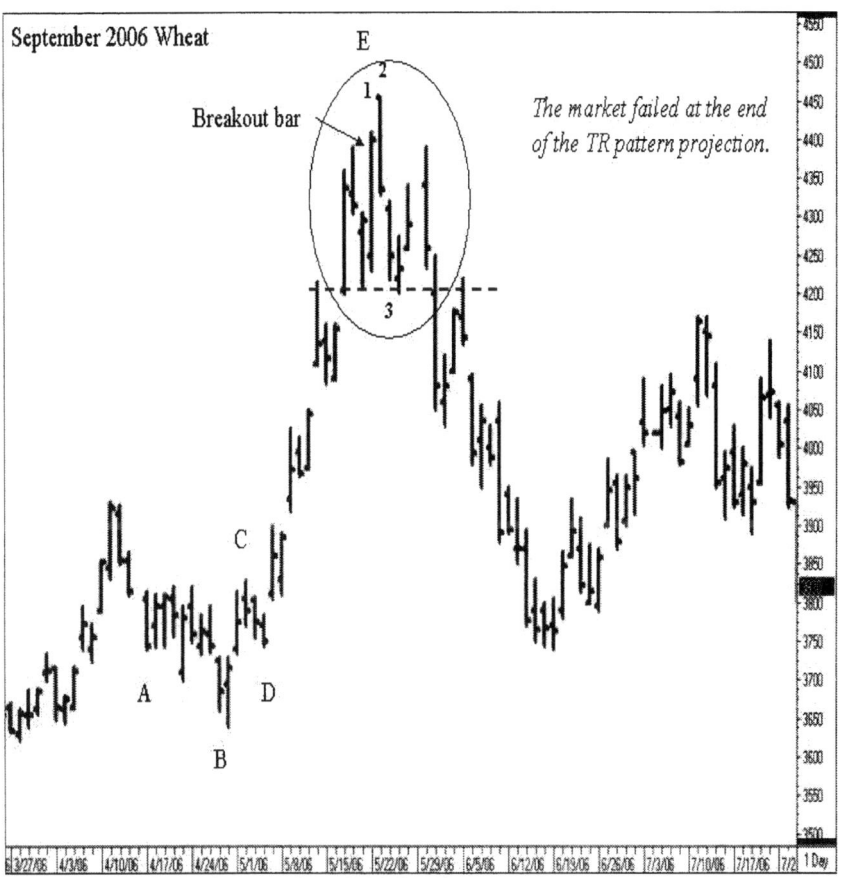

Figure # 6.18 – September 2006 Wheat

2-Day two – May 14 - The Japanese yen traded to a new low of .8712, but managed to close at .8761. The closing price was higher than the opening price and above the previous day's closing price.

3-Day three – May 17 - An early session rally failed to penetrate the pivot high and pulled back at the close. The day finished below the previous day's closing price, but remained above the contract low.

4-Day four – May 19 – So far the market had not given a clear signal of the next direction. After the third day, I would typically move the protective stop to just above the high of day three. That would put the protective stop at .8855. If the trend was going to continue lower it should continue lower from here.

5-Day five – May 19 - The Yen traded above the high of day three. This price action was enough to end any hopes of a continuation of the downward trend and corroborated the trend shift from bearish to bullish.

The market continued to rally over the next several days with only one slight pullback. As usual, the failed swing pattern was followed by a strong price move in the opposite direction.

Figure # 6.19 – June 2004 Japanese yen

Chapter 6 – Market Tells

Dell Inc. (DELL)

Figure # 6.20 - I wanted to show this chart of Dell Inc. and the swing pattern failure at (A) to (B) because this pattern is a little different than the previous patterns illustrated; it has three closes below the previous pivot low at (A). More often that not, this type of pattern would continue lower and provide a reliable trade signal, but DELL broke through the resistance and turned higher. Nevertheless, this is a very good illustration of the importance of moving the protective stop to the entry level after the third closing price beyond the previous pivot low.

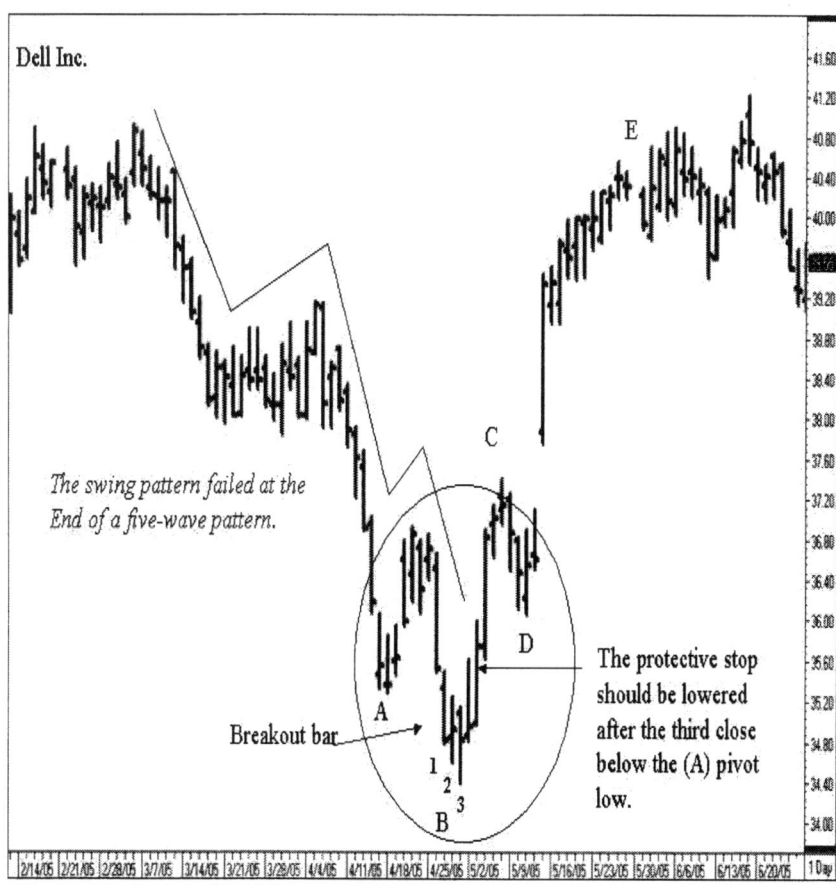

Figure # 6.20 – Dell Inc. (DELL)

Las Vegas Sands Corporation (LVS)

Figure # 6.21 - A major trend began with a swing pattern failure on October 19 – (B). LVS closed at 29.69 on October 18, just slightly above the previous low of 29.20 posted three days earlier. The next day opened lower and dipped to a new low of 29.08 before it turned higher and closed at 31.50. The October 19th close was above the previous three closes, but just shy of the 31.95 pivot high reached on October 17.

1-Day one – August 9 - Breakout bar – LVS opened lower and dropped to a new low at 29.08 before it turned higher and closed at 31.50. The close was above the previous three closes, but slightly lower than the pivot high of Reaction swing at 31.97

2-Day two – October 20 - The market ended the day as an inside day with a very narrow trading range. (An inside day typically suggests a continuation in the current direction.)

3-Day three – October 21 - LVS broke above the pivot high and closed at 32.35.

The failed swing pattern ended the downward trend and signaled a shift in the trend. Seven days later, LVS completed the TR pattern and entered a strong upward trend that peaked on the January 20 Reversal date.

One thing that should stand out after studying all the previous examples of the failed swing patterns, and the extensive price moves that follow, is the fact that many of them fall in the center of a TR pattern, usually marked a (B). That's right, they are an early "Market Tell" that a major TR pattern is in the making. Are you beginning to see how one price pattern leads into another price pattern? Having the foresight and understanding of this type of market behavior will provide insight into how a market should react after the previous pattern is complete. This knowledge will help you decide if the next reaction is characteristic of typical

Chapter 6 – Market Tells   201

market behavior or an atypical reaction. Then you can respond accordingly.

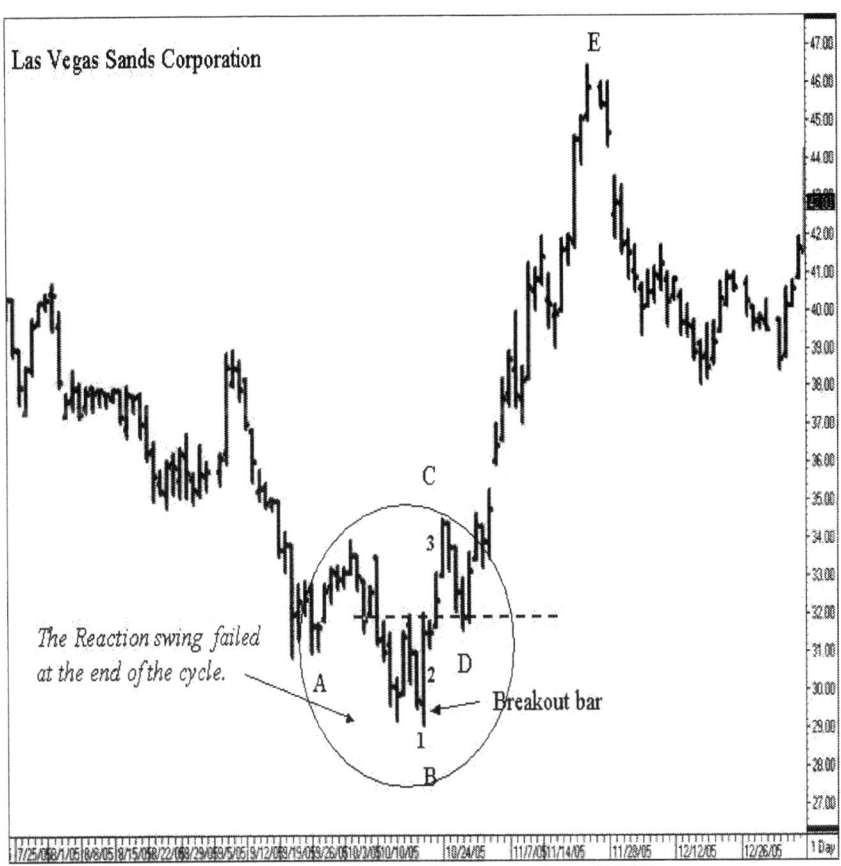

Figure # 6.21 – Las Vegas Sands Corporation (LVS)

Trail Day – Confirming the Reversal.

Projected Reversal dates are very specific and can be very precise in determining major turning points in the market. So far I have only used the Reversal dates to identify the most probable end of the move. Therefore, it would stand to reason that a Reversal date might also identify the beginning of a price move in the opposite direction. Usually, it is not advisable to for a trader to try to buy or sell before the trend change has been confirmed. It has always been tempting to try to pick the top or bottom of a major market move, but the risks are very high.

Once again, the Reversal date Indicator provides a "Market Tell" that can go a long way towards confirming a major high or low and provide a confirming price pattern at the major turning point. For this to happen, the specific criteria for the three major components of the Reversal date Indicator must come together. The key to the pattern is the "trail day"; the trail day is the date or price bar immediately following the Reversal date and it can be a very powerful directional indicator. The direction in which the market closes on the trail day is usually the direction of the next price move. In other words, if the trail day closes higher than the opening price, the market will usually continue to trade higher over the next few days. If the market closes lower than the opening price, the market will tend to trade lower. This falls right in line with the overall concept of the Time, Price and Pattern. The Reversal date suggests the Time is correct for a reaction in the market and the new high or low puts the market at the right Price level. The only thing left is the Pattern confirmation. Like everything else, the trail day must meet specific criteria for it to be a valid trail day confirming pattern. The rules are as follows for a major high.

1-The trail day must trade above the high of the reversal day and close lower than the opening price.

2-If the first criterion is met, a sell stop is placed underneath the low of the trial day. If the sell stop is filled the following day, a protective stop should be placed above the high of the trail day. From this point on, the individual trader can determine the degree of risk management they prefer.

3-If the trail day is an inside day (the entire trading range is inside the previous day's trading range), the following day must trade lower and not trade above the high of the trail day. The protective stop is treated the same.

Chapter 6 – Market Tells

4-All rules are reversed for a trail signal at a major low.

The Reversal date and confirming trail day combination is a leading indicator that uses the market action to identify a major turning point and trend shift. This allows me to enter the market at the beginning of a new trend and take advantage of the initial price thrust. Another advantage offered by a leading indicator is a specific stop placement. If the Reversal date has just confirmed a major high the protective stop is placed above the trail day high. A true reversal will not re-test a new high; therefore it will remain below the previous high. If the signal is going to fail, it will do so very quickly.

Let's look at the trail day signals that occurred after the Reversal dates in some of the markets we have already reviewed.

December 2004 Hogs

Figure # 6.22 - An eleven-day rally preceded the September 23 Reversal date. A short-term swing pattern formed right before the market surged to a new high on the Reversal date and closed at 71.20, near the high of the daily trading range. The trail day opened above the previous day's high and reached 71.80 before the market turned lower and closed at 70.82, below the opening price. The trail day directional indicator had just signaled a trend reversal and the beginning of a new downward trend that didn't end until December Hogs reached 63.50 on October 13.

December 2005 Dow Jones

Figure # 6.23 - The December Dow Jones made a new contract high on the November 18th Reversal date when the price pushed above the previous high made several weeks earlier. The Reversal date closed near the high of the daily price range. This is the point where a decision has to be made. Should the long position be closed out because the Reversal date has been reached and the market is sitting at a new high, or should the protective stop be

204   Chapter 6 – Market Tells

placed underneath the low of the Reversal date and the trade continued? If the latter is chosen, the trail day can be used as the final directional indicator.

Figure # 6.22 – December 2004 Hogs

The trail day opened above the previous day's high and continued higher into the close. The trail day directional indicator had just confirmed a continuation of the upward trend and the market continued higher over the following six days.

Chapter 6 – Market Tells

![December 2005 Dow Jones chart showing price action from 9/5/05 to 11/21/05 with points labeled A, B, C, D, and E. A note reads: "The Trail day closed higher than the opening price indicating more upside potential." An arrow points to the Trail day near point E.]

Figure # 6.23 – December 2005 Dow Jones

September 2003 Treasury Bonds

Figure # 6.24 - September T-Bonds reached a low of 109-12 on the July 22 reversal day (E). However, the market rebounded off the new low and closed near the high of the daily trading range. The next day—the trail day—T-Bonds continued higher and closed above the opening price. The market reversed the next day (F) and resumed the dominant downward trend.

In this case, the Reversal date made a new low, but the trail day did not trade below the low of the Reversal date before trading higher. Instead the trial day traded above the high of the Reversal date before the market resumed the downward trend. Therefore, the trail day did not meet the criteria for a reversal confirmation and the market continued in the same direction it was trading before the Reversal date.

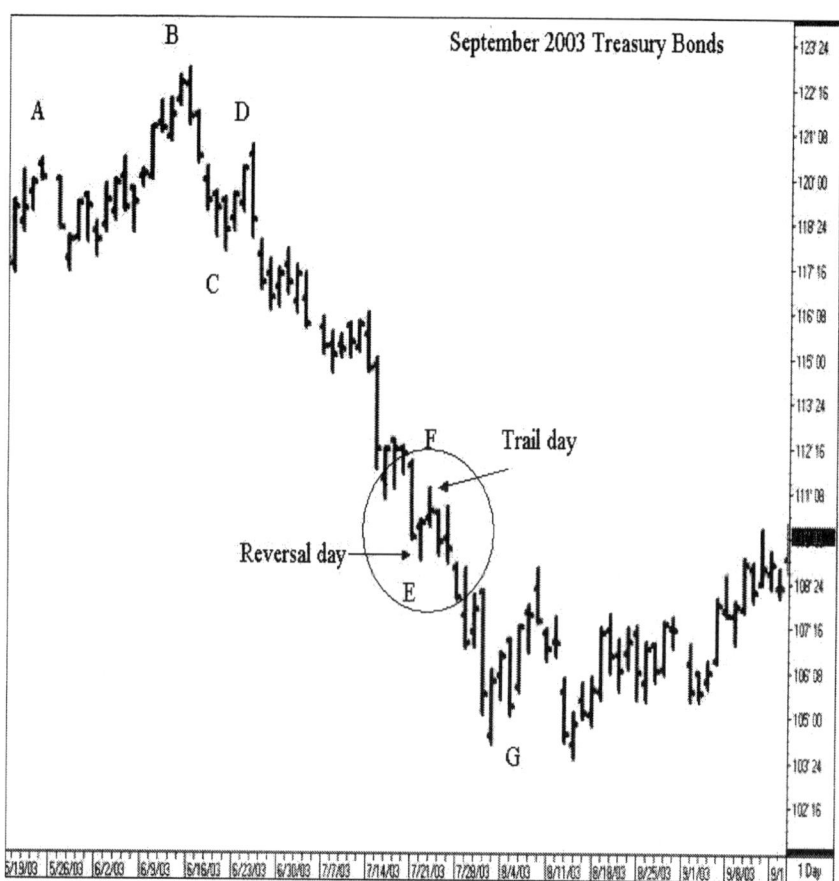

Figure # 6.24 – September 2003 Treasury Bonds

Microsoft Corporation (MSFT)

Figure # 6.25 - After the Reaction swing between (C) and (D) was confirmed, September 29 was projected as the next Reversal date. The market traded consistently lower over the next 17 days until it made a pivot low at 25.12 on September 23 (E). From this low,

Chapter 6 – Market Tells

MSFT traded higher until it peaked at 26.00 on the September 29 Reversal date (F). The Reversal date closed higher than the opening price and near the top of the daily trading range. Since the market had pushed higher into the Reversal date, I expected this to be the end of the correction and a resumption of the downward trend. The trail day—September 30—opened steady, but ended the day below the opening price, therefore the directional indicator was pointing to lower prices. However, the trail was also an inside day, and thus I wanted to see follow-through selling the next day to confirm the trail day pattern.

October 3 opened steady and closed below the opening price and below the previous three closes. This was enough to confirm the trail day signal and the resumption of the existing downward trend.

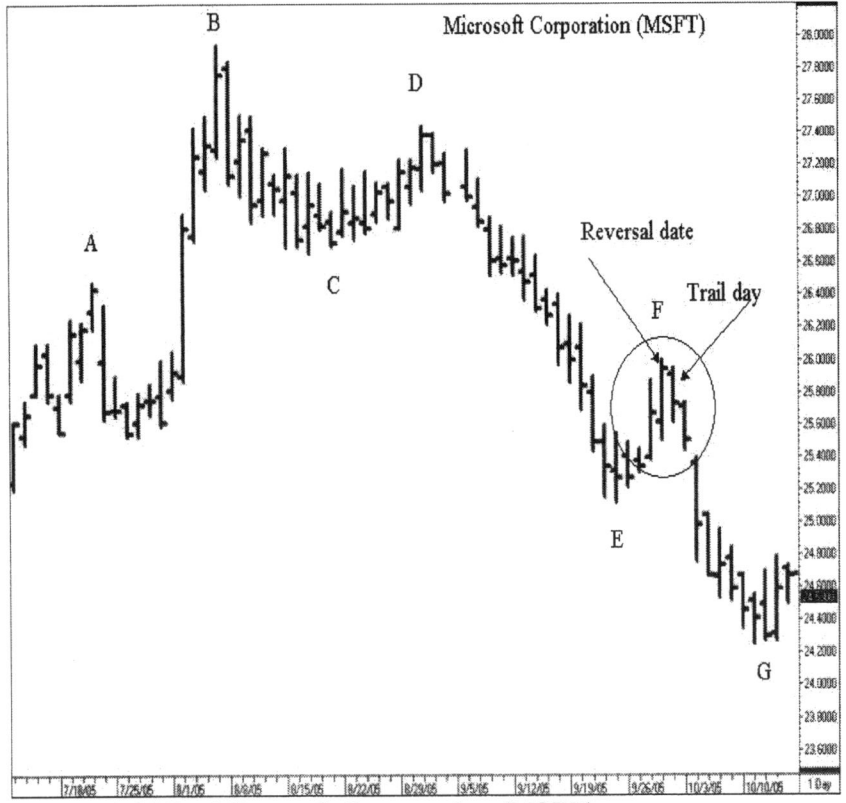

Figure # 6.25 – Microsoft Corporation (MSFT)

August 2005 Gold

Figure # 6.26 - August Gold reached a new 20-day high on the June 23 Reversal date. The trail day did not trade above the Reversal date high, but it did finish the day as an inside day with the closing price lower than the opening price. The preliminary indication was for the market to turn lower, but it was two days later before the market broke below the trial day low and closed below the previous low.

The trend reversed, as the trial day had suggested, and continued to trade lower over the next several days. The Reversal date and trail day combination had identified the major high and confirmed a significant reversal in the market.

The "Market Tells" forewarned of three great trading opportunities in the August Gold. A "Tell" appeared at both major highs and the low at (B). Can you identify them?

September 2006 Wheat

Figure # 6.27 - September Wheat rallied over $.50 cents in 12 days before it finally peaked at a new contract high of $4.41 on the May 22th Reversal date. The Reversal date was also the Breakout bar from the newly formed three-day Reaction swing. The market appeared poised for new highs. However, when the trail day did manage to push to a new contract high it failed to sustain the momentum. The market quickly turned lower and closed below the opening price. The trail day directional indicator said the rally was over and the Wheat should reverse and trade lower.

The next day, Wheat gapped lower and continued to trade for the remainder of the day where it closed below the previous three closing prices. The upward trend was over and the trial day pattern had confirmed a sell signal at the major high. Wheat continued lower without ever testing the trial day.

Chapter 6 – Market Tells

Figure # 6.26 – August 2005 Gold

September 2006 Cocoa

Figure # 6.28 - I have always found it interesting that fundamental news and the Reversal dates can work in harmony. The September Cocoa is a great example of this phenomenon. Political unrest in the Ivory Coast caused the Cocoa market to breakout and race to new heights in late June and early July, but the roaring bull market came to an abrupt halt on the July 10 Reversal date. The market peaked at 1,737 on July 10 and closed near the top of the daily trading range. July 11, the trail day, traded to 1,738, one point

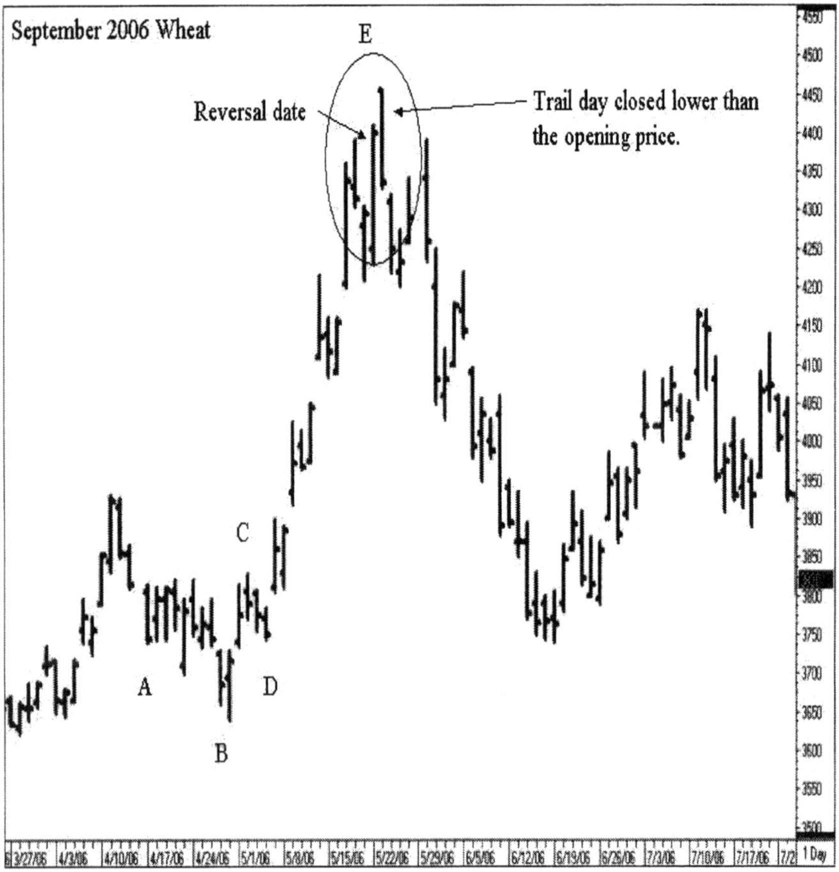

210 *Chapter 6 – Market Tells*

Figure # 6.27 – September 2006 Wheat

above the previous high, before it fell back and closed at 1,730, warning of an end to the rally. The next day gapped lower and marked the beginning of a significant market collapse.

The Reversal date, combined with the trail day directional indicator, provided advance warning of the major reversal and selling opportunity in the September Cocoa. The trail day directional indictor warned of this price reversal three days in advance of the 230-point plunge in September Cocoa!

Chapter 6 – Market Tells   211

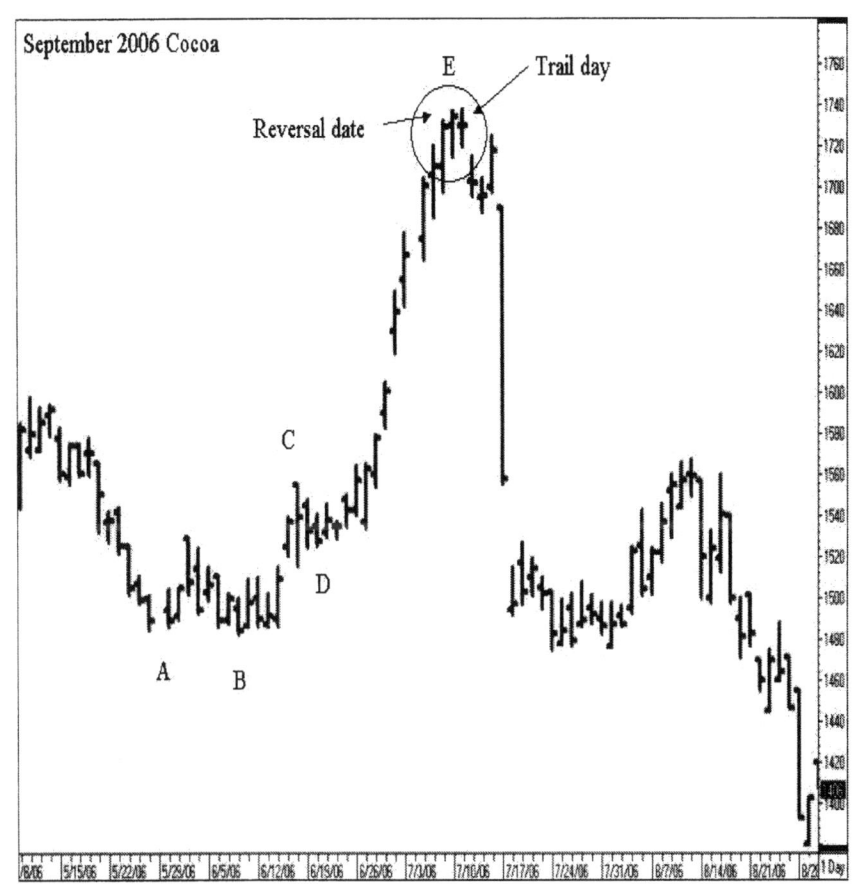

Figure # 6.28 – September 2006 Cocoa

December 2006 E-mini S&P 500 - 10 minute chart

Figure # 6.29 - The December E-mini S&P had peaked at 1347.75 on the projected 12:00 p.m. reversal bar. The market had closed higher than the opening price and near the high of the 10-minute bar. The trail bar pushed above the high of the reversal bar and closed below the opening price. The reversal bar had indicated an end of the cycle and the trial bar confirmed the directional change. The high of the trail bar proved to be the high of the daily price range and the S&P moved into a sideways-to-lower trading pattern until the close of the day.

Figure # 6.29 – December 2006 E-mini S&P 500 – 10 minute chart

Trident Microsystems Inc. (TRID)

Figure # 6.30 - TRID posted a low of 18.69 on the June 12 Reversal date and closed on the low of the daily trading range. This was not the lowest low because TRID had traded at 18.35 two day previously. The trail day dipped below the June 12 low, but stayed above the 18.35 low, before it turned higher and closed

Chapter 6 – Market Tells 213

above than the opening price, indicting a change of direction. TRID continued higher for two more days before it hit resistance. Although the market did follow through in the direction of the trail day, the new trend couldn't sustain itself. When the trail day did not trade below the previous low it did not meet the full criteria for a true trail day signal.

Figure # 6.30 –Trident Microsystems Inc. (TRID)

June 2004 Japanese yen

Figure # 6.31 - June Japanese yen traded to a new contract low on the May 13th Reversal date. The market had pushed below the prior

214   Chapter 6 – Market Tells

pivot low from three days earlier and closed at the bottom of the daily trading range. The new low was below the TC pattern, therefore the trend was reaching maturity and should be losing momentum. Based on this knowledge, I was on the lookout for a major reversal at this juncture.

The trail day quickly confirmed what I suspected when the Japanese yen traded to a new low before it turned and closed above the opening price. The Reversal date had just signaled it was time for a reversal. The new low suggested the market was at the right price level for a possible reversal and the trail day pattern confirmed a directional change at the end of the trend and the beginning of a new bullish trend. Everything had come together and the market responded accordingly.

Figure # 6.31 – June 2004 Japanese Yen

Billiton Ltd (BHP)

Figure # 6.32 - The importance of confirming the pattern and not anticipating the signal was illustrated in this chart of BHP.

BHP had reached a new high at 48.27 on the May 5th Reversal date and closed near the high of the daily price range. The trail day opened higher, but quickly turned lower, leaving the opening price as the high of the day.

The next day started with a steady opening followed by a rally to a new high. The market did not trade lower as indicated by the lower close on the trail day. On the other hand, the trail day was never confirmed because the following day did not trade below the low of the trail day. In other words, the sell stop placed below the low of the trail day would have never been filled and a short position would have never been entered.

Figure # 6.32 – Billiton Ltd. (BHP)

Final Thoughts

So far I have been using the same charts over and over to illustrate the different chart patterns and signals. I mention this because in the past I have had readers complain about different authors cherry picking a different chart for every example and suggesting they are only picking the perfect setup for the trade to make things look better than they really are.

First of all, I would like to say that yes, many of the charts are picked to illustrate the chart pattern or signal I am trying to describe. How am I going to describe the pattern or signal if I don't use a chart that illustrates the point I am trying to convey? I think it goes without saying that not every chart pattern or trading signal is going to work 100% of the time in every market situation. That is why it is important to wait for the correct setup and always use money management. The best offense is always a good defense.

Having said that, the reason I am using the same charts and markets over and over is to illustrate that I don't have to cherry pick a different chart for every pattern and every signal. Notice how the Reaction swing can be used to project future Reversal dates and the action/reaction lines can project future price levels all on the same chart. I can also use the "Market Tells" to identify and confirm the Reversal date signals on the same charts. In other words, I don't have to search through dozens of charts to find a good example of the pattern I want to describe. They are based on price action and can occur over and over in every market in every time frame.

Chapter 7

"If you don't have a plan for yourself, you will be part of someone else's plan" – American Proverb

The Reversal Date Trading Indicator and Option Trading Strategy

All that I have discussed thus far in this book seems great and it looks so easy, but the question you are probably asking now is what is the best way to trade the Reversal date Trading Indicator? That differs from trader to trader. One thing I have learned in my 20 years of working with thousands of traders is that everyone has their own style, even if they are following the same system or methodology.

Most traders are not aware or they do not want to admit that their trading style is affected greatly by their emotions. In my experience I have found that if you have 10 traders following the same trading system or method you will see 10 different results. Some traders are willing to take more risk than others, while others tend to take their profits quickly or overstay their welcome in a trade.

One of the benefits provided by the Reversal date Trading Indicator (RDTI) is the flexibility and variety of the different ways it can be used in trading. I consider the RDTI not so much as a trading system, but more of a trading methodology based on crowd psychology and pattern recognition. Trading systems are typically more stringent and are developed and tested under selected market conditions. While a system may perform well under certain conditions, when those conditions change—and they do—the results may suffer. On the other hand, a trading methodology is more dynamic and can adjust to the changing market conditions. I believe the RDTI is dictated more by the human emotions of fear and greed than by a predetermined set of trading rules.

Plan the trade – Trade the plan.

While the most common way to trade the RDTI is using futures contract or buying and selling the stock, another approach that should not be ignored is using options, either by themselves or in combination with a futures contract or stock.

When you buy an option you are buying time. Time for something to happen in the market; preferably that something is the thing you expect. As time passes and the market does not react, the option loses its value because there is less time for the market to make that expected price move. Therefore, timing the purchase or sell of the option is important. It is best to time the purchase or sell at the right time, i.e., right before a substantial market move. That is where the RDTI comes into play.

Using the TR pattern and the TC pattern to time the purchase or sell of an option may enhance the profitability of the trade. There are two things you know: the market will either make the expected price move soon after the purchase or sell of the option, or the signal will fail and the option should be exited quickly. That is all there is to it...the trade will either work quickly or not at all.

Long Options

Probably the most common option strategy is the simple purchase of an option. If you think the market will trade higher you buy a call option. If the signal is for the market to fall, you would buy a put option. That part is simple, but selecting which strike price to purchase can be a little confusing to new traders. The reasons

Chapter 7 – Options Trading Strategy

behind the strike price selections are as numerous as there are traders. It may be determined by the amount of money the trader wants to risk on the trade, or how much they are willing to pay. It can also be determined by the Time and Price projections. The list can go on and on.

Simply put, the long option strategy is to buy a call option one or two strike prices out of the money as soon as the trigger price is hit and exit when the futures price reaches the projected target price or Reversal date. If the trade fails to confirm by the three higher close rule, step out of the option with a small loss and wait for the next signal.

Of course, there are numerous option strategies that can be implemented, such as the Bull call spread or the Bear put spread and other combinations. However, it is not my intention to delve into the many different strategies. If you want to learn more about the most common and most useful option trading strategies I recommend you read the "Option Traders Playbook" by Joseph Kellogg. You can get more information on this excellent book at "www.tradersnetwork.com."

Short Option

Using options in conjunction with the Reversal date Trading Indicator may enhance performance and offer the ability to gain in either direction. One of my favorite strategies is a Covered Write. This strategy is set up by selling a call or put in combination with a long or short futures contract. The benefit is the potential for gain either way the market moves. Here is how the trade is set up for a bullish pattern.

Covered Write – What is it?

Without going into great details of how a Covered Write position works, I feel I need to touch on the basics. An option has a delta value, with indicates how much the option will increase or decrease in value in relation to an identical price move in the underlying futures contract. For example, an at-the-money option will typically have a delta of 50% and a futures contract will always have a delta value of 100%. Therefore, a $100 increase in the futures contract would increase the value of a long call option by $50.

Entering the position

Once a TR pattern and the TC pattern are formed, a call option is sold above the Reaction swing. As soon as the option is sold a buy stop is placed at the trigger price (above the high pivot of the Reaction swing) and the trade is set.

If the market continues lower and does not trigger the buy stop, the option will lose value and offer the potential for gain while the market continues the downward trend. On the other hand, if the market does turn higher it will hit the buy stop and enter a long futures position. As soon as the futures position is entered, a sell (protective) stop is placed underneath the low of the Reaction swing.

The long position is now a bullish Covered Write (a long futures position and a short call option) and offers you the potential to gain as the market moves higher. If the market continues to move higher you can either continue to hold the Covered Write until the maximum gain is achieved or exit the option and hold the long futures.

What is the Risk?

Nothing is without risk. If the market does not continue higher, after the futures position is entered, it may drop back to the protective stop and close the long futures position for a loss. However, the loss will be partially offset by the gain from the short call option. How much of the loss is offset depends on how long the short option is held.

The following examples will illustrate how this strategy works.

December 2006 Japanese yen

Figure # 7.1 - The December Japanese yen had been in a constant downward trend for several weeks before it formed a Reaction swing between September 18, (B), and September 21, (C). After the Yen established a high close of .8715 on September 22, it turned lower and confirmed a pivot high at (C) and a potential bullish TR pattern. It was time to set up the trade.

On September 26, the December Japanese yen .8750 call option traded for 70 points. Every point for the Japanese yen is worth $12.50; therefore the option had a value of $875 (70 x $12.50 = $875). So the first step was to sell the .8750 call option for 70 points and place a buy stop at .8750.

If the December Japanese yen continued lower a gain would be made and the short option would lose value. (When you sell an option and the market moves away from the strike price, the option will lose value. The lost value becomes a loss for the purchaser and a profit for the seller.)

Japanese yen continued the downward trend and traded below the previous contract low at (B). Instead of a TR pattern the Reaction swing turned out to be a continuation pattern. On October 13, the December .8750 call option closed at 17 points. The call option was sold at 70 and could be covered at 17 for a gain of 53 points or $662. The trade may have had more profit potential with just a short futures position, but opportunity to profit from a trend continuation would have been missed if the only order placed was a buy stop above the high pivot at (C). Combining the Reversal date Trading Indicator with short options offered the potential to gain either way the market moved. What more can a trader want?

222   Chapter 7 – Options Trading Strategy

Figure # 7.1 – December 2006 Japanese yen

November 2006 Crude oil

Figure # 7.2 - Between September 22 and September 27, November Crude oil formed a possible TR pattern after an extended downward move. The high of the pivot at (C) was 6400. At the same time the November Crude oil 6400 call option traded at 50. (One point in Crude oil equals $10.00 x 50 = $500.)

A sell order was placed to sell the November Crude oil 6400 call option at 50 and a buy stop entered at 6405 - the trigger price above the pivot high. Everything was in place if the market traded higher. However, the Crude oil gapped lower, the following day,

Chapter 7 – Options Trading Strategy

and continued lower into October 13. On October 13, the November 6400 Crude oil call option closed at 2 points. I had anticipated the market to trade higher and I was wrong. However, by using this strategy I was still offered the potential gain of $480.

Figure # 7.2 – November 2006 Crude oil

December 2006 Treasury Bonds

Figure # 7.3 - December T-Bonds had been in an extended bull market since mid-June, but accelerated near the end of September. The trend peaked at 113-11 on September 25, turned and closed lower for two consecutive days. The new swing pattern was near the end of a longer-term cycle and it could be setting up for a major reversal and there weren't any confirming signals indicating which way the market was going to break. But, that was all right... the trade was to be set for a price move in either direction.

On September 27, the December T-Bond 114-00 call option traded at 45. T-Bonds options trade in 1/64s. (One point is worth $15.62 x 45 = $703.) The trade is set up by entering two orders, the first order is to sell the December T-Bond 114-00 call at 45 and the second order is a buy stop at 113-15 – three points above the pivot high at (B). Once the option sell is confirmed the trade is set.

T-Bonds drop to a low of 112-01 on September 29 (C). From this low, the market rebounded off the pivot low and rallied over the next three days to (D). At this point,
T-Bonds were poised to test the high and possibly continue the current trend. If this happened, the buy stop was in place. However, the T-Bonds stalled at 113-05, on October 4 (D), reversed and continued lower. Ten days later the December 114-00 T-Bond call closed at 3 points... a potential gain of $656.

You may be looking at the T-Bond chart right now and saying to yourself, "That looks like a bearish TR pattern, shouldn't a sell stop be placed at the trigger price below the pivot at (C)?" Yes, a sell stop could have been placed below (C) and a short position added to the trade. There was also the option to sell a 111-00 put when the market bottomed at (C) and traded up to (D). It all depends on how aggressive the trader wants to be.

That's the benefit of using options in combination with the Reversal date strategy. There are plenty of different options on how the trade can be managed. However, there is one critical criterion that cannot be overlooked... the protective stops. If you sell an option and the market triggers the stop to enter a futures position, the protective stop must be in place. If the protective stop is not in place and the market turns against you, you will have two positions working against you. Every time I have gotten in trouble with a trade it is because the protective stop was not in place. I have learned it is much easier to get stopped out of a trade and re-evaluate it from the sidelines, than to think objectively when the market is running against you. I can re-evaluate the trade without the pressure of an increasing loss and make an objective decision.

Chapter 7 – Options Trading Strategy 225

Figure # 7.3 – December 2006 Treasury Bonds

December 2006 Cattle

Figure # 7.4 - On October 4, December Cattle broke out of a bearish Reaction swing and appeared ready to resume the prevailing downward trend. Although the market was poised to continue lower, selling the 88.00 put option would also prepare for a bullish reversal.

The December Cattle 88.00 put option traded at 165. (One point in Cattle is worth $4.00 x 165 = $660.) Once the option sell was confirmed and the sell stop in place at 89.50, the trade was set. The

Chapter 7 – Options Trading Strategy

Figure # 7.4 – December 2006 Cattle

following day Cattle dropped through the sell stop to trigger a short position against the short put and convert the trade into a Covered Write position.

Four days after entry, the short futures position was closed out at 87.47 for a gain of 202 points and the short 88.00 put option covered at 235. The futures position posted a gain of $808 dollars while the short option lost $280 for an overall gain of $528.

December 2006 Coffee

Figure # 7.5 - From early March through April, Coffee completed a five-wave zigzag connecting pattern that concluded with a TR pattern marked as (A)(B)(C) and (D) on the chart. The low pivot price of 113.70 at (C) was my focal point because it was the trigger to confirm a sell signal. I expected the TR pattern to confirm, but the trade could be set up to gain even if the market turned higher.

The low pivot at (C) was confirmed on May 2. The same day the December Coffee 110.00 put option traded for 875 points. (One point in Coffee equals $3.75 x 875 = $3,281.) Once the option sell was confirmed and the sell stop was placed at the trigger price below 113.50 (C), everything was in place for the next move in December Coffee.

The Coffee traded higher for a couple of days before it stalled beneath the previous pivot high (B) and turned lower. Five days later the sell stop was hit to trigger the sell signal. The position now had a short futures position in conjunction with the short 110.00 put option that should continue to gain as the market moved toward the next Reversal date scheduled for May 26.

December Coffee closed at 104.80 on May 26 and the December 110.00 put option closed at 1,310. The potential gain from the short futures position was 870 points or $3,262. The loss on the short put option was 435 points (1310 − 875 = 435) or $1,631. So the overall trade offered a possible net gain of $1,631 ($3,262 - $1,631 = $1,631).

In this example, the short put option was held for the duration of the trade, but that is not necessary for this strategy to work. It really depends on the individual, how they choose to manage this type of trade. For example, after the sell signal was confirmed, the trader could use the three-lower-close rule and exit the option with a small loss and hold the short position. This, of course, would increase the profit potential, but also increased the risk if the market turned higher. That is just one of the reasons I like the strategy; it offers several choices on managing the trade.

228   *Chapter 7 – Options Trading Strategy*

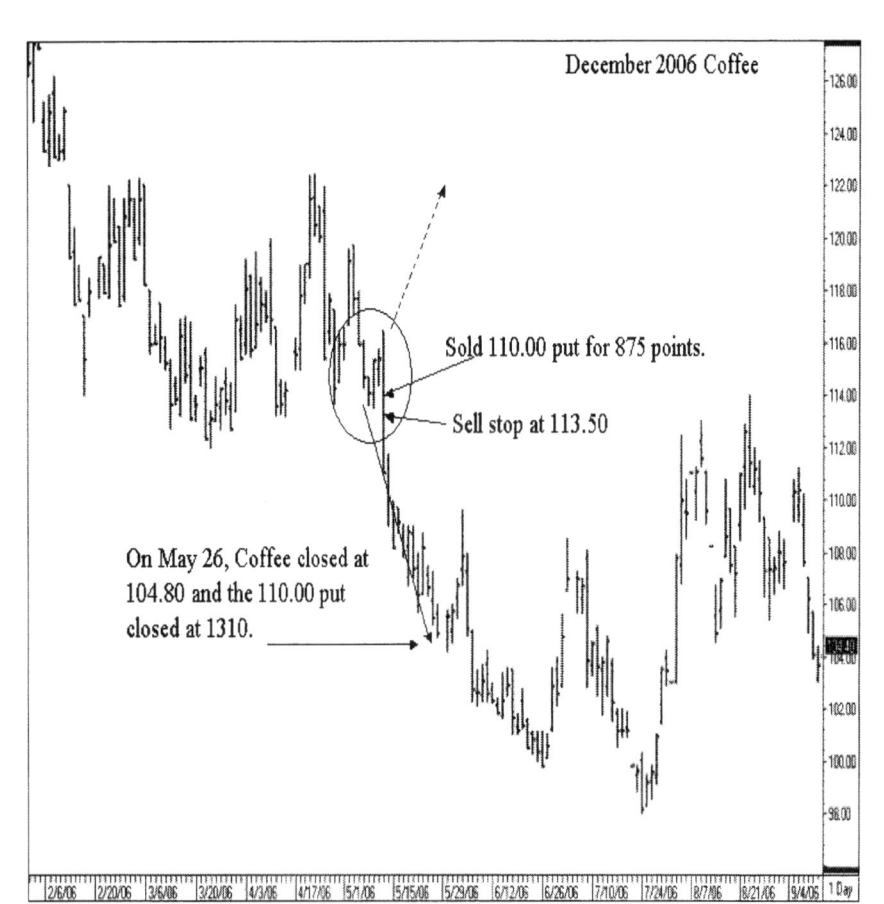

Figure # 7.5 – December 2006 Coffee

[Chart annotations: December 2006 Coffee; Sold 110.00 put for 875 points.; Sell stop at 113.50; On May 26, Coffee closed at 104.80 and the 110.00 put closed at 1310.]

January 2006 Soybeans

Figure # 7.6 - January Soybeans had drifted steadily lower after the fourth of July. Talk of ideal growing conditions and a possible record crop kept pressure on Soybeans throughout the summer. November Soybeans reached a low of $5.50 ½ on September 12 – two days prior to the projected Reversal date of September 14. The succeeding two trading days both ended with a close higher than the previous day. Since the market had traded higher into the September 14th Reversal date, it set up a bearish Reaction swing and the possibility of another push to a new contract low. On the other hand, the Reaction swing was at the end of a cycle and the trend could be ready to shift. Everything suggested the timing was right to sell a put option and prepare for a reversal. Let's see how the setup played out.

On September 14 – the projected Reversal date – the January Soybean $5.40 put option traded at 11 cents. (One cent in Soybeans equals $50.00 – 11 x $50.00 = $550.00). Once the option sell was confirmed and the sell stop placed underneath the September 12 low of $5.50 ½, the trade was in place and prepared for the next move in Soybeans, whichever direction the market broke.

It turned out that the bearish cycle was over as Soybeans traded higher into September 21 before falling back during the following two trading sessions. However, the sell stop below the pivot low was never in danger as the two-day correction ended and the market moved sideways over the next six trading sessions. The short option did its job.

As the market chopped back and forth, a potential TR pattern began to show up. The high pivot at (C) and the low pivot at (D) had formed a possible Reaction swing with a trigger price above the $5.75 high at (C). On September 4, Soybeans surged forward and broke above $5.75 and triggered a buy signal... the TR pattern had been confirmed. On January 4, the January $5.50 put option closed at 6 cents. It was decision time – should the option continue to be held? The TR pattern had been confirmed and the trend had shifted from a downward trending market to a new upward trending market. Would it be best to take the 5-cent gain and offset the short option? Either way, the signal worked out very well. Nine days later, January Soybeans closed at $614 1/2 and the $5.40 put closed at 2 1/4 cents.

Do you see what I mean about the flexibility this strategy offers? Each trade signal can be evaluated and treated differently, depending on the market price action. But remember, it is equally important to make sure the money management protection is always in place.

230   *Chapter 7 – Options Trading Strategy*

Figure # 7.6 – January 2007 Soybeans

December 2006 10-Year Treasury Notes

Figure # 7.7 - The December T-Notes had been in a steady upward trend for about five weeks when the market began to correct and form a Reaction swing. This looked like a potential continuation pattern, but what if the market did not continue higher? Let's see how this option strategy would have worked in the Ten-year Notes.

The pivot high of 106-21.5 occurred on August 4 (E) and was followed by a six-day correction to (F). On August 11 the December 107-00 T-Note call option traded for 31 points. (One point in the T-Notes options equal $15.62 – 31 x $15.52 = $481.) As soon as the option sell was confirmed the buy stop was in place at 106-23, just above the pivot high.

Two days later – August 16 – T-Notes traded above the pivot high and triggered the buy stop to enter a long futures position at 106-23. Four days after the long future position was initiated, the market had closed above the pivot for three consecutive days, therefore the protective stop should be moved to the entry. On August 29, the T-Notes dropped back and traded through the protective stop to close the long position at the entry price. After the long futures position was closed the short option was no longer covered and at risk if the market continued higher. There are two things that can be done at this point: place a buy stop above high, hold the short option and wait for the market to continue lower or close the option and end the trade. The option closed at 45 on August 29.

November 2006 Crude oil

Figure # 7.8 - On August 29, November Crude oil had just completed a successful TR pattern and staged a small two-day correction from the Reversal date. Most likely, the short-term correction was just a pause before resuming the downward trend, but it could also be the low before another rally. So the trade was set up to be ready whichever direction the market decided to move. Let's see how it worked out.

The pivot low was 69.80 on August 29. The November Crude oil 69.00 put option traded at 160 on August 30. (One point in Crude oil equals $10.00 x 160 = $1,600.) As soon as the option sell was confirmed and the sell stop placed at 69.80, the trade was set.

The sell stop was triggered on September 5th as the Crude oil gapped lower and began a rapid descent over the next several days. The position was now a Covered Write consisting of a short November Crude oil 69.00 put option at 160 points and a short futures position from 69.80. At this point it was very important that

Chapter 7 – Options Trading Strategy

Figure # 7.7 – December 2006 Ten Year Notes

the protective stop be placed above the pivot high of the current Reaction swing at (F). Crude oil had been experiencing some high volatility so the protection was vital. It should also be noted that the $1,600 of premium collected from short put option did offer some protection should the market suddenly turn higher and run your protective stop. Having said that, let's get back to the trade and see how it played out.

Crude oil continued to trade lower into the next projected Reversal dates of September 12 and September 22. On September 12th the Crude oil closed at 64.90 and the 69.00 put option closed at 510 for a potential gain of $4,900 on the futures position and a $3,500 loss on the option, netting a gain of $1,400.

Chapter 7 – Options Trading Strategy 233

Figure # 7.8 – November 2006 Crude oil

Once again, the individual trader can decide if he prefers to keep the extra protection offered by holding the short option or giving up the protection by closing the option soon after the futures position is entered. Each approach has its own pros and cons.

December 2006 Silver

Figure # 7.9 - I am including the chart of December Silver because it offers good examples of both a trend continuation and a trend reversal.

The confirming Reaction swing of a TR pattern had formed between May 19 and May 29. The pivot low of the pattern was $12.19 on May 22. Two days after the low the December Silver $12.00 put option traded at $1.30. (One cent in Silver equals $50.00 x $1.30 = $6,500.) As soon as the option sell was confirmed a sell stop should be placed at $12.17, underneath the pivot low at (C). Two days after the Reaction swing peaked on May 29, Silver slid through the sell stop. The short $12.00 put option was now covered by a short futures position from $12.17.

The reverse/forward count projected June 15 as the next Reversal date and Silver bottomed at $9.64 just two days prior to the June 15th Reversal date. December Silver closed at $10.15 on June 15 and the $12.00 put option closed at $2.49. Therefore, at the close of the June 15th Reversal date, the combination of the short futures position and short put option offered a potential gain of $4,050.

After posting a low on June 14, Silver traded higher during the two next trading sessions and set up another possible bearish Reaction swing. Not knowing whether this was a continuation pattern or a major low, I looked at the December Silver $9.50 put options. On June 15 the option was trading at 81 cents. (.81 x $50.00 = $4,050). As soon as the option sell was confirmed a sell stop should have been placed underneath the June 14 low of $9.64.

But that sell stop would have never been challenged, as Silver continued to climb until it reached $11.92 on July 12. On the same day the $9.50 Silver put closed at 37 cents for a potential gain of $2,200 from the short option, all because on June 15 the trade was set up to take advantage of a market move in either direction.

Chapter 7 – Options Trading Strategy

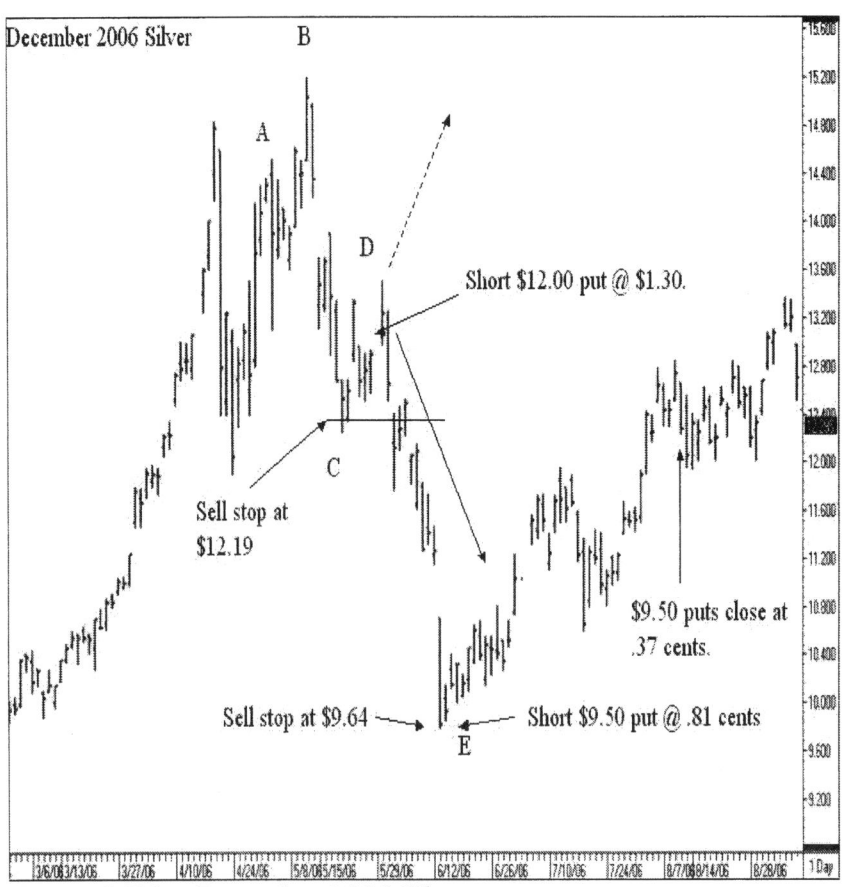

Figure # 7.9 – December 2006 Silver

Chapter 8

"You can observe a lot by watching"
Yogi Berra

Bullish and Bearish Divergence

When I first started trading in the late 70's I received my price charts through the mail every Monday or Tuesday and then I would update the rest of the week by hand. It was a great way to learn about price patterns and market behavior because I could watch the patterns unfold as I updated the charts every morning.

At the top of the chart page was the Relative Strength Indicator, also known as RSI, and the Slow Stochastic (SSTO) indicator was on the bottom of the chart. This was my first introduction to technical indicators. At the time these were probably the two most popular indicators and continued to gain popularity as computers became more available.

While I do consider myself a dedicated student of technical analysis, I am not a strong proponent of using technical indicators exclusively. There is a huge difference between trading with a method based on market behavior and price action versus one derived from technical indicators. Although many books and trading systems will lead you to believe otherwise, technical indicators are lagging in nature. Since they are derived from price alone and generated based on a time frame and formula that smoothes out the data, the indicators have a built-in lag time. This makes it difficult for an indicator to predict a significant price move in advance, but they can offer a good confirmation of a move already in progress. Lastly, indicators often require subjective interpretations that can create problems for novice traders.

Having said all that, I now want to say that there is one indicator that I will use under certain circumstances. That indicator is the Slow Stochastic, but I don't use it on a stand-alone basis because of its tendency to give false signals. However, there is one technique I will use in conjunction with selected price patterns...bullish or bearish divergence.

Divergence occurs when the market is making new highs or new lows, but the SSTO fails to match the new highs of the new lows. In other words, when the market trades above the previous pivot high, there should also be a corresponding new high in the SSTO. If the SSTO fails to trade above its previous high it suggests - even though the market is moving higher – that the underlying momentum is beginning to weaken and a major turn is imminent.

The Slow Stochastic (SSTO) is based on the theory that, as prices move higher, the daily closes should reflect the high of the daily range. Likewise, as prices decrease, the daily close tends to accumulate closer to the low of the daily range. SSTO calculations are based on the rate of change in the daily high, low, and close. The SSTO chart needs two lines and three values. The three values are: the raw value, %K, and %D. These values are plotted on a scale of 0 to 100. When the raw value and the %K are plotted on the same chart, the result is "fast stochastic." The fast stochastic shows you many up and down swings in a very short time period. When the %K and %D are plotted together you have a "slow stochastic" that smooths out the data. I'm not going to take the time to describe the formula for the SSTO because it is available on most technical charting software. Even though you do not have to calculate the formula, you will have to decide the number of time periods to use. The lower the number of periods used, the more swings in the SSTO. Therefore, more signals. A higher number of time periods will smooth the indicator and generate fewer signals. The default setting on most technical charting software is at 14 days as its parameter. I prefer 20 days because I believe it generates better trading signals for the longer-term trend changes. As everybody has his or her own preferences, you should test different time periods to see which one matches your trading style.

Chapter 8 – Bullish and Bearish Divergence

This means, in an upward trending market, the closing price should be near the highs, and during a downward trending market the closing price should be near the lows. If the closes are near the highs the trend remains strong; therefore, as the market peaks the indicator should be at its highest level. As long at the market is making higher highs the SSTO should also make a higher high.

Although the stochastic indicator can be used in different ways, many novice traders have only a limited understanding of how to use them. The most common use is to sell when the indicator reaches overbought – above 75 – or buy when the indicator reaches oversold – below 25. This method may be the most common usage, but I found out very quickly that it is not the most effective use because it can give many false signals. Strong trending markets can stay above 75 for long periods of time and even fluctuate below 75 and then turn higher. There are even trading systems designed around the tendency of the SSTO to dip below 75 and turn higher. This is typically a sign of strength in the market and can be followed by a price surge to new highs.

Using the SSTO as a Timing Indicator.

Divergences in momentum indicators is a gauge that has been around for quite some time and is used on a wide variety of indicators, such as the RSI and MACD, as well as the Slow Stochastic. Although using divergence as a timing tool can be useful, it is not the Holy Grail. Just like all other technical indicators, I feel it works best when used in conjunction with charting patterns. Even though there are many different ways to trade using the SSTO, there is only one way I like to use it, and that is when the market is showing either a bullish or bearish divergence in conjunction with a pattern sequence that typically leads into a TR pattern.

The Three Drives to a High or Low.

In the book "Street Smarts" by Linda Radske and Larry Connors, Linda described a chart pattern consisting of three consecutive pivot highs each pushing higher than the previous pivot point. She described how the pattern has a tendency to appear near the climax of the trend. Of course, three lower lows would also appear at the end of a downward trend.

The three successive higher pivot highs or three successive pivots lows will usually occur in a relatively short time period. Knowledge of this pattern can give you a warning before the pinnacle is reached. Linda nicknamed this pattern "Three Little Indians."

I like to keep a close eye on the last two thrusts or pivots because they will typically form the (A) and (B) pivot points of a TR pattern. The added appearance of bullish or bearish divergence increases the probability of the pattern confirming a major reversal. It is just another tool to help confirm the reversal.

The rules to identify bearish divergence are very simple. If the market is making a series of lower lows the SSTO should also be making corresponding lower lows. If instead, the second or third low in sequence does not correspond with a new low on the price chart, it suggests the market is beginning to gather underlying strength that is not yet reflected in the price and a major low could occur soon.

Let's look at a few examples of bullish and bearish divergence using the Slow Stochastic in conjunction with the TR pattern.

December 2004 Coffee

Figure # 8.1 - The December Coffee chart provides two good examples of bullish divergence in conjunction with three lower lows. The first divergence occurred between April 13 and April 30. The Coffee made a pivot low at 76.10 on April 13, marked as (1), followed by another dip to 74.30 on April 22, marked as (2). Six

Chapter 8 – Bullish and Bearish Divergence

days later, on April 30, the market dropped to 74.00, marked as (3) on the chart. The Coffee had posted three consecutive lower lows, but the same lower lows were not reflected in the SSTO. The April 22 pivot low was followed by another lower low on April 30, but the new low on April 30 was countered by a higher low on the SSTO, therefore revealing bullish divergence. The April 30th low held and acted as a springboard to the 1,000-point rally that followed.

The second appearance of divergence occurred in early August. The December Coffee had traded to a low of 69.60 on the July 30th Reversal date (4), but the market wasn't ready to bottom yet. Coffee went on to make another new pivot low on August 5 (5), followed by the third new pivot low on August 16 (6). Meanwhile, the SSTO bottomed on August 2 and followed with two higher lows on August 5 and August 13. While the market was making new lows on the price chart, the momentum was beginning to build in front of a market reversal. The TR pattern was confirmed after the August 19 pivot low and Coffee shifted from a downward trending market to an upward trending market. Notice how the SSTO dipped between August 17 and August 19, while the bullish Reaction swing was formed.

August 2005 Gold

Figure - # 8.2 - The pivot low on May 16 - marked as (1) - was followed by another lower pivot five days later on May 23, marked as (2) on *Figure # 8.2*. The two new lows corresponded with two lower lows on the SSTO. But the market sentiment was about to change when the Gold gapped to a new contract low of $415.80 on May 31 (3). While the price chart reflected a new low the SSTO was moving higher. The SSTO did turn lower to mirror the new contract low, but its low was higher than the previous two. The new low at (3) was followed by a sharp rally into June 6, which was the beginning of a bullish Reaction swing and that confirmed the bullish TR pattern.

242 *Chapter 8 – Bullish and Bearish Divergence*

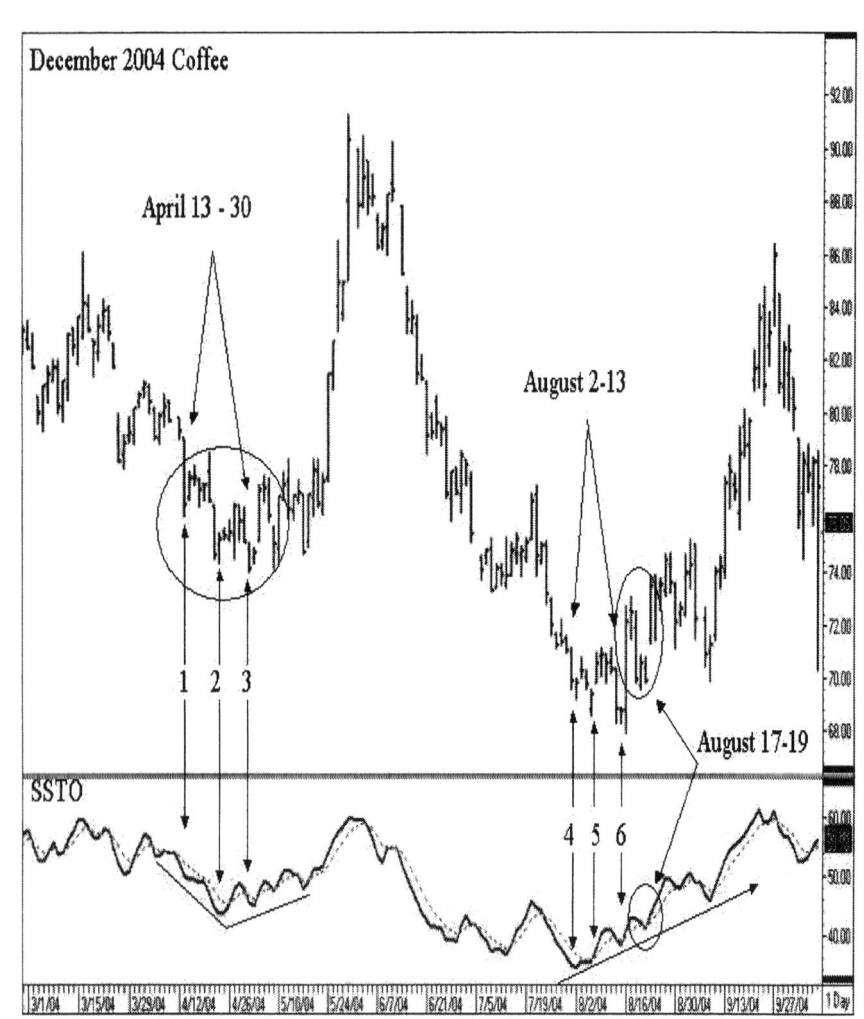

Figure # 8.1 – December 2004 Coffee

The bottom in August Gold was preceded by three successive lower lows on the price charts and the ensuing bullish divergence in the SSTO. The Gold moved off the bottom and proceeded to form a bullish Reaction swing between June 6 and June 9, which was reflected in the SSTO as a short-term dip before turning higher.

If you look to the far right of the chart you see another bearish divergence pattern begin to develop.

Chapter 8 – Bullish and Bearish Divergence

Figure # 8.2 – August 2005 Gold

Las Vegas Sands Corporation (LVS)

Figure # 8.3 - The chart of LVS presents a classic example of the three drives to a high collaborated by bearish divergence. During the two-week period between February 17 and March 6, LVS made three successive higher highs while the corresponding SSTO peaked at the second high and failed at the third high. The third high, in the SSTO, was considerably lower than the previous high and the divergence made a clear statement that the momentum had shifted from bullish to bearish and the market responded by trading lower.

244　*Chapter 8 – Bullish and Bearish Divergence*

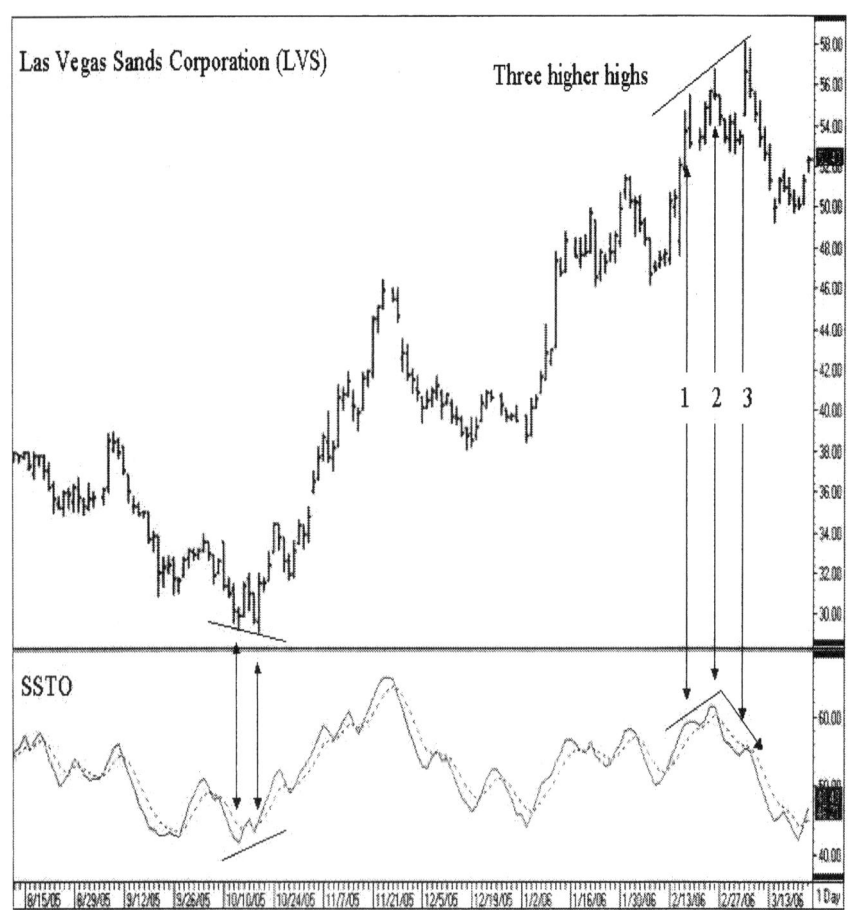

Figure # 8.3 – Las Vegas Sands Corporation (LVS)

Dell Inc. (DELL)

Figure # 8.4 - The bullish Reaction swing did not appear until May 6 and May 10, but the SSTO foretold of a pending trend change a week earlier. Although the market did not make the ideal three successive lower lows on the price chart, it did have two lower pivot lows on April 18 and April 29 – marked as (A) and (B) on the chart – before turning higher. However, if you look down to the SSTO it is very clear that the April 29 low was higher than the April 18 low, suggesting bullish momentum had entered the

Chapter 8 – Bullish and Bearish Divergence 245

market. This pattern forewarned of a pending climax of the downward trend and set the stage for a rally into May 6 (C). Note: Notice how the %K line dipped towards the %D line and then turned higher when the Reaction swing between (C) and (D) was confirmed.

Two days before the May 30th Reversal date (E), DELL reached the first of three successive higher highs marked as (1)-(2)-(3) on the chart. The corresponding SSTO indicator showed three lower highs occurring at the same time. The rally ended and DELL moved into a choppy sideways trend for the next several weeks.

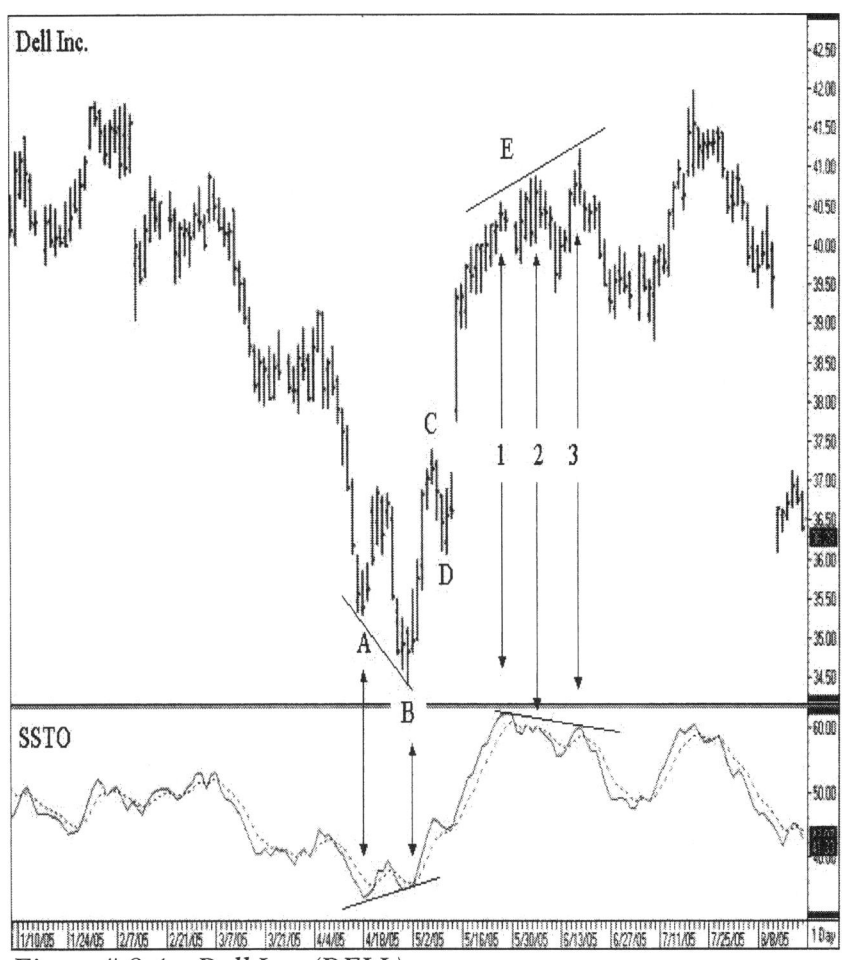

Figure # 8.4 – Dell Inc. (DELL)

March 2006 Wheat

March Wheat posted a pivot low on November 7, 2005 – marked as (1) on *Figure # 8.5*. This low was the beginning of a Reaction swing that projected a future Reversal date for December 9 at (3). March Wheat went on to make two more lower lows – marked as (2) as (3), with the last low occurring on December 9. Meanwhile, the December 9 low (3) in the SSTO was higher than the previous low (2) that occurred on November 11. March Wheat went on to rally over 40-cents in the next three weeks.

Figure # 8.5 – March 2006 Wheat

June 2005 Crude oil

Figure # 8.6 - June Crude oil made a major trend change during late March and early April 2005. The market made three consecutive higher highs leading into the peak. I have marked the last two consecutive highs as (A) and (B) because they represent the beginning of a TR pattern. The corresponding SSTO indicator peaked when the Crude oil reached a high of 58.60 on March 17 (A). From this high, the market pulled back over the next week, before it pushed to a new high of 59.32 on April 4 (B). However, the related high in the SSTO (B) was considerably lower than the previous high (A). The bearish divergence, in conjunction with the TR pattern, forewarned of the pending trend change.

Figure # 8.6 – June 2005 Crude oil

December 2006 Dow Jones - (30-minute chart)

Figure # 8.7 - The December Dow Jones 30-minute chart posted three successive higher highs between September 20 and September 21 with the final peak reaching 11,720. During the same time period the SSTO indicator made three lower highs, suggesting an imminent climax to the current upswing and set up a potential TR pattern - marked as (A) and (B). On September 21, the Dow Jones turned lower and formed a new Reaction swing between 8:50 a.m. CST (C) and 9:50 a.m. (D). The TR pattern was confirmed and projected a drop into 2:20 p.m. the same day (E).

Figure # 8.7 – December Dow Jones – 30-minute chart

Chapter 8 – Bullish and Bearish Divergence

The Dow Jones hit a low of 11,583 between 2:20 p.m. and 2:50 p.m. and formed a TC pattern. Once again, the bullish divergence, in combination with the three drives to the high, foretold of a pending change in momentum before the TR pattern began to form. Note: If you look to the far right of the chart you will see another divergence pattern beginning to form.

March 2006 Coffee

In Figure #8.8, March Coffee offered two good examples of divergence appearing before a significant trend change. The first example appeared between October 20 and November 9. The Coffee had made two successive higher highs, followed by a sharp price drop. During the same time period the SSTO posted consecutive lower highs in front of sell-off.

Although the earlier divergence was a good forerunner to the early November reversal, Coffee offered a classic three thrusts to a trend climax between January 9 and January 30. As the market pushed higher and higher - with the final high occurring on the January 30 Reversal date - the SSTO indicator failed to correspond and posted three successive lower highs at the same time. The bearish divergence worked as a perfect precursor to the TR pattern and the major reversal.

December British Pound (60-minute chart)

Figure # 8.9 - The 60-minute chart in the December British pound offers an example of bearish divergence at the beginning of a downward trend followed by bullish divergence at bottom of the trend. The first example occurred between September 21 and September 22, with the third price peak reaching 1.9081 at 2:00 p.m. CST on September 22. The corresponding high (3) in the SSTO indicator was considerably lower than the second peak on September 21 (2). The market had reached a new high, but the SSTO was already trending lower and suggested the British pound

250   Chapter 8 – Bullish and Bearish Divergence

had reached a critical price juncture and would soon follow the SSTO on its downward path.

Figure # 8.8 – March 2006 Coffee

The British pound continued to trade lower, but between September 28 and September 29, the market posted three successive lower pivot lows. Each time the price chart dropped to a new low, the corresponding SSTO indicator made a higher low. After the British pound posted its third consecutive new low the market reversed and formed a bullish Reaction swing. The number (2) and (3) low were also the beginning pivots of a bullish TR pattern that later confirmed the bottom and triggered a strong rally.

Chapter 8 – Bullish and Bearish Divergence   251

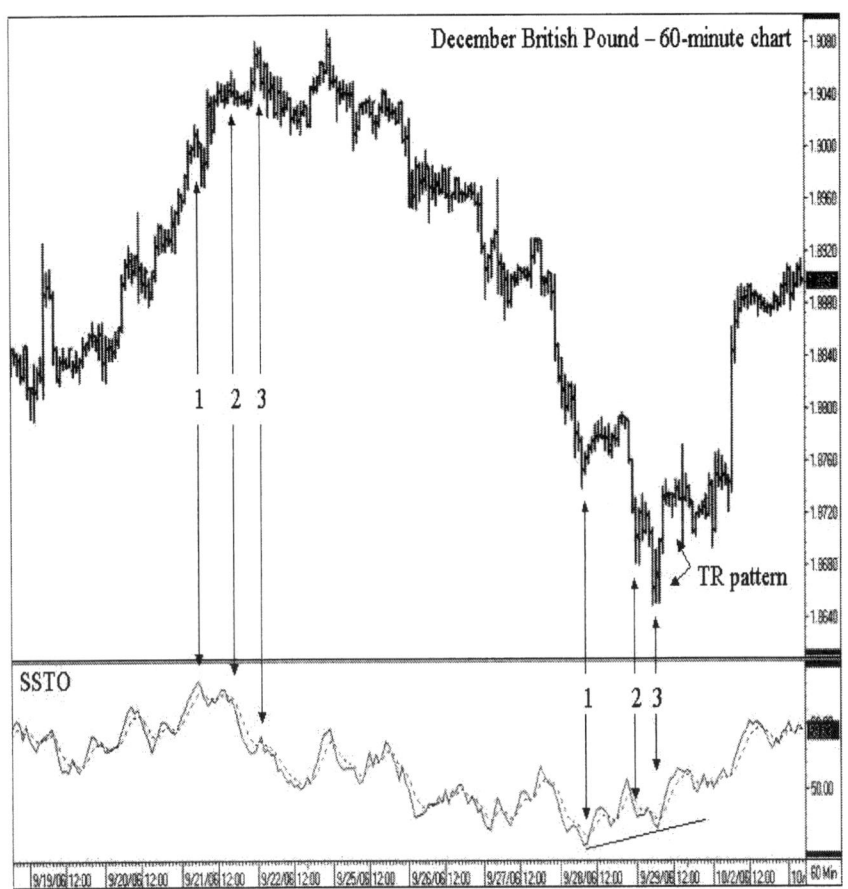

Figure # 8.9 – December British Pound – 60-minute chart

Combining Chart Patterns with Technical Indicators.

Although this pattern does not appear frequently, it is worth learning and adding to your pattern toolbox. As I have illustrated throughout this book, I typically do not use a lot of technical indications because of their lagging nature. Since momentum indicators are based off price only and calculated from past price action, the market change is usually already in progress when the confirming signal is triggered by the indicator. I believe incorporating the price in the momentum indicator, with price patterns, will add the necessary ingredient to catch reversal earlier.

This also removes the need for subjective interpretations of the indicator to determine an entry or exit.

You may read in other books about technical analysis, that the standard way to use the SSTO indicator is to sell when the indicator moves above 75 and turns lower or buy when the indicator moves below 25 and turns higher. I have learned the hard way this can be a costly way to use the SSTO because of its tendency to generate false signals when used on a stand-alone basis. In my years of experience, I have found bullish or bearish divergence in the SSTO can portend significant trend reversals when used in conjunction with the TR patterns.

Although I used the SSTO indicator in all the examples, most momentum indicators such as the RSI, CCI or MACD will offer the same divergence patterns. I simply use the SSTO because it was my first introduction to technical indicators and I am most familiar with its characteristics. I have worked with many traders throughout the years that prefer other indicators and use them in the same manner. Once again it comes down to individual preference.

Chapter 9

"Time is nature's way of keeping everything from happening at once." - Woody Allen

Trading With Different Time Frames

There are count-less different technical indicators used by traders in an attempt to predict future price movements, and since every person has a different trading style the same indicator can be used in different ways or different time frames, depending on their particular view of the market. For example, a long-term trend trader may prefer a weekly chart while the swing trader may feel more comfortable with a daily chart. Both traders may use the same technical indicator, but in different time frames. The patterns and confirming signals may be the same, but the results can differ depending on the time frame from which you view the chart.

Traders may benefit from widening their point-of-view by using more than one time frame. Each time frame can offer a different perspective and reveal a pattern or signal not seen on the other time frame.

I am sure you have all see a movie or read a story about someone finding a treasure map or a mysterious code that reveals very little at first glance, but once the different levels are peeled away and examined closer, more clues begin to appear. Price charts can work in the same way. For example, as a swing trader you may not see a buy/sell pattern on a daily chart, but once you drop down to a 60-minute or 30-minute chart, a pattern may appear that was hidden in the longer-term view. Had you stuck to only one time frame, you would have missed the pattern entirely.

The hidden Reaction swing offers early entry

If you know what to look for and where to look, a hidden Reaction swing can offer an early entry signal after a major turning point and before the regular Reaction swing even begins to form. This is an opportunity to enter the market after a major high or low reversal – usually marked as (B) in the TR pattern - and before the beginning of the first Reaction swing – marked as (C). The only way to find the hidden Reaction swing is to drop down to the lower time frame once the correct "Market Tell" is seen on the daily chart.

The Counter-Close

The "Tell" I am referring to is called the "counter-close". The counter-close is a price bar where the closing price is in the opposite direction of the previous close. In other words, if the market were trending higher, a counter-close would close lower than the opening price. If the market were trending lower, the closing price would be higher than the opening price.

On the daily chart, a one-day counter close is not enough to confirm a Reaction swing and set up an entry signal, but a 60-minute chart may reveal a nicely formed Reaction swing and offer a potential signal that is hidden from view on the daily price chart.

A counter-close can appear anywhere in a trend, but there are only two places I look for the "Tell" and that is after a major high or low reversal and near the 20-day SMA after a TR pattern or TC pattern. In *Figure # 9.1* I have you can see what a counter-close looks like in a downward trending market and an upward trending market. The following chart examples will better illustrate how to find the counter-close and the hidden Reaction swing and how it can be incorporated into your trading strategy.

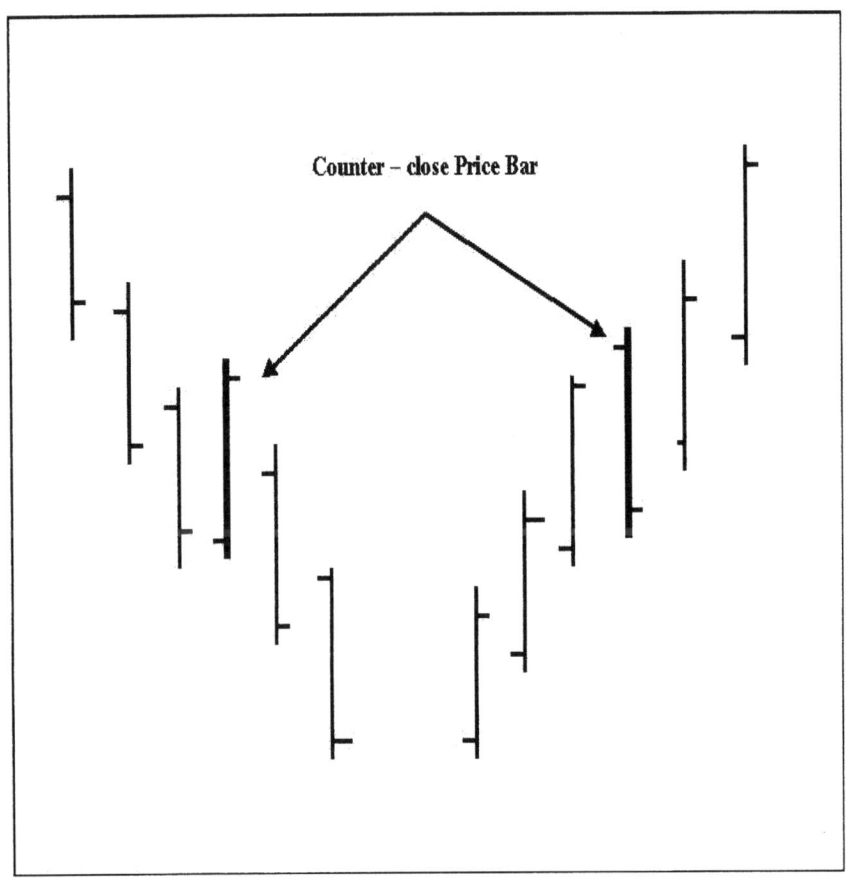

Chapter 9 – Trading With Different Time Frames 255

Figure # 9.1 – One-day Counter-Close

December 2006 Hogs

Figure # 9.2 - During the last two weeks of October, the December Hogs completed a pattern of three successive lower lows. After the third low, Hogs closed higher for two consecutive days and ended on the 20-day SMA. The following day—October 24—opened steady and closed lower than the opening price. The opening price was 60.10 and the closing price was 59.85. The lower close was counter to the previous two price bars and the daily price range straddled the 20-day SMA.

On the daily chart a one-day pullback is not enough to form a Reaction swing, but the 60-minute chart told a different story. As the October 24th daily price bar was trading against the previous two-day trend, a bullish Reaction swing had formed above the 20-bar SMA on the 60-minute chart. Based on this pattern, a buy stop could be placed at 60.40, just above the pivot high of the Reaction swing – this would also be above the high of the one-day counter-close on the daily chart.

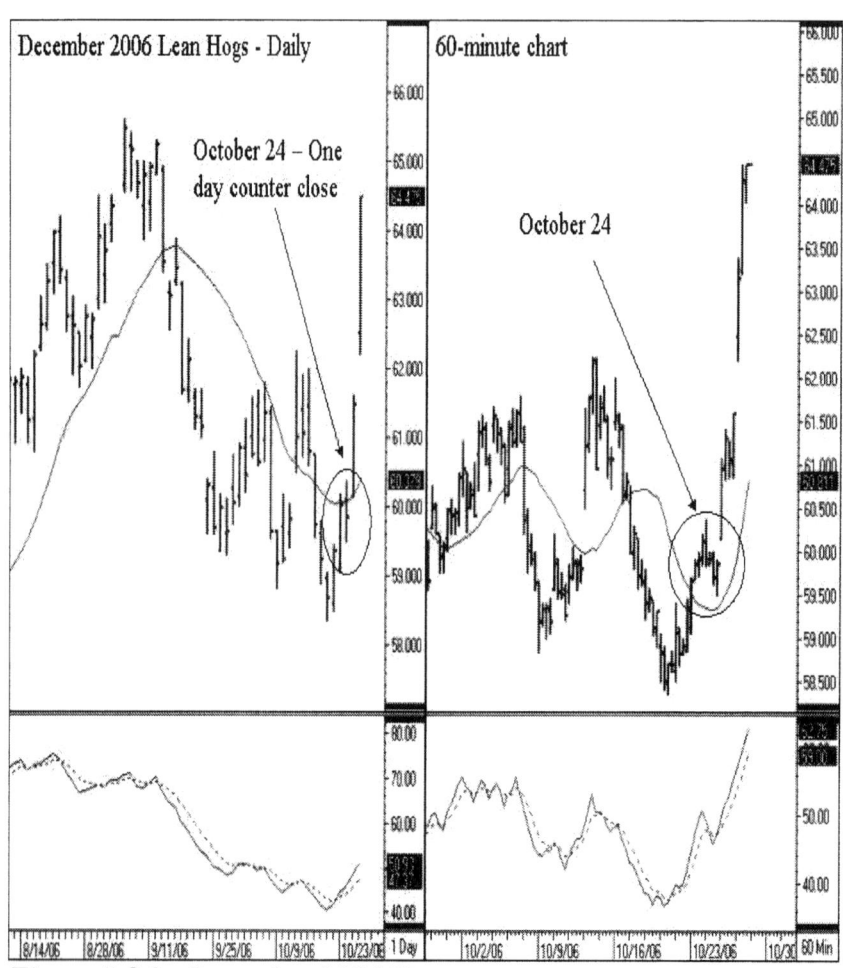

Figure # 9.2 –December 2006 Hogs

October 25 opened slightly higher and traded above the 60.40 trigger price within the first hour of trading. The upward price surge continued throughout the next day as the Hogs reached 64.47. The hidden Reaction swing signal offered a potential gain of 440-points in two days! A reaction never appeared on the daily chart and the buy signal would have been missed entirely if by not looking at the 60-minute chart.

December 2006 Cotton

Figure # 9.3 - Cotton began to form a possible TR pattern with the (A) pivot low on October 11 and another low pivot low of October 18 (B). After posting a low on October 18, Cotton reversed and closed higher for three consecutive days and finished above the 20-day SMA.

The October 24 trading session opened at 49.90 and closed at 49.57 on the 20-day SMA. The close was below the open and against the newly established trend. The market needed another lower close, in order to form a Reaction swing, but that wouldn't happen.

The SSTO indicator was showing slight evidence of bullish divergence, but it was not enough to suggest the market was gaining bullish momentum. Since the one-day counter close was not a bullish Reaction swing, the daily chart didn't identify a trigger price for a buy signal, therefore it was time to look at the counter-close price bar in a shorter-time frame.

The 60-minute chart revealed stronger divergence in the SSTO and a bullish Reaction swing had formed just above the 20-bar SMA. The TR pattern was ready and the trigger price was above the pivot high of 50.41. October 25 opened steady, but wasted little time before climbing higher and traded through the trigger price. The daily chart had only a one-day pullback and never formed a Reaction swing pattern; it was hidden in the lower time frame.

258 Chapter 9 – Trading With Different Time Frames

Figure # 9.3 – December 2006 Cotton

December 2006 Cattle

Figure # 9.4 - A bullish TR pattern confirmed a bottom and a Reaction swing had formed between October 13 and October 20, marked as (C) and (D) on *Figure # 9.4*. The October 23 breakout bar triggered the buy signal at 88.50 and closed above the 20-day SMA. October 24 opened at 88.60, slightly lower than the previous days close, and ended the day at 88.35. The day ended as an inside day with the close below the 20-day SMA. The closing price was lower than the opening price and also counter to prevailing trend.

Chapter 9 – Trading With Different Time Frames

In this example the TR pattern had already triggered a buy signal, but the market had not carried through on the following day. This could mean the signal is doomed to fail and turn lower. However, the price pattern on the 60-minute chart was much more encouraging. The first thing to stand out was the bullish divergence revealed in the 60-minute SSTO that did not show up in the daily SSTO. The 60-minute chart also revealed a bullish Reaction swing above the 20-bar SMA.

The following day - October 25 - opened steady, then traded lower until it found support at the 20-bar SMA. The support held and the market began to climb into the close. However, it was the higher opening on October 26 that caused the market to accelerate. October 26 closed at 90.70 considerably higher than the 88.95 trigger price.

Figure # 9.4 – December 2006 Cattle

November 2006 Natural Gas

Figure # 9.5 offers a good example of a counter-close after a major low. Following a persistent downward spiral November Natural gas posted a new contract low on September 28 with a slight hint of bullish divergence on the SSTO. The following day closed higher than the opening price and against the downward trend. At first glance this could be considered a counter-close signal bar. However, it does not meet the criteria of being at the 20-day SMA and it never triggered a sell signal because the market never traded below its daily low.

However, the next day—October 2—was a different story. The market opened higher and closed lower. This was the opposite – counter – to the previous day so it can be considered a counter-close day. At the same time the SSTO showed bullish divergence, but the chart pattern wasn't suggesting much more...until you look at the lower time frame.

The 60-minute chart looked a lot different. The first thing that jumped out was the three lower lows in conjunction with strong bullish divergence in the SSTO. Secondly, October 2 had formed a bullish Reaction swing straddling the 20-bar SMA. The Reaction swing was formed on the 60-minute chart, but it is still treated the same as a Reaction swing on the daily chart. In other words, the market had retraced more than 60% from the previous price swing high; therefore it was considered to be inside the buy window. The buy window was breeched on October 3 when the market traded to a low of 5.460. Since the 60% rule was in effect, the trigger price was above the high of the price bar that entered the buy window; therefore the trigger price was 5.605. Three hours into the October 3 trading session, Natural gas surged higher and triggered the buy signal at 5.605 and continued higher until it peaked at 6.800 on October 9. The signal offered a potential gain of over $10,000 in only 20 hours of trading.

Chapter 9 – Trading With Different Time Frames   261

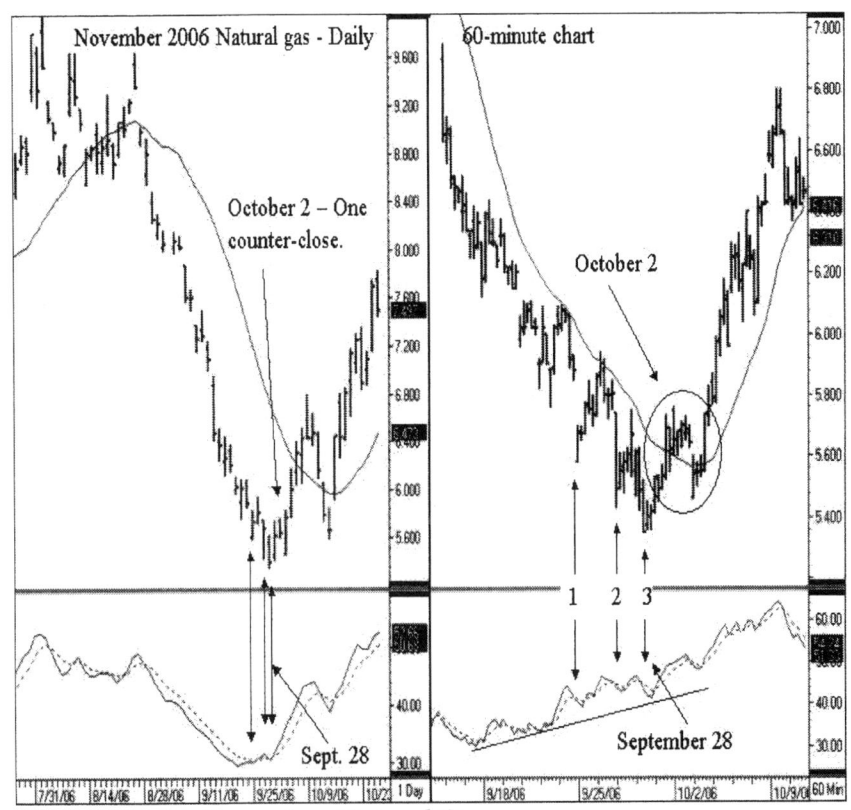

Figure # 9.5 – November Natural Gas

The pivot high on October 9 was the beginning of a Reaction swing that later triggered another buy signal with substantial profit potential. But, if it had not been for the "Market Tell" provide by the counter-close pattern, the early entry buy signal, at the very beginning of the bullish trend, would have been missed. That's the real advantage of the using counter-close pattern in conjunction with different time frames to identify market signals. Unless you look at all the available information you may see the whole picture.

December 2006 British Pound

Figure # 9.6 - The December British pound posted a low close of 1.8645 on October 11. This was the third lower close of a series that had unfolded over the past several days. The next day, after opening higher, the market began a six-day climb that ended with two consecutive closes above the 20-day SMA. The following trading session – October 23 – traded lower and closed below the 20-day SMA. This was counter to the previous trading sessions, but was not enough to form a bullish Reaction swing.

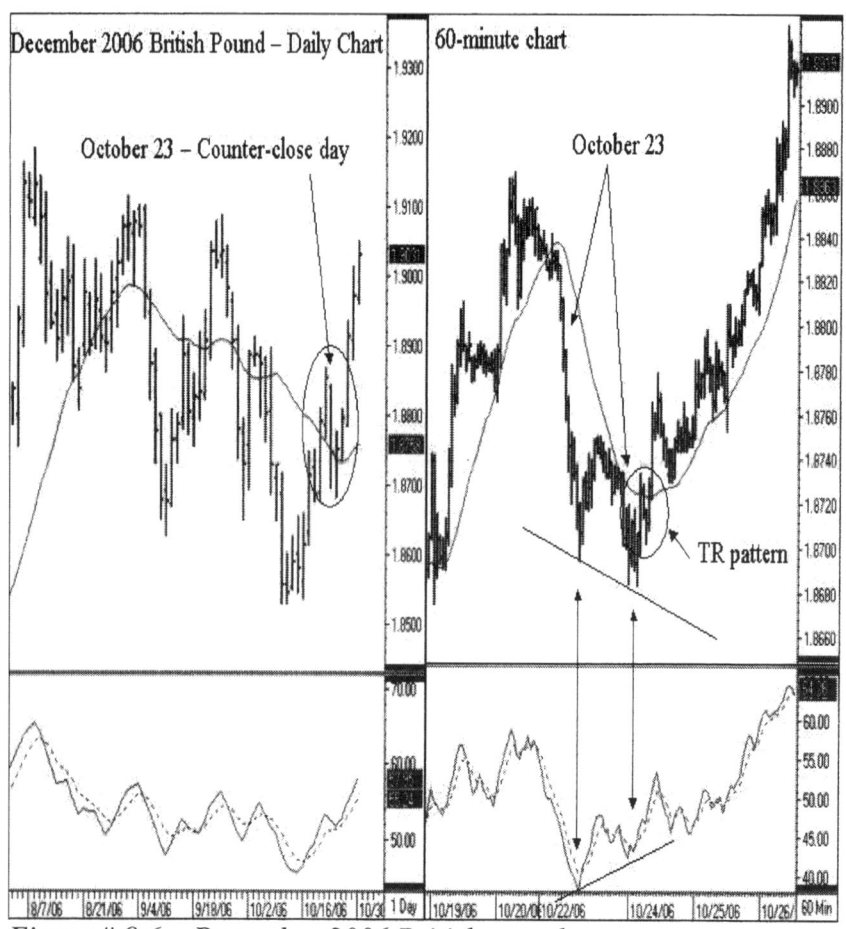

Figure # 9.6 – December 2006 British pound

The 60-minute chart offered a lot more information. The SSTO showed bullish divergence, but the retracement was not complete. The British pound continued slightly lower into October 24, but bottomed early in the session, where it formed a bullish Reaction swing underneath the 20-bar SMA. *(Note: The low was posted just two hours after the reversal bar projected from the TR pattern that formed between 9:00 a.m. and 1:00 p.m. CST on October 20.)* Between 9:00 a.m. and 10:00 a.m. the market traded through the 1.8740 trigger price and confirmed the buy signal. The British pound continued higher over the next several days and reached 1.9108 on October 31. This Reaction swing was hidden in the 60-minute chart and would not have been found if you were only looking at the daily chart.

Las Vegas Sands Corporation (LVS)

Figure # 9.7 - LVS provided two excellent hidden Reaction swing signals. The first example occurred after a sharp three-day rally that pushed the market to a new high on of 78.90 on June 30. The market paused on Monday, July 2 and closed slightly lower after trading in a very narrow price range. The market was closed on July 4, but LVS traded lower again on July 5th. The market attempted to rally on the next day, July 6th and reached as high as 77.00 before stalling. However, the market did end as a counter-close because the closing price was higher than the opening price. In this case, the market was closed on July 4 and left a gap on the chart, which could be considered as day one, of a three-day Reaction swing. However, just to be sure I took a look at the 60-minute chart and sure enough, there is a hidden Reaction swing forming on the 20-bar SMA. I marked the Reaction swing as (C) and (D) on the 60-minute chart.

LVS opened at 77.23 on July 7. The higher opening was above the 60% retracement level and inside the sell window, so the trigger price was below the low of the Signal bar. That put the trigger price at 75.70. On July 7, between 10:30 a.m. and 11:30 a.m. CST, the price dropped through the trigger price to confirm the early sell signal and close at 73.08.

This is where it gets interesting. The hidden Reaction swing triggered the early sell signal at 75.70 on July 7 and the market closed at 73.08. The following two trading sessions both closed higher than the previous trading session and formed a bearish Reaction swing on the daily chart.

The Reaction swing reached as high as 74.92 before it peaked and turned lower, but the trigger price was 71.30, underneath the pivot low at (C). This was still a very good trade signal because the market continued lower after the sell was triggered and reached a low of 59.39 on the Reversal date projected from the daily TR pattern.

However, the hidden Reaction swing from the 60-minute chart offered an early entry considerably higher that the entry provided by the daily Reaction swing signal.

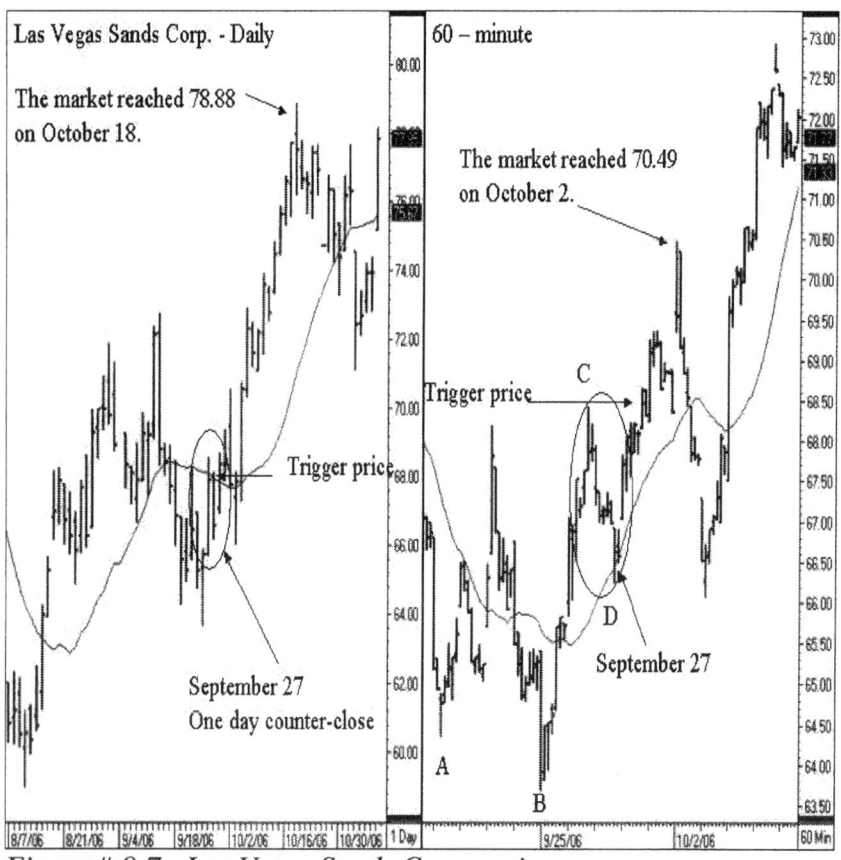

Figure # 9.7 - Las Vegas Sands Corporation

Chapter 9 – Trading With Different Time Frames 265

Las Vegas Sands Corporation (LVS)

Figure # 9.8 - The second example occurred in late September. LVS had just completed and eleven day correction and turned higher after a failed swing pattern on September 25. The following day shot higher but hit resistance after it breeched the 20-day SMA. The next day ended as an inside day with the closing price lower than the opening price ... a one-day counter-close. The one-day pullback was not enough to form a Reaction swing on the daily chart, but the 60-minute chart revealed a hidden Reaction swing.

The 60-minute chart is much more illuminating as it displayed a potential TR pattern forming above the 20-bar SMA. The market had made a high pivot at 68.42 on September 26 and pulled back to the 20-bar SMA, where it posted a low pivot at 1:30 p.m. CST on September 27. The pattern was confirmed the following day when LVS traded above 68.42. However, the market paused as the daily chart tried to form a Reaction swing but never met the criteria before it pushed to new highs. The market peaked at 78.88 on October 18 and began to form a new Reaction swing. The TR pattern was hidden inside the daily chart but could not be seen unless you dropped to the lower time frame of the 60-minute chart.

The daily chart did not confirm a Reaction swing until five days later when the market was already trading above 71.00 ... 250 points higher than the trigger price provided by the hidden Reaction swing.

December 2006 Crude oil

Figure # 9.9 - The December Crude oil had been in an unrelenting downward trend for almost four months, but began to show signs of losing momentum. After posting the fourth consecutive new low on October 31, Crude turned and traded higher during the next four days. On November 6, the market peaked at 60.55, just above the 20-day SMA and followed with a counter-close day on November 7. The market was set up for a possible TR pattern buy signal, but

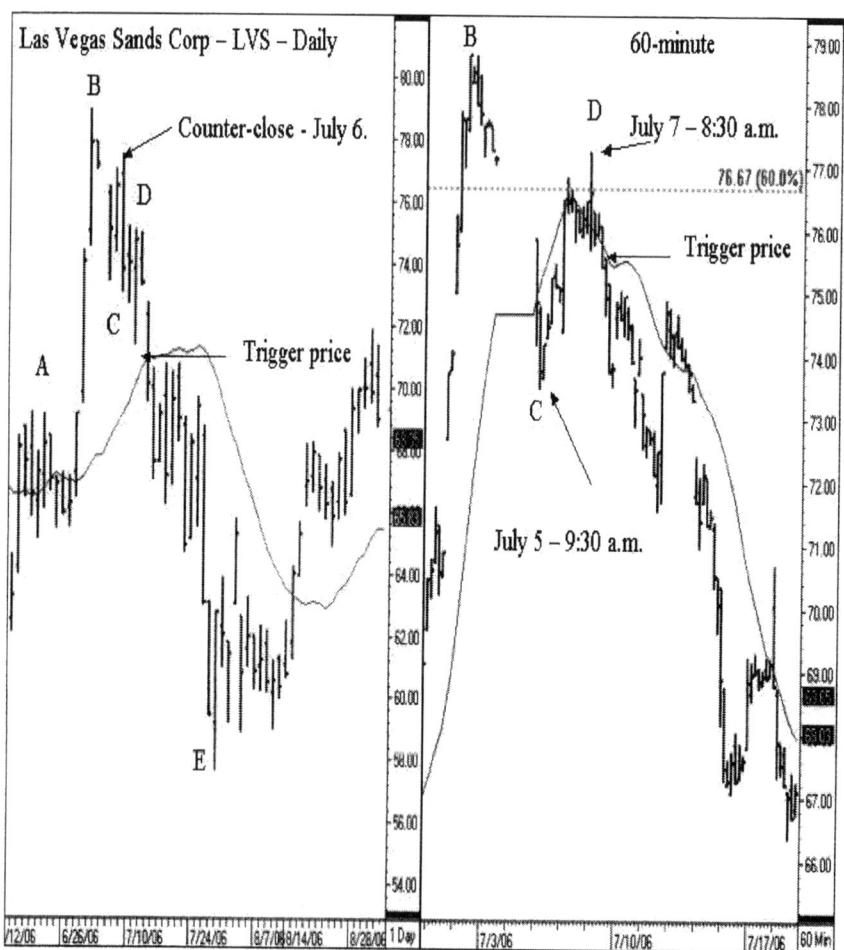

266   Chapter 9 – Trading With Different Time Frames

Figure # 9.8 – Las Vegas Sands Corporation (LVS)

the market needed another lower close to set up the Reaction swing. However, the following day opened slightly higher and closed above the open. This meant the I would have to wait another day for a Reaction swing to form in order to give me the buy signal I needed to enter a long position. Or does it?

The 60-minute chart revealed a bullish Reaction swing pattern had begun above with a pivot high at 60.55 on November 6 and ended with a low pivot at 1:00 p.m. CST on November 7. The market moved off the pivot low and traded toward the trigger price of 60.60, but didn't reach it on November 8. The signal was

Chapter 9 – Trading With Different Time Frames   267

triggered at 60.90 when the Crude opened sharply higher on November 9.

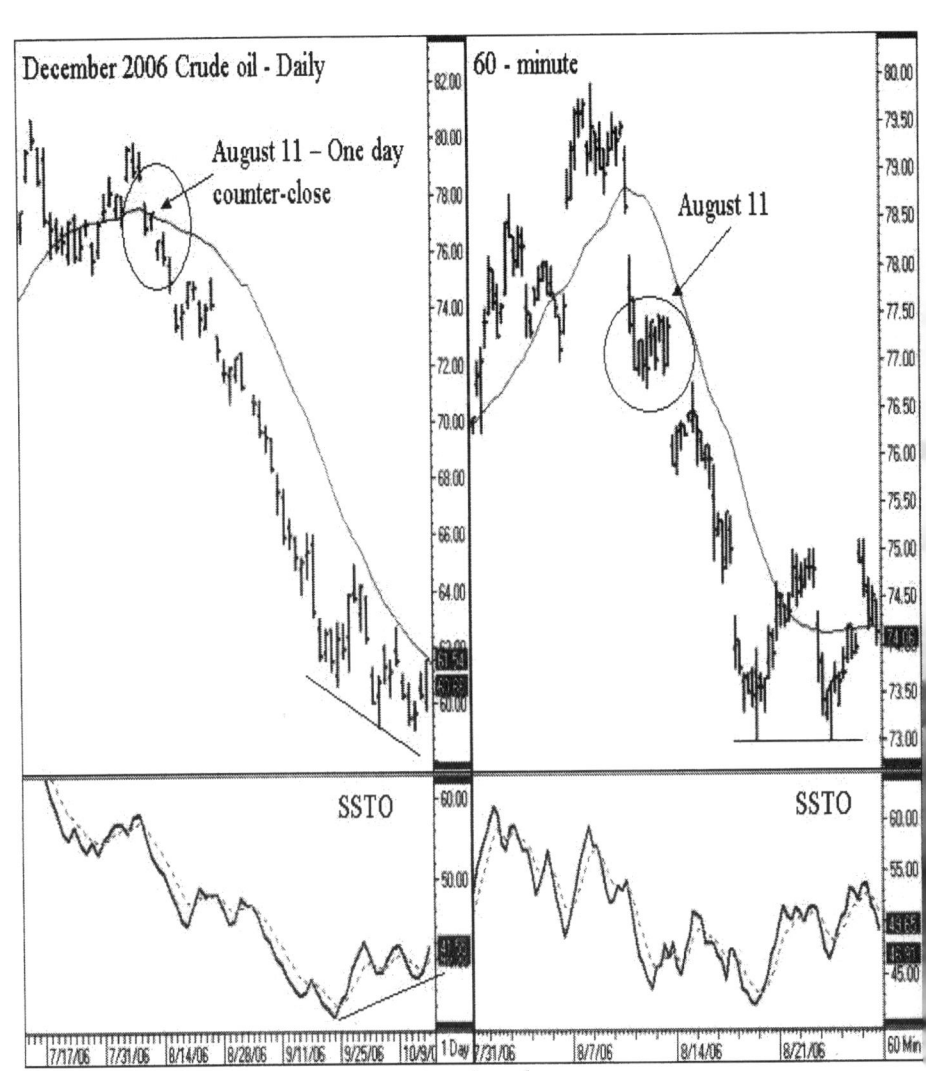

Figure # 9.9 – December 2006 Crude oil

Benefits of the Counter-Close

The counter-close pattern can be a very beneficial pattern to add to your trading playbook. Some traders use it exclusively because it appears often, as illustrated by the fact that three of the examples illustrated occurred on the same day, October 24. Another benefit is the tendency for a quick price surge right after the signal is confirmed. However, like other pattern set ups you must learn the criteria and make sure the set up is correct and always manage the risk. One mismanaged trade can eliminate a lot of good trades.

Chapter 10

"A year from now you may wish you had started today"
Karen Lamb, author

Some Final Words

After you have read this material and studied the charts, you may be filled with such enthusiasm that you feel you are ready to conquer the markets. However, before you set out to do just that, I want to share with you another important rule: *never force a chart pattern or signal*! Unfortunately, in our enthusiasm to be right, traders are sometimes tempted by irregular patterns and formations. Instead of waiting for the correct formation, they tend to force the trade from a pattern that slightly resembles a specific pattern. Since chart trading involves risk, even if you have a perfect pattern, using your creative imagination and wishful analysis can lead to unsatisfactory results. There are more than enough markets to trade that you will almost always find a market with an identifiable Reaction cycle about to begin or end. Remember, patience and research will be rewarded.

Always let the market tell you what it is going to do--let it do its own forecasting. If the market is not behaving as you think it should, get out and wait for the market to prove itself before re-entering the trade. Once you are out of the trade, you can re-evaluate the trade. It is easier to re-evaluate a trade from the sidelines than from a position with a large loss. If it is still a good trade, you can always re-enter. That extra commission spent is always cheaper than riding a bigger loss.

I suggest that you take the time to re-read and review this book from the beginning before attempting to apply the methodology. It is vital that you understand all the components of the Reaction swing and the concept of the reverse and forward count before you can move on to Action/Reaction lines and the projection of Price.

Take the time to understand and practice the concepts. You will be glad you did! When you fully grasp the concepts in this book, you will never look at the market the same. Imagine the confidence you will feel knowing how the market should react and unfold.

What I have written and illustrated in this book is the result of years of study, research and experience. In the many years that I have been involved in trading, I have found one thing to be true: every day is different, and any actions you take and decisions you make will depend upon the experience and knowledge you have acquired. This experience and knowledge will consciously or subconsciously affect every aspect of your trading.

A very wise trader once told me, *"amateurs look for perfection, and professionals look for performance!"* Remember, not every pattern or cycle will work or form perfectly – trading is not an exact science. Even with perfect setups there are going to be losing trades, but the concept is sound and over a period of trades your confidence will grow, and with that comes success.

If you have questions, there is help available.

You may have questions that the book just can't answer. This is okay... you can always pick up the phone and give me a call or you can send me an e-mail. Either myself, or one of my trained and licensed staff will be happy to answer your questions.

If you want more information you can call **Traders Network** at 1-800-831-7654 and I will have them send you a complete information kit. This kit contains everything you need to begin trading; this includes software for online trading, charts, quotes, news and account access. Traders Network even has a Tech help line!

You will need this!

Just for reading this book you will receive a two-month trial subscription to *The Traders Market Views (TMV,)* now in its 20-year of publication. This electronic publication is sent out every

Monday, Wednesday and Friday and is packed timely market insights and recommendations. This is my free gift for buying this book. *Don't pass up this offer!*

This will allow you to compare your projections with mine - what better way to test your knowledge! Remember, if there is a question, you know where to get the answer.

The *Traders Market Views* is yours *free* - but first you must call to sign up at
1-800-831-7654 or visit my website www.tradersnetwork.com

Advanced Swing Trading DVD and Online Seminar

In this 90-minute DVD John Crane clearly describes his original Action/Reaction trading method. With the help of numerous real-world examples, he delineates his system and shows how to consistently project tops and bottoms.

Evaluating Risk
Investors/traders should understand that there are risks associated with trading futures. The Commodity Futures Trading Commission (CFTC) requires that prospective customers be provided with risk disclosure statements. Historic performance results should be reviewed with the understanding that past performance is not an indicator of future results.

Resources for Traders & Recommended Reading

"Trading from the Inside" by Joseph Kellogg
You don't have to be a Wall Street Insider to trade like one! Trading from the Inside is a must read for every commodity trader. Mr. Kellogg packs all he has learned about trading into this book. He breaks down trading and clearly explains how to read charts, how to interpret technical indicators, and how to master trading psychology. The path to market freedom is knowledge. This book

is full of wit and war stories and should be a part of every trader's library.

"I found it direct, clear, and informative. You seldom see something so successfully straight forward."
-Stocks & Commodities Magazine
242 pages - $49.95 – ISBN 1-931611-00-9 - You can order online at www.tradersnetwork.com or by calling 1-800-521-0705 or 1-800-831-7654

"The Option Traders Playbook" by Joseph Kellogg
The Option Traders Playbook will answer your option questions and help you develop option strategies to meet your trading goals. This easy to understand guide is illustrated with graphs and charts that go beyond the mechanics and the basic trading strategies of the commodities market; this guide delves into the market pitfalls to avoid. The strategies taught inside this course will open up a whole new way of looking at the futures and options markets. After taking this course, your eyes will be open, and your trading will never be the same.
175 pages - $49.95 - You can order The Option Traders Playbook online at www.tradersnetwork.com or by calling 1-800-521-0705 or 1-800-831-7654

Trading Tools

Market Center Direct (MCD) Online Trading Software
Market Center Direct has revolutionized futures trading on the Internet. From the live quote page and real time data to the easy order placement and order log confirmation, click on Bonds and instantly send a Bond order; click on E-mini and you instantly get a chart; click on Corn and you instantly get the FWN Grain news. Other built-in features include: real-time equity statements, messaging with your broker, and tracking all your orders. Market Center Direct is the ultimate trading software for active and

beginning traders. With MCD, you have access to quotes from all the U.S. markets directly on your computer via the Internet.

Traders Market Center (TMC) Web Based Trading Software

Traders Market Center takes MCD to a new level. No longer will you have to install or configure your computer. You can gain access to TMC from any computer by logging into our customer website. You have MCD's functionality with even less fuss. You will get real-time quotes & charts, equity information, research, and order tracking all from our Traders Network website.

Trade Simulator

Trade Simulator is a powerful commodity trading software tool that is built to help teach both beginners and experienced traders how to trade commodities. You will learn how to properly trade and gain "real-market" experience without the risk! In just a few hours you will gain months of trading experience! *Trade Simulator's* database comes equipped with 17 years of real market history that covers 22 markets. Analyze daily, weekly, and monthly charts with 14 of the most popular technical indicators.

A *Futures Magazine* comparison of trading simulators gave *Trade Simulator* the edge saying, *"It offers more indicators, more control over parameters, and it's the easiest to use."*

"Overall, Trade Simulator is fun and instructive...(and) a good introduction to tracing's decision-making process...making Trade Simulator a real deal."
-Stocks & Commodities Magazine

The Trade Simulator can be ordered online at www.tradernetwork.com or by calling 1-800-521-0705 or 1-800-831-7654.

Reversal Tracker Trading Software

Many trading systems are ambiguous about when to buy -- and give no indication of when to sell. With Reversal Tracker, you get clear, precise, easy-to-read signals on every trade. Trade signal confirmations clearly define where to buy and where to sell with precise Time and Price projections.

Reversal Tracker will work with any freely traded market anywhere in the world. It is an easy way to make logical trading decisions, based on the purest market data known: price movement and market behavior.

The system's buy and sell signals are calculated by a proprietary, back-tested algorithm based solely on real-time or end-of-day price data - giving you timely, specific, and objective signals for every trade. Proprietary indicators set optimal stops for seeking maximum profits. Reversal Tracker shows traders the course a market will take in the future if the prediction is correct.

The two chart examples illustrate the type of signal and analysis provide by the Reversal Tracker software. For your trial offer call 1-800-521-0705 or visit www.tradersnetwork.com

Chapter 10 – Some Final Words

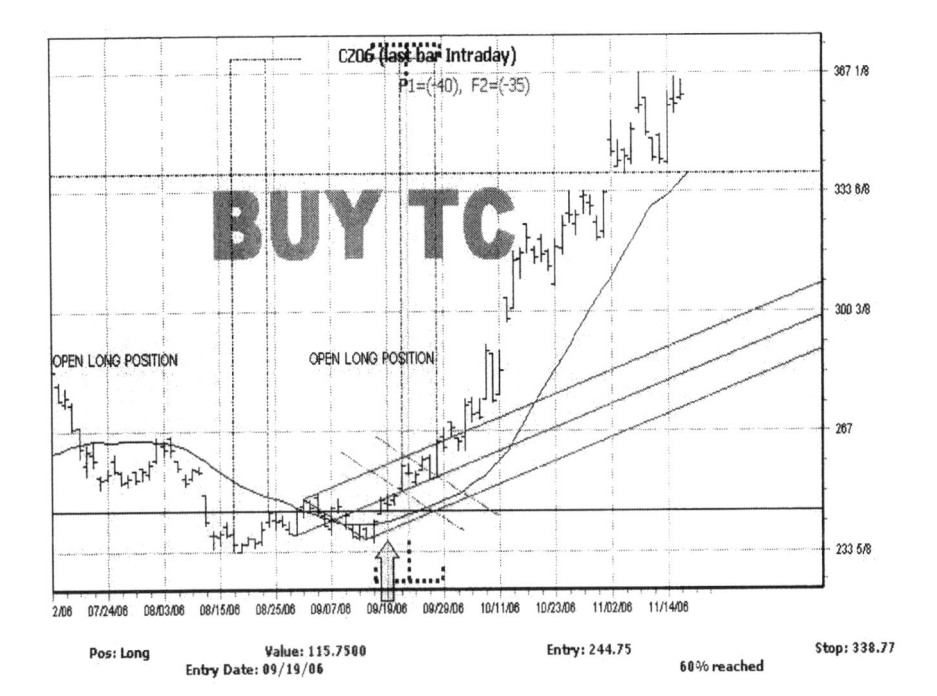

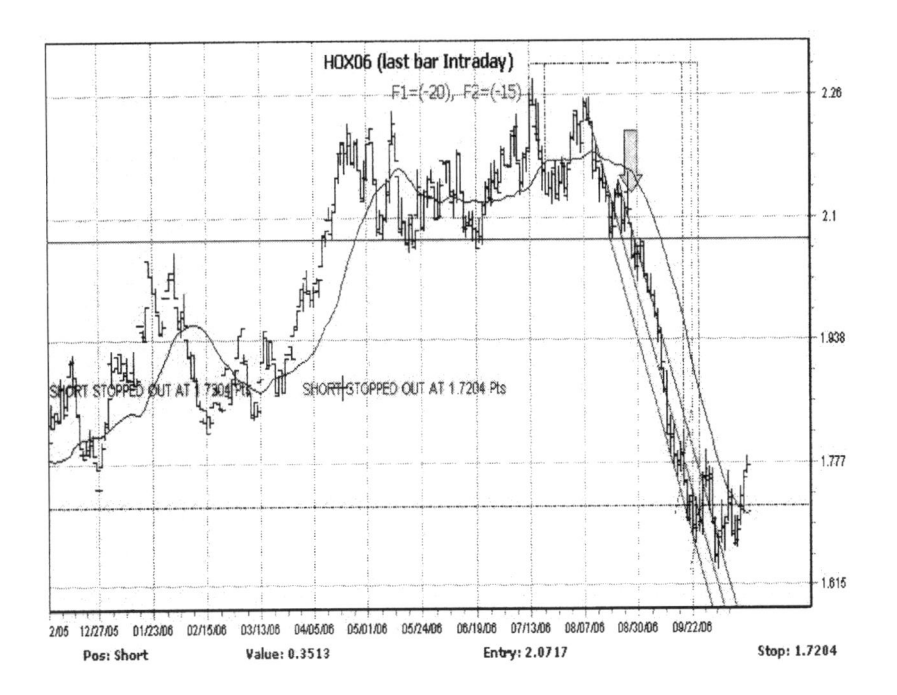

Pos: Long	Value: 115.7500	Entry: 244.75	Stop: 338.77
	Entry Date: 09/19/06	60% reached	

| Pos: Short | Value: 0.3513 | Entry: 2.0717 | Stop: 1.7204 |

Index

A-B-C correction - 62, 150, 158, 159
   Hog example – 158-159
   Five-wave pattern – 159, 190
Action lines – 10, 13
Action/Reaction lines – 106, 107, 118, 120, 121, 122, 124, 125,
Action/Reaction theory - 14
Andrews, Alan – 106, 110
Andrews Pitchfork – 106, 109-110
Babson, Roger – 21, 106
Bearish divergence – 237, 238, 239, 240, 242, 243, 247, 249, 252
Bearish trend - 24
Breakout bar – 29, 35, 42, 48, 57, 60, 67, 77
Broker, picking - 272
Bullish divergence – 240 - 262
Bullish trend – 45, 168, 214, 261
Buy signal, confirming – 29, 44, 46, 56
Buy window or zone – 39, 40, 44, 46, 55
Calculating – 38, 39, 109,
Center line – 106, 107, 108, 109, 110,
Charting software – 39, 109, 110, 238
Chart patterns – 12, 15, 27, 170, 216, 251
Charts – 80, 103, 149, 170,
Closing prices and Reaction swing – 27, 28, 56, 59
Confirming – 34, 40, 52, 59,
Consolidation pattern – 31, 47, 72, 123, 130, 152, 159, 182
Connecting patterns – 149, 227
Corrections. See Retracement – 17, 57, 70, 87,
Covered write – 219, 220, 226, 231
Cycles, natural - 10
Downward trending market – 32, 33, 35, 57, 59, 89, 90,
Elliot Wave Theory – 10, 149, 150
Extending, count - 101
Failed swing patterns – 188, 189, 190, 194, 198, 200, 265
Fast stochastic - 238
Five-wave pattern – 159, 190
Forward count – 31-35, 41, 44, 46, 48, 51-53, 60, 61, 63-65, 67
Futures trading – 271, 272
Gann, W.D. – 10, 21
Gap – 60, 64, 65, 67, 70, 74, 75, 77, 78,
Holidays – 32, 35, 44, 60, 65, 69, 70, 72, 75
Human emotions – 86, 218
Identifying, see Reversal dates – 36, 85

Index

Indicator – 14-17, 23-25, 42, 43, 48, 52, 58, 59, 72, 80, 84, 93, 106, 111, 148, 202-204, 207, 208, 210, 217, 219, 221, 237, 238
Kellogg, Joseph, books by – 219, 271-272
Knowledge of market - 5
Learning and practicing concepts – 9, 15, 270
Long-term trend – 87, 91, 253
Major reversal pattern - 127, 210, 214, 224
Major trend – 36-37, 84, 200, 247
Market Center Direct - 272
Market correction – 49, 57, 156, 161
Median line study - 106
Misinterpreting Reaction swing - 36
Money management – 8, 10, 42, 86, 98, 216, 272
Moving average – 15, 43, 44, 58, 64
Options – 218, 219, 221, 224, 231, 234, 272
Options Traders Playbook, The – 219, 272
Patterns, see Charts Patterns
Performance, looking for – 106, 219, 270, 271

Poker, trading compared to - 169
Price – 7, 9, 10-19
Price action – 13, 17, 18, 22, 23, 46, 63-64, 67, 78, 94
Price charts, patterns in – 170, 237, 240-242, 244, 250, 253, 254
Price correction – 24-25, 30, 32
Price target – 23, 113, 115, 117, 133
Pivot point – 24, 28, 29, 33, 36, 38
Protective stop – 8, 19, 38, 42, 44, 47, 48, 51
Reaction cycle – 14, 26-27, 150, 158, 167, 191, 193, 269
Reaction line – 106, 107, 109-116, 118, 120-126, 128, 129-131, 133
Reaction swing – 14, 22-25, 29, 31-37, 42-50, 52-55, 58-61
Reading resources - 271
Retracement – 24-26, 38, 52, 54-55, 57, 59, 63, 69, 78, 81, 87, 90-91, 97, 150, 262-263
Reversal date – 14, 23-24, 26, 29-30, 35-36, 42-43, 46-50
Reverse count – 31-35, 44, 48, 52-53, 56, 60-61, 63-64, 67

Index

Risk disclosure statement - 271
Sell signal, confirming – 29, 38-39, 41, 47-48, 52, 56-57, 64, 67, 72, 90, 94-95, 97, 116, 118-120, 122, 123-124, 126-127
Sell window – 26, 38-41, 47-48, 50
Shorter time frame, trading in – 253-254, 257, 260-261, 265
Signal bar – 38, 40-41, 44, 47
60 percent retracement level – 38, 52, 57, 63, 69, 78, 263
Slow stochastic – 237-240
Slow stochastic technical oscillator (SSTO) – 237-248
Software. Also see Charting software – 109, 238, 270, 272-274
Supply and demand law – 10-11, 13, 17
Support and resistance levels – 23, 25, 118
Swing trading - 271
Target price – 113-115, 118-126
Technical analysis – 10, 12, 14, 27, 237, 252
Technical indicators – 15-16, 43, 58, 237, 239, 251-253, 271, 273

Tells – 169-170, 188, 191, 208, 216
Three Little Indians - 240
Three-wave pattern - 158
Time – 14, 21, 48, 88
Time duration - 112
Trade components of – 14, 202, 269
Traders Market Views – 270, 271
Traders Network – 270, 273
Traders Network website - 273
Trade Simulator - 273
Trading – 5, 6, 8, 10, 11
Trail day – 61, 64, 201-210, 212-215
Trend – 6, 11, 15, 17, 18, 22-24, 26
Trend continuation pattern – 50, 74, 80, 87-90, 118
Trend exhaustion - 88
Trend line - 15
Trend reversal pattern – 36-37, 57, 90, 107
Trigger price – 41-42, 51-52, 55, 61, 68, 74, 77-78, 80, 84, 90, 92, 95, 97, 100
Upward trending market – 26, 28, 32-33, 59, 87, 89-90,
W bottom – 37, 150
Zigzag patterns – 150, 158-159, 167-168